CLUES

HB77.S65   CC CS
SPENGLER, ORIGINS OF ECONOMIC THOU

I CUM 00 0091470 H

☞ **W9-BRK-534**

HB
77
S65

Spengler, Joseph
John, 1902-

Origins of economic
thought and justice

JUL   2000

DATE	JUN	2004
JUL X X 2015		
	JUN 0 9	
WITHDRAWN		

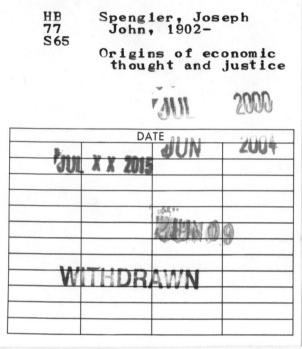

DUE DATE
10/01/07

© THE BAKER & TAYLOR CO

POLITICAL AND
SOCIAL ECONOMY SERIES
Edited by
C. Addison Hickman and
Arthur H. Ford

Joseph J. Spengler

Origins of Economic Thought and Justice

Southern Illinois University Press
Carbondale and Edwardsville

Feffer & Simons, Inc.
London and Amsterdam

Cumberland County College Library
P.O. Box 517
Vineland, NJ 08360

HB
77
S65

81-50

Copyright © 1980 by Southern Illinois University Press
All rights reserved
Printed in the United States of America
Designed by James Wageman

Library of Congress Cataloging in Publication Data

Spengler, Joseph John, 1902–
   Origins of economic thought and justice.

   (Political and social economy series)
   Bibliography: p.
   Includes index.
   1. Economics—History.   2. Economics—Moral
and religious aspects—History.   3. Distributive
justice—History.   I. Title.   II. Series:
Political & social economy.
HB77.S65   330'.09   79-27026
ISBN 0-8093-0947-5

*To Gertrude Arbogast, Elizabeth Boston,
and the memory of
Frank Spengler and William Wenrick*

Contents

Acknowledgments

I am greatly indebted to the Rockefeller Foundation which made it possible for me to obtain clerical and research assistance. I am indebted also to the works of many scholars whose studies have made possible this inquiry into the interpretation of the development of economic thought with that of man's concerns respecting economic justice, especially in the ancient world.

Ms. Barbara Culbertson, Mrs. Virginia Skinner, and Mrs. Margaret Moore have contributed greatly to the preparation of several versions of portions of this study and the shaping up of the final manuscript.

My wife, Dorothy, has done a great deal to facilitate completion of this as of other of my works. She has freed me of many chores which would otherwise have interfered with my completion of this study. She has also provided me with inspiration by surrounding me with flowers of exotic origin.

Thanks are due also to Joyce Atwood and her staff for the fine editorial work done on my manuscript by the Southern Illinois University Press.

I wish to thank the following publishers for their kind permission to quote from the books listed below:

Clarendon Press, Oxford, England, and Random House, Inc., New York, *The Basic Works of Aristotle*, 1941, and *The Dialogues of Plato*, 1937.

Columbia University Press, New York, *Records of the Grand Historian of China*, translated by Burton Watson, 1961.

Doubleday and Co., New York, *History Begins at Sumer*, by Samuel N. Kramer, 1959.

Oxford University Press, New York, and Oxford, *Paideia: The Ideals of Greek Culture*, by Werner Jaeger, 1943–45, and *The Oxford Translation of Aristotle*, edited by W. D. Ross, 1925.

Princeton University Press, *A History of Chinese Philosophy*, by Fung Yu-lan and translated by Derk Bodde, 1952.

Acknowledgments

University of California Press, Berkeley, *The Ancient Economy*, by M. I. Finley, 1973.

University of Chicago Press, *Letters from Mesopotamia*, by A. Leo Oppenheim, 1967, and *Ancient Mesopotamia*, by A. Leo Oppenheim, 1977.

JOSEPH J. SPENGLER
December 10, 1979
Durham, North Carolina

Introduction

Science, at least science in a world relatively free of risk and uncertainty, presumes the existence of order.[1] "There can be no living science unless there is a widespread instinctive conviction in the existence of an *Order of Things*, and, in particular, of an Order of Nature."[2] While a few individuals felt such a conviction, their number was small, and it did not arise in parts of the world (e.g. Asia) where the conceptions of God were "too arbitrary or too impersonal."[3] "Geniuses such as Aristotle, or Archimedes, or Roger Bacon must have been endowed with the full scientific mentality, which instinctively holds that all things great and small are conceivable as exemplifications of general principles which reign throughout the natural order."[4] The number of persons answering to the description of scientist was conditioned, of course, by the degree to which a spirit of inquiry prevailed as it had among the earlier Greeks but not among the Romans, Egyptians, Jews, and Babylonians.[5]

Economically oriented ethics entailed a conception of right and an area within which a right was enforceable. Greek authors, we shall see, developed the idea of every man's being given his due, at least within the jurisdiction of a man's city. Under the Roman Empire, however, this right was extended to its borders and thus became one of the greatest legacies of that empire. However, inasmuch as a man's due might be conditioned by the need to preserve order and promote efficiency, a stable ethical solution might entail balance among the separate principles of equity, order, and efficiency—a balance easier to attain in technologically static societies.

---

[1] Novelty, of course, imposes the need to theorize and anticipate novel situations, a task often beyond man's powers.

[2] A. N. Whitehead, *Science and the Modern World*, p. 3.

[3] Ibid., pp. 6–7, 18–19. On the genesis of "Nature as Norm," see *A Documentary History of Primitivism and Related Ideas*, ed. Arthur O. Lovejoy, et al., 1, ch. 3.

[4] Whitehead, *Science*, p. 7.

[5] C. N. Cochrane, *Christianity and Classical Culture*, pp. 143, 148–49, 413–14; H. W. Household, *Hellas, the Forerunner* 1: 44–47.

My concern in this collection of studies is to sample writings in China, India, the Middle East, and the Mediterranean world—writings that bear upon regnant opinion respecting economic behavior and justice. Many of the opinions dealt with reflect local economic conditions at a time when empirical conditions were not yet favorable to the development of anything like modern economic science. Even so, similar problems tended to give rise to somewhat similar solutions reflective of constraints often associated with similarity in the problems calling for solution. Presumably the available range of solutions to a typical problem was narrow and hence allowed but limited uniqueness in response.

While economic science as we know it is essentially a product of European civilization with some of its origins dating back to the Graeco-Roman and medieval worlds, economic relationships were participated in and observed in a number of parts of the ancient world. What may be called its "origins" lie mainly in what Benjamin I. Schwartz,[6] following the example of Karl Jaspers, calls "the age of transcendence," the first millennium before Christ. For this millennium "witnessed the emergence within the orbit of the 'higher civilizations' of certain major spiritual, moral, and intellectual 'breakthroughs'" in the Middle East, India, China, and Greece. Our concern in the present study therefore has been to examine manifestations, not of economic science, still less than four centuries old, but of some economically oriented opinions in the pre-Christian millennium, in China, India, the Middle East, and especially the Graeco-Roman world. Attention is devoted as well to the contribution of pre-Christian insights to the subsequent development of economic thought. Much of what we find in early writers is describable as proto-economics, incomplete visions of imperfectly conceptualized worlds dominated by sociophysical parameters much more constraining than today's of the nature and range of man's options.

Economic discussion presupposes concern with man's engagement in the satisfaction of his physical and related needs. We shall not be concerned, however, with the origins of man's modes of engagement, individual or institutional, in the satisfaction of these needs. Indeed, as Carl Menger pointed out in his *Grundsätze der Volkswirtschaftslehre* (1871), productivity-favoring institutions could and did come into existence spontaneously—e.g., the institution of money—evolving in response to man's tastes and conditions affecting his satisfaction; they were not dependent upon the state or collectively for existence, though communal activity could affect their evolution. Robert Nozick's account of the origin of the state in his *Anarchy, State and Utopia* (1974) bears some resem-

---

[6] B. I. Schwartz, "The Age of Transcendence," in symposium on *Wisdom, Revelation, and Doubt: Perspectives on the First Millennium B.C.*, *Daedalus* 104.

blance to Menger's account of the often somewhat spontaneous origin and evolution of economic institutions. Suggestive also is Menger's view that economic theory deals with the conditions under which men engage in activity directed to the satisfaction of their needs.

While at least three conditions must coexist if economic discussion is to emerge, the presence of a fourth is essential to the emergence of concerns respecting what may be called economic "justice." (1) An economic problem arises "whenever scarce means are used to satisfy alternative ends." (2) When solution of this problem "involves the cooperation and interaction of different individuals," solution becomes a concern for the science of economics.[7] (3) While the solution achievable will be conditioned by a society's institutional arrangements and the concrete nature of the problem, it is through consideration of alternative solutions, together with their comparative costs and advantages, that an appropriate analytical apparatus may be brought into being. There is, as will be seen, much to be said for the view that the structure and preconditions of such an analytical apparatus did not really begin to be systematically perceived until in the seventeenth century. (4) The concept of economic justice took shape much earlier therefore than did the concept of an apparatus of economic analysis, since the chosen solution of a concrete economic problem that involved individual interaction could entail a different distribution of costs and benefits than might available alternative solutions. Whence customs and eventually codes evolved, the function of which was to rule out solutions that entailed too inequitable a distribution of costs and benefits and perhaps threatened the stability of the state or collective system that afforded means of support and enforced ruling customs or codes.

As is shown later on, thought about a social subject, having evolved into a social science, may eventually acquire a life of its own, relatively independent of society's sociophysical parameters.[8] The content of economic thought was not initially independent of the sociophysical parameters of the society within which it developed, nor did it ever become completely independent even in modern times.

The protoeconomist resembles Schumpeter's economist in that he has a "Vision or Intuition," a mixture "of perceptions and prescientific analysis."[9] He resides in a world endowed with certain options, certain possi-

[7] On economic science and its natural origins, see Milton Friedman, *Price Theory: A Provisional Text*, pp. 6–7, and William Letwin, *The Origins of Scientific Economy: English Economic Thought 1660–1776*.

[8] E.g., see my "Population Phenomena and Population Theory," in *Research in Population Economics*, ed. Julius Simon, pp. 197–215.

[9] J. A. Schumpeter, "Science and Ideology," *American Economic Review* 39: 345–59, esp. pp. 350–51.

bilities and probabilities, that is, with concrete existing conditions. While these conditions may be differently perceived by different economic observers, the perceptions of diverse individuals are likely to have much in common. However, even if individuals perceive sets of related phenomena in quite similar fashion, they may differ in how they choose from among these perceived phenomena and tie them together in what are intended to be explanatory models. Defective perception and conceptual orientation may therefore influence both the content of the set of related phenomena perceived and how an explanation is induced out of these phenomena. Until a pattern of generality, albeit crude, is detected in the diverse phenomena perceived, the perceiver remains a perceiver quite removed from a protoeconomist.

We may say that the content of economic thought at any time can be influenced by a society's sociophysical phenomena which condition the individual's exploitable range of choice. This influence will be greater, of course, insofar as economic thought is empirically and objectively rather than subjectively oriented. Relevant also is the adaptability of a language and writing materials in use to the representation and analysis of economic phenomena, a quality of language that varies with its nature and its state of development. Careful study of the languages utilized in the ancient world, together with their comparison with modern languages, would reveal differences in their initial adaptability to economic analysis and/or in their capacity for developing in keeping with the needs of such analysis.[10] For example, ambiguity of terminology could impair analysis. Illustrative is the impact of ambiguity of the term "nature" upon ancient Greek attempts to use "nature" as a norm.[11]

The relevant parameters of ancient as of modern economics may be classified into those which are physical in character, those descriptive of a society's organizational dimensions, and those bearing upon the interpersonal distribution of decision-making power. These parameters are interrelated, of course, in that societal organization and societal decision-making are likely to interact and that physical parameters condition the options and the range of choice respecting both organization and operative decisions. Of course, the impact of all three sets of parameters is affected by the general state of a society's physical environment in that it conditions not only man's dependence upon elements of his physical environment but also his capacity as an organizer and a decision maker. Physical parameters were more important in ancient times, both because

---

[10] E.g., see Arthur F. Wright, "The Chinese Language and Foreign Ideas," in *Studies in Chinese Thought*, ed. A. F. Wright, pp. 286–303, and bibliography; also references in ch. 2, n. 27.

[11] Lovejoy, et al., *Primitivism*, pp. 110–13, also pp. 447–56.

man was quite constrained by them and because his visions reflected these parameters in much greater measure than a twentieth-century economist's models directly reflect the world he envisions. As yet insignificant roles were played by the creators and appliers of economic thought.[12]

[12] Cf. my "Economics: Its History, Themes, Approaches," *Journal of Economic Issues* 2: 5–30.

Origins of
Economic Thought
and Justice

1

The Rudiments of Economic Thought

For they all seek their own.
St. Paul, *Phil.* 2:21

Economic thought consists in a variety of percepts and concepts made in response to sets of conditions and problems—responses that after the passage of many centuries became transformed out of specific observations into organized sets of observation and finally a science of sorts. Evolution moved initially from ad hoc empirical observations to *sets* of observations, such as those that guided ancient business firms and influenced ethical theory; only after the passage of many centuries did economic science begin to take shape. In this chapter we examine the kinds of problems and conditions to which response was made.

A. Protoeconomics

Economic behavioral propensities in the form of want satisfaction, of opportunity-and-utility augmentation, or of maximization *subject to physical, institutional, and other contraints*, may be taken to be roughly universal in the large. For, as Lotka observed, "However erratic human desires may appear in detail, in the gross they display a species of uniformity, of law, of constancy; a fact recognized long ago by Adam Smith, who 'considered a science of economics possible because of a few outstanding traits of man which guaranteed self-preservation while also promoting the welfare of society at large.'"[1]

[1]A. J. Lotka, *Elements of Physical Biology,* pp. 385, 386. See also S. N. Kramer, *History Begins at Sumer*, chs. 11, 15–16, and my *Indian Economic Thought: A Preface to Its History*, pp. 42–46. R. A. Schwartz shows that even personal philanthropic behavior rests largely upon an economic base. See his "Personal Philanthropic Institutions," *Journal of Political Economy* 88:1264–91; but compare Marcel Mauss, *The Gift*, p. 126 n. 85, also pp. 73ff., where he contends that only in Western societies did man become an "economic animal." See also H. A.

Universality of propensity as defined does not result in substantive similarity of outcome, however, insofar as tastes, values, and institutional and other constraints differ. These constraints must be taken into account, particularly by economists who rest their analysis entirely on market-oriented capitalistic models despite the nonparallelism between this type of model and models appropriate to agrarian and nonindustrial economies. Furthermore, as Finley implies, the suitability of a model may be conditioned by philosophical, ideological, and related circumstances as well. For, in his discussion of the uniqueness of the Western world wherein capitalism eventually came to flourish, Finley observed: "The Graeco-Roman world was essentially and precisely one of private ownership" whereas "the near Eastern economies were dominated by large palace- or temple-complexes, who owned the greater part of the arable, virtually monopolized anything that can be called 'industrial production' as well as foreign trade (which includes inter-city trade, not merely trade with foreign ports), and organized the economic, military, political and religious life of the society through a single complicated, bureaucratic, record-keeping operation for which the word "rationing," taken very broadly, is . . . [a] one-word description."[2]

It is not surprising that even in the West observation of the response of individuals to prices and price changes did not lead to perception and conception of a market-oriented *price-system* that rationed and allocated goods, services, and inputs. Outside the West conditions were less conducive to the genesis of such a conceptual model. Emphasis in ancient "economic" discourse was upon the relevant, upon instruments, arts, and acts of management by the individual or the bureaucratic decision-maker—that is, upon accounting, market information, judgment, fi-

---

Simon's distinction between maximization and satisficing as ends in his *Models of Man*, pt. 4 passim.

[2] M. I. Finley, *The Ancient Economy*, pp. 28–29; also M. W. Fredericksen's review, "Theory, Evidence and the Ancient Economy," *Journal of Roman Studies* 65:164–70. The word "freedom" had no equivalent in any ancient "Near Eastern language," including Hebrew, or any "Far Eastern language," Finley finds (p. 28, p. 182 n. 38), also references in n. 8 below. See also N. Georgescu-Roegen, "Economic Theory and Agrarian Economics," reprinted in his *Analytical Economics*, pp. 359–97, on incompatibilities between the theory of the capitalist system and that of a noncapitalist economy. See also L. Dumont, *Homo hierarchicus: An Essay on the Caste System*. This system did not exist in the ancient world, not yet having replaced what Finley calls "orders and status" (ch. 2, p. 185 n.20, and passim). F. M. Cornford notes that the "very word *cosmos* was a political term among the Dorians, before it was borrowed by philosophy to denote the universal order," a situation later reversed when societal organization was regarded as a miniature copy of the cosmos, *From Religion to Philosophy*, pp. 53, 211.

nance—together with collective restraints and the philosophy and ethic of behavioral control; it was not upon how a price system could keep a multitude of individual decision-makers interacting in ways such as tend to maximize the aggregate output/input ratio. One engaged in production or trade will emphasize what seems pertinent thereto whereas philosophers and officials will deal with moral and public administrative issues (e.g., property, taxation, legal rules, just price, conditions affecting political order), with the last three long dominating what was written from a community point of view. After all there must have been general agreement with St. Paul's observation (*Phil.* 2:21) that a man is egocentric and self-serving.

Managerial skill and economic wisdom arose out of concrete economic experience and became a part of economically oriented custom and tradition (e.g., man must very early have learned, as one reads in 2 Esdras 7 [58], that "what is plentiful is of less worth, for what is more rare is more precious"). This made for rational future-oriented behavior of the economic sort, on the part both of the private decision-maker and of the bureaucrat living in a simple, noncomplex and technologically nondynamic economy relatively free of repercussions flowing from bad local decisions in complex, connectedness-ridden economies of the modern type. Of main use to many ancient-world decision-makers besides record keeping techniques, information on weights and measures, the state of markets, physical risks, legal rules, banking conditions, and business risks, was technological information about goods.[3]

When economics really began to become economics remains subject to dispute, in part because of difference in opinion respecting what constitutes "economics." Thus while Harro Bernardelli finds some of the beginnings in L. Pisano's *Liber Abaci* (1202) he suggests that in Babylonian temples priests interested in the mathematical implication of fertility worship probably had rudimentary notions.[4] Elements of management theory are even older.[5] While most would agree, however, that the origin

[3] I base this impression in part upon medieval manuals and correspondence. E.g., see R. S. Lopez and I. W. Raymond, *Medieval Trade in the Mediterranean World*, esp. pt. 5; R. S. Lopez, "Stars and Spices: The Earliest Italian Manual of Commercial Practice," *Economy, Society, and Government in Medieval Italy*, ed. David Herlihy, et al., pp. 35–42; S. D. Goitein, *A Mediterranean Society*, 1, esp. pt. 3. W. F. Leemans, *The Old-Babylonian Merchant*, chs. 1, 3. See also F. L. Pryor, *The Origins of the Economy*.

[4] Harro Bernardelli, "The Origin of Modern Economic Theory," *Economic Record* 37: 320–38, esp. pp. 320–22, 332–33; also Finley, ch. 1.

[5] C. S. George, Jr., *History of Management Thought*, pp. xiii, xiv, 1–26. See also Thorkild Jacobsen, *Toward the Image of Tammuz*, ch. 13; Joseph H. Vlaemminck, *Histoire et doctrines de la comptabilité*, pp. 13–29, on Sumerian and

of economics, defined as the study of economic behavior within a system of relations, does not antedate the seventeenth century, such dating rests upon the definition of "economics."

Today's economist probably is better equipped to understand ancient economic behavior than so-called ancient economics. He needs, however, to understand the set of institutions within which economic activities were carried on in order to comprehend that which was written about. For what is set down in indigenous terms in accounting records or "philosophical" accounts is not expressed in terms reflecting the modern economist's categories of thought. Even so, he may find it of interest to explain what is set down as well as the behavior to which it relates, for since he is well equipped with theory and method he may hit upon more fundamental explanations of the ancient phenomena described, together with accompanying ethical principles and administrative rules.[6] He may also come across close parallels between various situations in an ancient-world economy and some encountered in today's world. For, given the finitude of economic behavior, economic situations, and relevant combinations of behavioral propensity and situation, analogues are bound to appear.

Protoeconomic wisdom, ancestor of vintage economic theory, was inductive in origin, in part the product of what H. A. Simon calls "satisficing" rather than "maximizing" behavior within a context of ethical principles[7] and rules customary or administrative in character.[8] With the emergence of larger temples, partnershiplike business associations, fully individual and alienable property, together with enlarged and essentially autonomous communities, economic problems must have increased in number and scope along with specialization. Associated with this increase in economic problems must have been growing pressure to move from what Brunner has called an "administrative system coupled with domi-

---

Egyptian accounting. See also C. H. W. Johns, *Babylonian and Assyrian Laws, Contracts and Letters*, chs. 20, 29.

[6] E.g., see Eli Ginzberg, "Studies in the Economics of the Bible," *Jewish Quarterly Review* 22: 343–408.

[7] E.g., the Maori proverb, "Give as much as you receive and all is for the best." See Marcel Mauss, *The Gift*, p. 69. See also on Zoroastrian emphasis upon truth and honesty in Magan A. Buch, *Zoroastrian Ethics*, chs. 4–6.

[8] George Dalton, "Theoretical Issues in Economic Anthropology," *Current Anthropology* 10: 63–102, esp. pp. 66–74, 96; idem, ed., *Primitive, Archaic, and Modern Economies: Essays of Karl Polanyi*. "Every primitive society recognizes in some way that fellow citizens have mutual obligations which do not extend to aliens, and in the societies which have the least government these obligations are concerned with the limits of the use of force." So observes Lucy Mair, *Primitive Government*, p. 35.

nantly collective property" toward "a system of markets associated with the institution of private property."[9] For insofar as the administrative apparatus of state could not be continually modified in keeping with increase in economic complexity, the power to decide and transact would tend to devolve downward to individual entrepreneurs, business associations, and guildlike bodies.

While what may be called economically-oriented writing seems to have emerged with the construction of legal codes and the application of customary or group (e.g., guild) principles to concrete problems, it could not continue to map well on economic reality as the latter experienced increasing freedom from centralized control. Put tersely, economic thought could and presumably did evolve out of inter-decision-maker transactions and their increase in number, complexity, and technological or organizational implications.

In archaic societies transactions took place not only within the local community and among local communities but also between the political center (i.e., king, temple, elite, etc., about which the local communities were assembled) and either other political centers or foreigners. "The local constituents pay tribute to the political center . . . and usually receive from the center military protection, juridical services, and emergency subsistence in time of famine and local disaster."[10] A redistributive role may thus be performed by the centralized polity and political authority. There was need, therefore, for rules and guiding principles, preferably for written rules and laws, usually in keeping with "natural law," or superior principles of right, that bore transcendental sanction.[11]

Rules were required not only by governing officials of the more or less bureaucratic states that came into being, they could also prove useful to those engaged essentially in private trade. Rules and inferences relating to trade and pricing bore closest resemblance to what later became classical economics. Presumably many of those most concerned about rules operative within what may be called the private sector did not always look with favor upon rules emanating from the bureaucratic state and hence sought preferable guiding principles. After all there must have

[9] Karl Brunner, "Knowledge, Values and Choice of Economic Organization," *Kyklos* 23: 558–79, esp. pp. 561–62.

[10] Dalton, pp. 73–74.

[11] China was an exception. See Derk Bodde, "Basic Concepts of Chinese Law: The Genesis and Evolution of Legal Thought in China," *Proceedings of the American Philosophical Society* 107: 375–98, esp. pp. 377–79, and Bodde and Clarence Morris, *Law in Imperial China*, pp. 9–11, 48–49. But see on "Tao" Joseph Needham, *Science and Civilisation in China* 2: 36ff., 491–93, ch. 18. The function of Western natural law is treated by C. G. Haines, *The Revival of Natural Law Concepts*.

been many counterparts to the Panjab proverb: "As famine from the desert; so comes evil from a Brahman."[12] Whence both merchants' law and a private merchant's analytical apparatus tended to come into being as the private sector developed, posed problems, generated experience that could be reduced to terms of rules, custom, and stability-generating common law, and revealed what amounted to simple economic guides or principles essential to economic survival and success.

Economically oriented or implicit economic ideas came to repose in essentially bureaucratic writings, in private (as well as public) accounting records and guides to the conduct of mercantile and engineering activities, and in essentially philosophical discussions of ethics, politics, and economic activity.

B. Universals

While ancient-world cultures varied with country and region there underlay most if not all ancient polities a number of common conditions and problems, or *universals*. These *universals*, while differing substantively, were similar in form and in impact on politicoeconomic behavior and its analysis.

(1) *Scarcity.* That (as Thomas Hobbes was to demonstrate in his *Leviathan*) the unconstrained wants of men in groups exceed their collective capacity to satisfy, was occasionally stated explicitly by ancient writers and almost always recognized implicitly in their legal codes, systems of constraint, and conceptions of cosmic order. The presence of scarcity in all societies functioned as a necessary precondition to the development of constraining and rationing institutions (e.g., law), the study of which gave rise to jurisprudence, political science, ethical philosophy, economics, and later sociology.[13] For in the absence of what amounted to rationing arrangements in preliterate as well as in literate societies group survival would have proved very difficult if at all possible.[14]

(2) *Specialization and Exchange.* Economics could not emerge until after local or regional specialization had taken form and made exchange, especially commercial exchange, necessary, since the needs of complex

---

[12] Sir Denzil Ibbetson, *Punjab Castes*, p. 218. See also M. Rostovtzeff, *The Social and Economic History of the Hellenistic World* 2: 896–97, 914; A. L. Oppenheim, *Letters from Mesopotamia*, pp. 78–82, 96–105; S. N. Kramer, *History Begins at Sumer*, ch. 7.

[13] E.g., see T. E. Holland's definition of "jurisprudence" in his *The Elements of Jursiprudence*, 12th ed., chs. 1–2, 5.

[14] On the development of institutions to cope with the Principle of Scarcity see J. R. Commons's *Institutional Economics* and *Legal Foundations of Capitalism*.

organizations could not be satisfied by very simple forms of exchange.[15] Some "intrafirm" exchange accompanied the development of temple organizations and state economic undertakings, perhaps in part because intrafirm exchange was found more economical[16] then than now, given all the difficulties that then beset a great deal of commerce.

(3) *Money.* Exchange could not become complex or extensive in the absence of money. For barter not only imposed severe limitations on trade in general, it also limited the functioning of redistributive mechanisms and of arrangements for "reciprocal" exchange. M. A. Copeland believes that a money economy first developed in Mesopotamia, in the third millennium B.C., as a concomitant of temple record keeping, public works, fairly extensive division of labor, and borrowing and lending.[17] What is important in the present connection is that with exchange, money, lending in terms of money as well as of goods, and "financial" institutions came explicit prices and probably the beginnings of a sense of a price system—in other words, the object of what eventually became economic inquiry in the West.

(4) *Political Stability.* The advantages associated with exchange could be fully realized only if there was adequate security, if rules of ownership were effective, and if exchange itself was in accordance with something like that which classical writers implicitly and medieval writers explicitly called commutative justice and distributive justice. All this is evident in early all-covering legal codes (e.g., Hammurabi's) which not only reflect custom but are complemented by customary law which is analogous to common law and responsive to significant changes in circumstances. Greek thought on these matters, become Roman partly as a result of Cicero's influence, was well expressed by Sohm in his treatise on Roman

[15] E.g., see Colin Renfrew, *Before Civilization,* pp. 116–18, 189, 191, 211–12; M. D. Sahlins, "On the Sociology of Primitive Exchange," in *The Relevance of Models for Social Anthropology,* ed. M. Banton, pp. 139–238; K. Polanyi, "The Economy as Institutional Process," in *Trade and Market in the Early Empires,* ed. Karl Polanyi, C. M. Arensberg, and H. W. Pearson, pp. 243–69. The extent of specialization may be inferred from the number of terms referring to occupations and professions. S. D. Goitein found about 450 mentioned in the medieval "geniza" records, far more than in ancient Rome; *A Mediterranean Society,* p. 99.

[16] Cf. R. H. Coase, "The Nature of the Firm," *Economica* 4: 386–405.

[17] M. A. Copeland, "Concerning the Origin of a Money Economy," *The American Journal of Economics and Sociology* 33: 1–18; also his "Foreign Exchange in the 4th Century, B.C.," ibid. 36:205–16; also Leemans, *The Old-Babylonian Merchant,* ch. 2. See also Upendra Thakur, "Early-Indian Mints," *Journal of Economic and Social History of the Orient* 16:265–95, and "A Study in Barter and Exchange in Ancient India," ibid., 15:297–315. By the fifth century B.C. the minting of coins, widely known already a century earlier, had "spread over the whole civilized world" (p. 315).

private law which, as did Middle Eastern and other earlier codes, reveals the law-generating influence of scarcity as envisaged by Thomas Hobbes. Careful comparison of ancient non-Western codes or their equivalents with Greek and Roman codes or their equivalents should reveal how much they contain in common and in what respects concepts of justice in ancient Western and non-Western civilizations were similar. Sohm wrote as follows:

> Justice is a principle regulating the distribution of things valued by men—awarding them to some, denying them to others—and it is, at the same time, a principle whereby man's worth is appraised. Justice gives to "everyone that which is his," that which (in other words) is due to him according to his worth. . . .[18] All law exists in order that the people may live and be strong, and the power of law over the individual is rooted in that subordination of the individual life to the common life which is demanded by morality. The people claim back from the individual the life which it gave him. *Populum vivere necesse est, te vivere non necesse est.* Law apportions to each individual that which is due to him as a member of the people, and due to him, moreover, for the sake of the people. Herein lies the true significance of the *suum cuique*, in its legal sense.[19]

It was the function of juristic law to make "the moral freedom of the individual . . . possible"—"of private law to transform [men] into a community of free individuals."[20] Earlier "primitive law" (the *dharma* of the Indians, the θέμιδ of the Greeks, the *fas* of the Romans) was bound up with the belief "that the gods shield what is right and punish what is wrong." Later "the law set by the gods" is replaced by "law made by the State."[21]

Presumably what was required politically and economically was exchange in keeping with accepted rules of justice since otherwise dissatisfaction threatening to political stability might develop. Juristic law thus made for economic freedom and hence for the advantages we associate with the free market, probably in greater measure under flexible common or customary law than under rigid written law; it also conditioned the emergence of capitalism and its economics.

[18] Rudolph Sohm, *The Institutes*, p. 22. This is the third edition of the translation and is based upon the 12th German edition, 1905. Justinian's *Institutes* had opened with Ulpian's principle, "Justitia est constans et perpetua voluntas jus suum cuique tribuens." See H. O. Taylor, *Ancient Ideals* 2:54, 340; also Cornford, pp. 19, 119.

[19] Sohm, p. 24.

[20] Ibid., p. 22 n, p. 25.

[21] Ibid., p. 22. Cf. Holland, ch. 5.

(5) *Parameters of State*. The magnitude of a representative region within which most trade was carried on—an area including a number of essentially local markets as in Mesopotamia between 2500 and 2000 B.C.—[22] was limited by a variety of physical and other constraints. Among them may be included agricultural yields and hence size of trading surpluses and nonagricultural populations, cost and speed of transport, pattern of urbanization, size of polity and population, physical risks, cultural and related barriers to economic development, strength of apparatus of state, and so on. These had become complex and varied by the emergence of the Roman Empire.[23] Such limits are reflected in the vision or model a bureaucrat or an "economist" has of the concrete economy within which economic behavior or its so-called principles are finding expression.

(6) *Longevity of records*. What we know of man's thoughts and behavior in the past is conditioned by the longevity of the written records in which these thoughts were set down, together with the degree and correctness with which perishable records were copied and transmitted. For, since some records are much more perishable than others and hence differ in survival power, the conspectus of the records available to us today may not correspond closely to the conspectus of records originally produced. Moreover, there usually is a likelihood that at the time records are initially being made some thoughts will be set down rather than others, with the result that the representation of man's thought and behavior is biased both at the start and later on.[24] It is possible also that the frames of reference within which ancient thought and practice were oriented

[22] See Copeland, "Origin of a Money Economy," pp. 6–9. On markets and money lending see Leemans, *Old-Babylonian Merchant*, pp. 15, 43–44, 125. The maximum rate of interest for barley loans was 33⅓ percent and for silver loans 20 percent (p. 14). While navigation downstream on waterways was easy, towing barges upstream was at a rate of about 5 miles a day compared with around 20 downstream (pp. 1–2).

[23] E.g., see my Indian Economic Thought, ch. 1; also Colin Clark and M. R. Haswell, *The Economics of Subsistence Agriculture*. On technological limits see, e.g., Henry Hodges, *Technology in the Ancient World*; M. E. L. Mallowan, *Early Mesopotamia and Iran*. See also Richard Duncan-Jones, *The Economy of the Roman Empire: Quantitative Studies*; A. H. M. Jones, *The Roman Economy*; C. A. J. Skeel, *Travel in the First Century After Christ*.

[24] See J. J. Spengler, "Laissez Faire and Intervention: A Potential Source of Historical Error," *Journal of Political Economy* 57:438–41. Over 4,000 years ago the need for accuracy in transmission of language was stressed by Ptah-Hotep. "If there be an emissary not from one noble to another, be exact after the manner of him that sent thee, give his message even as he hath said it." *The Instruction of Ptah-Hotep and the Instruction of Ke'gemini: The Oldest Books in the World*, with introduction by B. G. Gunn, trans., p. 45.

may be exposed to radical change in the course of time with the result that ancient meaning may be perverted, or that records when copied may be incorrectly transcribed or summarized.[25]

(7) *Adequacy of Language*. Language conditions thought while thought, responding to observation, perception, and conception relating to the changing world of affairs, tends to bring about increase in the lexical content and adequacy of language. Not only may the state of language make for inadequate categorization; it may also lead to misdirection of thought, to search for Jabberwocks, and so on.[26] Thinking economically could progress, therefore, only within the limits of the language available and its capacity to absorb superior terminology from other languages.[27] Neglect of the institutional context within which exchange takes place can lead to misinterpretation of ancient terms.

(8) *Factors*. It is commonly remarked that until the eighteenth century and perhaps not until the nineteenth century, only two factors of production were emphasized in a generic sense, namely, labor and land. For discourse at some levels this two-factor approach was roughly adequate; it did not, however, make for supple enough discourse when a multiplicity of professions was involved. Accordingly, ancient economic discourse was improved when land as well as labor was appropriately broken up into economically dissimilar components associated with complexity of trade.[28]

(9) *Macroeconomic views*. Ancient authors writing from a bureaucratic point of view sometimes conceived of polities in optimum terms, the dimensions of which were mainly physical and demographic.[29] In the West, according to Singer, the concept *oikonomia* was enlarged and ex-

---

[25] The problem here referred to is treated in a contemporary setting by Karl Brunner, n. 9, above.

[26] E.g., see A. J. Lotka, ch. 1.

[27] See my discussion of language in "Notes on the International Transmission of Economic Ideas," *The History of Political Economy* 2:133–51. See also Arthur F. Wright, "The Chinese Language"; P. Gopal Sharma, "Problems of Hindi Terminology," *Asian Studies*; 6:383–94; Kurt Singer, "Oikonomia, An Inquiry into Beginnings of Economic Thought and Language," *Kyklos* 11:29–55; K. R. Veenhof, *Aspects of Old Assyrian Trade and its Terminology*, pt. 5, pp. 348–49; Cornford, p. 141. Polybius, in Book 3 of *The Histories*, warns that his translation of the first treaty between the Romans and the Carthaginians (508 B.C.) might be inaccurate because the language of the Romans had changed so much during the four succeeding centuries.

[28] One gets a sense of the variety of medieval commerce from S. D. Goitein's *A Mediterranean Society*. See n. 3, above.

[29] E.g., see my "Kauṭilya, Plato, Lord Shang: Comparative Political Economy," *Proceedings of the American Philosophical Society* 113:450–57, esp. p. 453.

tended from estate to polity and even to cosmos, that is, to well-constituted wholes ordered by a manager.[30]

C. Inferential Approach

One may indirectly infer how ancients thought and behaved or were supposed to behave economically. Such inferential approach may yield two kinds of information. It may tell us much about the implicit plans and models in keeping with which economic activities were ordered and carried on. It may also serve as a check upon the validity of purported principles of economics put forward to explain economic behavior or to guide it.

Among the bodies of information which may, by inference, reveal principles describing or guiding "normal" economic behavior in literate societies, the following are identifiable:

(1) *Accounting Records*. These may reveal much about the conduct of business and hence in some measure disclose the rationale underlying this conduct.

(2) *Legal Codes and Systems*. These reveal constraints to which economic behavior was subject. They thus permit inferences respecting both how freely private enterprise could function and the degree of fear of exploitative behavior (e.g., monopolistic pricing, defrauding workmen, etc.) on the part of private or public enterprisers, together with operative underlying behavioral tendencies and their control. Comparisons of codes may reveal the degree to which the "economic" content of codes overlaps.

(3) *Ethical and Related Religious Literature*. From this one may deduce inferences similar to those mentioned under (2) and the extent to which analogues of competition condition economic behavior (e.g., fear of divine wrath or disturbance of cosmic harmony).

(4) *Data on Public Administration*. These may be interpreted to reveal the "vision" which the administrator has of the economy and models adapted to governing the behavior of those subject to regulation. These data may also reveal the role supposedly played by incentive in the behavior of managers and of those employed or regulated by administrators.

(5) *Data Gathered by Economic Historians*. These may be interpreted to complement interpretations included under (1) to (4).

[30] Singer; Finley, pp. 26–27, also ch. 6. For an account of estate management see Michael Rostovtzeff, *A Large Estate in Egypt in the Third Century B.C.* There is some comparable material in Rostovtzeff, *The Social and Economic History of the Hellenistic World* 2:267–331, also 1:78, 134–35, on monetization of barter trade. See also F. M. Heichelheim, *An Ancient Economic History*, pp. 1166–93.

(6) *Protective Measures and Mechanisms which Guard the Community* against famine that could arise because of seasonality of crops and crop failures (e.g., measures taken in so-called storage economies).

(7) *Public Works*. Data relating to these, especially in bureaucratic states when labor and other inputs need to be drawn from the private sector, add to ordinary information assembled under (4).

(8) *Writings of Scribes, Administrators, and Political Philosophers*. These reveal assumptions and philosophical beliefs regarding the "forces" which "naturally" stabilize politicoeconomic behavior and the degree to which they need to be reenforced by the apparatus of state. These writings also reveal the degree to which a spirit of inquiry flourishes.

(9) *Models*. These may be constructed on the basis of legal codes, to permit analysis of the probable effects of indicated economic regulations as well as provide fuller insight into the ultimate objectives of such regulations.

(10) *Counting Boards and Numbers*; their history and use.

Unfortunately, while bodies of information such as are listed above may inform us how ancient authorities measured specific economic phenomena (including economic behavior), they do not enable us to transform the information into elementary treatises descriptive of rudimentary economic "science" as then held. For such a treatise had not yet been contemplated.

D. Uncertain Future

Uncertainty permeated the ancient world in far greater measure than today's world. Political instability was more pronounced. Man not only had less control over his physical environment but sometimes exaggerated the costs associated with its supposed instability and proneness to disorder. Human societies were subject to periodic pestilence. Moreover even under ordinary circumstances life expectancy at birth was low and death was omnipresent. In short the world in which man found himself was likely to be subject to so much instability and disorder that his capacity for the effective planning of his future would be quite limited. This in turn would affect the role assigned to rationality by analysts of behavior and increase the importance attached to the role of deities and divination. The likely shortness of life tended to telescope individual planning periods and discourage investment relating to the present while encouraging that relating to passage to the next world.

Illustrative of belief in the instability of the physical world is Polybius's report (*Histories*, bk. vi, par. 1) that it was "reasonable" to suppose that floods, pestilence, crop failure could happen as in the past and reduce the race of man almost to extinction. The Stoics believed that the earth was doomed to periodic disasters, a possibility referred to also in Plato's *Timaeus*. Resource depletion did not enter notably, however, into Aristotle's and Xenophon's discussions of natural resources.[31]

Of greater importance than belief in future catastrophic resource depletion must have been the impact of uncertainty owing to periodic pestilence and persistent high mortality and very low (by modern standards) life expectancy. For example, given a male life expectancy at birth of 32.5 years—a higher level than sometimes was achieved in the ancient world—about 48 percent of these born would attain age 35, about 35 percent, the age of 50, and nearly 13 percent the age of 70. A male stationary population based upon a life expectancy of about 32.5 years would consist of about 30 percent under 16, about 18 percent over 50, and about 5 percent over 65. Given a male life expectancy at birth of about 74 years, about 97 percent would attain age 35, nearly 95 percent would attain age 50, and 71 percent, age 70. A male stationary population based upon a life expectancy of 74 years would consist of about 20 percent under 16, about 34 percent over 50, and about 16 percent over 65.

E. Factor Structure

The factor structure of ancient economics limited the options open to a society and hence to a potential economist's vision. The potential sources of output were essentially two, labor and land. Land was immobile and economic power gravitated into the hands of the owners of land, concentrating power via labor in these hands. Meanwhile trade, especially international trade, provided only limited escape from subservience to the landowning class. The resulting economy was free in too limited a degree to catalyze the formation of economic theory in the modern sense.[32]

---

[31] S. T. Lowry, "The Classical Greek Theory of Natural Resource Economics," *Land Economics* 41:203–8.

[32] Cf. Louis Dumont, *From Mandeville to Marx: The Genesis and Triumph of Economic Ideology*, pp. 5, 34, and *Homo hierarchicus*, pp. 199–202, 209–12.

2

Mesopotamia and the Beginning
of Economics

*Mesopotamian man evolved a civilization equal in
range and endurance to any of the great civilizations in history.*
A. L. Oppenheim, *Letters from Mesopotamia*

*The first millennium before Christ . . . witnessed
the emergence within the orbit of "higher civilizations" of certain major spiritual, moral, and intellectual "breakthroughs."*
B. I. Schwartz, *Daedalus*

I have chosen Mesopotamia to represent the economic cultures in the
Middle East because of its fundamental contribution to the development
of civilization in the Near East and the world of the Greeks, where a basis
for economic thought[1] first came into existence.[2] For as Margueron observes, the "Greek miracle [was] made possible only by the contribution
of the Orient, both as regards its religious thought and its scientific dis-
coveries."[3] Even so, as Oppenheim observes, "All told, very few and

[1] Throughout the book the term "economic thought" will be used rather than
"economic science," which may be viewed as a subcategory of economic thought
and restricted to models or analogues of market-oriented, price-system-domi-
nated, capitalistic economies peopled by "free" rather than "hierarchical" men.

[2] "The state of Iraq and other adjacent regions of today's Iran, Turkey, and Syria
contain the core of that part of the ancient Near East in which Mesopotamian
civilization held sway from the beginning of the third millennium B.C. into the
first millennium A.D. Mesopotamian civilization also exercised influences of varying reach and intensity beyond—at times far beyond—the present borders of
these nations." See A. Leo Oppenheim, *Letters From Mesopotamia*, p. 1. Mesopotamia proper differed from Canaan lying to the West in that the "economic life
and importance" of the Canaanite cities (e.g., Sidon, Tyre) "stemmed primarily
from trade rather from the exploitation of their agricultural resources and the
extension of their control over areas larger than those necessary for support." See
Mason Hammond, *The City in the Ancient World*, ch. 9, p. 91.

[3] Jean-Claude Margueron, *Mesopotamia*, p. 180. "If we think of Greece as the
cradle of modern thought," Margueron writes, "it is because Greece was able to

these mainly secondary cultural achievements of Mesopotamian civilization were preserved and incorporated in the general trend of development that ran westward. This is also true of Egypt, the other representative of the great and primary civilizations of the ancient Near East."[4]

Descriptions of early economics in terms of the concepts constituting modern economics tend to be misleading regarding their character and to make it appear that the ancients comprehended economic concepts and relationships and were able to build thereon an analytical superstructure conducive to analysis and generalization of principles.

Our exact knowledge of the "economic life of ancient societies"—even that of old Mesopotamia after writing and record-keeping had developed—is quite limited and we know almost nothing corresponding to (say) Alfred Marshall's economics, for the ancients lacked concepts corresponding to "economy" and the elements (e.g., the abstract term "market") constituting an economic system (e.g., conglomeration of interdependent markets) and its adjustment mechanisms.[5] One may, of course, search ancient literature, legal and otherwise, for implicit and explicit statements of relationships between instances of economic behavior and particular changes in economic-conduct-determining variables.

Out of such statements one may possibly construct implicit ancient models of sorts—often models shot through with gaps and uncertainty as to meaning. There is danger that we may lose sight of ancient meaning when we lift statements out of subjective and objective contexts that we do not well understand. Even if we do not lose meaning we do not know to what extent unphilosophical ancient observers looked upon various bits of information as transformable into an explanatory model of the total economy or an exemplary part. Moreover, if the behavior of man and his world is subject to great disorder and uncertainty, owing to the erratic behavior of deities and rulers, he is not disposed to conceive of his immediate socioeconomic environment as orderly and quite responsive to rational direction.

---

pass beyond the stage of individualism and attain the universal: but it was the Mesopotamian world that took the first steps, produced the first great civilization and bestowed its benefits on its neighbours and successors" (p. 180).

[4]A. Leo Oppenheim, *Ancient Mesopotamia*, rev. ed., p. 73. On continuing redistribution of political power in the Near East see E. R. Bevan, *Ancient Mesopotamia*.

[5]On lack of economic concepts in ancient times see M. I. Finley, *The Ancient Economy*, esp. ch. 1, and his "Aristotle and Economic Analysis," *Past and Present* 47:3–25; also Louis Dumont, "On the Comparative Understanding of Non-Modern Civilizations," *Daedalus* 104:153–72, esp. p. 158 on the differential impact of unmovable versus moveable wealth. But see also I. M. Diakonoff, ed., *Ancient Mesopotania*; H. Limet, "Les metaux à l'epoque d'Agade," *Journal of the Economic and Social History of the Orient* 25:3–34, esp. p. 3.

Of course, what constitutes beginnings turns on one's definition of economics and economy and on the degree of generalizability conferred on simple common sense, such as that foodstuffs are cheap when abundant. Thus the word *oikonomia* had to do with management of sorts, not with what "economics" signifies today.[6] Hence what was written of *oikonomia* bore little resemblance to a modern analytical and prediction-oriented study of the market-coordinated response of diverse individuals to perceived scarcity within a multi-decision-maker universe of activity—a universe sharply distinguishable from that confronting a single-decision-making Crusoe, at most under the partial governance of a rudimentary exchange system.[7] The virtual universality of man's self-serving motivation is, of course, taken for granted, given recognition of it over the centuries in many cultures in the form of proverbial expressions[8] and in literature touching upon behavior describable as economic.[9] This literature also reflects intercultural differences in the framework within which lives were ordered, "welfare" sought, the degree to which law was believed to be of divine rather than human origin, and the interests of those capable of decision-making were pursued.[10]

[6] E.g., see Finley, pp. 17–21, 26; Kurt Singer, "Oikonomia," *Kyklos* 11:29–55; Harro Bernardelli, "The Origins of Modern Economic Theory," 37:320–38; Karl Menninger, *Number Words and Number Symbols*, pp. 422–31. See also Barry Gordon on the contribution of "ability to reason about social relationships in a generalised or abstract form," together with the opportunity to reflect "on living in a sophisticated economic environment" in *Economic Analysis Before Adam Smith: Hesiod to Lessius*, ch. 1; and E. A. Havelock, *The Liberal Temper in Greek Politics*, ch. 13, on the contrast between the views of Aristotle and those of his "liberal" contemporaries. According to S. C. Humphreys, "what we call rational discourse is not a cultural specialty of the West, but a necessity for any complex and mobile society." See "'Transcendence' and Intellectual Roles: The Ancient Greek Case," *Daedalus* 104:91.

[7] See H. M. Robertson, "Robinson Crusoe Economics," *South African Journal of Economics* 1:24–35; and for the view that society consists in interacting individuals seeking to maximize personal advantage, Frederik Barth, *Models of Social Organization*.

[8] "The early proverbs of man reveal the beginnings of social thought." See Emory Bogardus, *A History of Social Thought*, p. 22. On motivation in prehistoric exchange see Philip L. Kohl, "The Balance of Trade in Southwestern Asia in the Mid-Third Millennium B.C.," *Current Anthropology* 19:468–70.

[9] E.g., see W. G. Lambert, *Babylonian Wisdom Literature*; selections from ancient Indian and Sumerian literature in my *Indian Economic Thought: A Preface to Its History*, pp. 42–46; S. N. Kramer, *From the Tablets of Sumer*, pp. 154–55, also p. 158 on keeping up with the Joneses, a disposition that, according to J. M. Keynes, makes man's wants very difficult to satiate. See Keynes, *Essays in Persuasion*, pp. 365–68; see also Marshall D. Sahlins, *Stone Age Economics*.

[10] E.g., see Henri Frankfort, et al., *Before Philosophy*, esp. chs. 4, 7; Joseph

A. Preconditions

The coming of economics into being depended upon two principal conditions. First, there must be present a sufficiently large number of free decision-makers living and behaving economically who without necessarily intending it bring into being a local economy capable also of trading with other local economies. Such development process resembles Nozick's explanation of the origin of the state in response to the nonviability of anarchy due to its inability to prevent violation of the rights of some by others.[11] For in the absence of an economy emerging needs cannot be met effectively.

Second, even given an economy, the launching of economic discussion calls for the presence of individuals (e.g., philosophers) capable (a) of observing directly and/or indirectly how individuals or groups with economic decision-making power behave vis-à-vis other such decision-makers, and (b) of developing an analytical superstructure on the basis of their immediate apprehension, observations, and systematizing inferences. Differences in capability (b) account for intercountry differences in the treatment of similar economic matter and, in some instances, in ethical orientation. Apparently the training and work of the scribes was too oriented to record-keeping and concrete administration to give rise to well-articulated philosophical overviews and interest in a system embracing *inter alia* such units or branches of activity as those with which individual scribes or civil servants had become closely identified.[12] Indeed, the concerns and perceptions of philosophers did not often embrace enough of the market place and economic world to lead them to see it as a system other than as a potentially strife-ridden world requiring strong government to insure tranquility, particularly if the character, content, and style of their language were poorly adapted to the representation and facilitation of economic analysis.[13]

Needham, *Science and Civilisation in China*, 2; Derk Bodde, "Basic Concepts of Chinese Law: The Genesis and Evolution of Legal Thought in Traditional China," pp. 375–98, esp. pp. 377–79. See also under "ethics" and "law," Kramer, *History*, ch. 14; Clyde Kluckhohn, *Anthropology and the Classics*, ch. 3; and P. S. V. Kane, *History of Dharmasastra*, 5 vols.

[11]Robert Nozick, *Anarchy, State, and Utopia*, chs. 2–3; also K. Menger, *Problems of Economics and Sociology*.

[12]On the scribe see H. F. Marrou, *A History of Education in Antiquity*, pp. xiv–xx, also bibliography, pp. 469–71; S. N. Kramer, *History*, chs. 1–3, 6; A. Leo Oppenheim, *Ancient Mesopotamia*, rev. ed., ch. 5, and "The Position of the Intellectual in Mesopotamian Society," *Daedalus* 104:37–46; James B. Pritchard, ed., *Ancient Near Eastern Texts*, pp. 431–34; Margueron, pp. 173–79.

[13]E.g., the Sumerians did not pursue secular knowledge for its own sake, a view that may have come into the world with the Ionian Greeks. See J. Hawkes,

Commercial activity conceived of in terms of permanency[14] and resulting in diverse economic institutions seems to have developed quite clearly in the Mesopotamian (or "cuneiform") world, a source of much influence in the surrounding world. There private property was widely recognized, as were "the rights of the individual in relation to society and the cosmos," with the result that the development of law was shaped in part by the needs of commerce,[15] especially for written legal documents consonant with sanctioned norms and protection of the individual. Whence the law and legal concepts of surrounding countries reflected Mesopotamian influence.[16]

The study of man and his behavior, particularly with the assistance of a conceptual apparatus, was not, however, undertaken in the Mesopotamian world. "To the Mesopotamian the crucial and urgent subject of study was the entire universe, without any interposition of self between the observer and the observed. There probably has never been another civilization so singlemindedly bent on the accumulation of information and eschewing any generalization of enunciation of principles. Thus all phenomena subject to contemplation . . . could be known and understood in their apparent features and characteristics."[17]

The First Great Civilizations, p. 223. The Sumerians never evolved a "system of philosophy" or an "explicit system of moral laws and principles" into which to incorporate specific moral injunctions. See S. N. Kramer, *The Tablets of Sumer*, pp. 96–97. Scribes, though held in high esteem, were not philosophers. Chinese authors did not undergird ethical practice with natural law as did Western authors. E.g., see Derk Bodde, "Basic Concepts," pp. 337–79. Cf. also Thorlief Boman, *Hebrew Thought Compared with Greek*, and M. C. Astour, *Hellenosemitica*. On norms see A. O. Lovejoy, "'Nature' as Norm in Tertullian," *Essays in the History of Ideas*, ch. 16. The Sumerian approach was dominated by the particular to the neglect of the general. Cf. N. Georgescu-Roegen, *The Entropy Law and the Economic Process*, pp. 28–32, on differences between East and West respecting the particular and the general.

[14]"Friendship lasts for a day, business connexions forever," reads a Sumerian proverb. W. G. Lambert, p. 259.

[15]E.g., see Kohl, pp. 463–89.

[16]E.g., see Bodde, "Basic Concepts," pp. 378–79; E. A. Speiser, "Early Law and Civilization," *The Canadian Bar Review* 31:863–77, and "Cuneiform Law and the History of Civilization," *Proceedings of the American Philosophical Society* 107:536–41, esp. pp. 537–38; W. F. Leemans, "The Role of Landlease in Mesopotamia in the Early Second Millennium," *Journal of the Economic History of the Orient* 18:134–45; G. R. Driver and John C. Miles, *The Babylonian Laws* 1:111–245, 469–78. See also "Advice to a Prince," in W. G. Lambert, pp. 110ff., also his introduction.

[17]J. J. Finkelstein, "Mesopotamian Historiography," *Proceedings of the Ameri-*

Of the three vantage points from which early "economics," forerunner of the study of scarcity-oriented human behavior within an appropriately defined matrix of conditions,[18] may be approached—that is, exchange, administration of an economic organization, and ethical and legal constraints to which economic behavior is subject—exchange is potentially most informative, particularly in respect of ancient economies.[19] For it focuses attention upon the dynamic role of trade, upon the determinants and fairness of exchange, and upon the behavior of exchangers in response to their own interpretations of relevant present and future conditions. Exchange presupposes specialization and occasional salable surpluses, which, along with traders and trading organizations and continuing trade, give rise to an "economic nexus"[20] of sorts and hence to standard measures, monetary media, economic motivation, "economic man,"[21] and protoeconomic thought. Production for markets was a likely sequel to exchange when the output of particular products could be made to exceed local requirements as often was the case in ancient economies.

The role played by exchange in the ancient world was conditioned not only by transport and physical and institutional constraints but also by what was subject to optimization,[22] by whether optimization was defined in less rigorous terms of "satisficing," with the content of what "satisfices" subject to change, and by the relations between real income and status viewed as competing or complementary objectives of economic behavior and exchange.[23]

---

can Philosophical Society 107:461–63, also pp. 464, 466. See also pp. 471–72, on how the Chinese, "starting with a set of beliefs and concepts very similar to those of the Mesopotamians" introduced rationalism, as did the Greeks, while the Mesopotamians remained true to "elemental empiricism." In China and India science did not, as it did in Greece, realize the utility of logic for classifying factual knowledge. See N. Georgescu-Roegen, *The Entropy Law*, p. 30; and *Analytical Economics*, pp. 9–12.

[18] See P. A. Samuelson, *Foundations of Economic Analysis*, pp. 8–10; also H. A. Simon, *Models of Man*, chs. 14–16.

[19] See J. A. Sabloff and C. C. Lamberg-Karlovsky, eds., *Ancient Civilization and Trade*: Raymond Firth, ed., *Themes in Economic Anthropology*. Cf. J. M. Buchanan, "What Should Economists Do?" *Southern Economic Journal* 30:213–22.

[20] P. H. Wicksteed, *The Common Sense of Political Economy*, ch. 5.

[21] Although Marcel Mauss asserts that "it is only our Western societies that quite recently turned man into an economic animal," he may be underestimating the role of traders in earlier societies. See *The Gift*, pp. 73ff.; also Kohl.

[22] E.g., cf. K. J. Lancaster, "A New Approach to Consumer Theory," *Journal of Political Economy* 74:132–57.

[23] The key to simplifying the choice process is "the replacement of the goal of *maximizing* with the goal of *satisficing*, of finding a course of action that is 'good

Given that an individual acts "from only two motives: (a) desire for real income and (b) desire for status,"[24] the relative weights of these two motives will vary accordingly as an economy is dominated by a free market, or subject to ascription and influences emanating from a hierarchical politicosocial system which reduces exchangeability between "income" and "status" except insofar as "status" may be a spill-over complement to growth of "income."[25] The character of ascription is conditioned, of course, by the size of an autonomous community, together with its system of communication, with the result that the role of the market system tends to be positively associated with the size of an isolated sovereign community, or with the extent of a trading area when participating traders are from a number of countries that constitute a kind of commercial region such as Western Asia and the Mediterranean world in pre-Christian times. An ascriptive system may, of course, partially undermine itself in the longer run when, by excluding able persons from acceptable status, it forces them to engage in competitive economic activities and accumulate the wealth, skill, and power which made ascribed status as such less attractive than alternatives achievable in a "free market."[26] In the shorter run, however, an ascriptive system tends to weaken a dynamic private sector by diverting talent into bureaucracies which are likely to be less creative and dynamic than the private sector.

Economics as an instrument of analysis was very slow to develop despite early manifestations of economic behavior. This was true even in the Middle East where as already noted we find economically oriented organizations in the third millennium B.C., media of exchange and banking, writing, accounting, record-keeping, and regulations essential to the conduct of transactions subject to consummation over time.[27] Fitting lim-

---

enough.'" See Simon, *Models,* pp. 204–5. But cf. Fritz Machlup, "Homo Oeconomicus and His Classmates," in *Phenomenology and Social Reality,* ed. Maurice Natason, pp. 1238–39. See also N. Georgescu-Roegen, *Analytical Economics,* pp. 187–92; W. A. Weisskopf, "The Image of Man in Economics," *Social Research* 40: 546–63.

[24] H. W. Arndt, "Prestige Economics," *Economic Record* 48: 584–92. See also Kramer, *Tablets of Sumer,* p. 158.

[25] On ascription see Talcott Parsons, *Sociological Theory and Modern Society,* pp. 14–16, 496–500; N. J. Smelser and S. M. Lipset, eds., *Social Structure and Mobility in Economic Development,* chs. 1, 4–5; Marion Levy, *Modernization and the Structure of Society* 1, chs. 5–6, and passim. See also Marc Bloch, *Feudal Society.*

[26] E.g., see M. Levy, "Contrasting Factors in the Modernization of China and Japan," in *Economic Growth: Brazil, India, Japan,* ed. Simon Kuznets, Wilbert E. Moore, and Joseph J. Spengler, eds.

[27] E.g., see F. M. Heichelheim, *An Ancient Economic History.* Cf. Frederick L. Pryor, *The Origins of the Economy.*

ited observations into terms of a demonstration-oriented larger explanatory (and hence somewhat predictive) system was very slow to develop, initially in the so-called ancient world and in the world immediately following. As a result "scientific economics" did not really begin to emerge until the Renaissance when science began to flourish (due to the development of mathematics, according to Morris Kline),[28] but not to the exclusion of elements of Graeco-Roman and medieval "economic thought" that often were reflected in later writings about economic transactions and issues.[29] As one moves backward in time therefore, it is aspects of economics and relations between economic behavior and ethical and political considerations that increasingly command one's attention.

B. Excursus on Early Mathematics

Inasmuch as the beginnings of mathematics were empiricist even as were those of economics, inquiry into the history of early mathematics may contribute to our understanding of the beginnings of economics. Of course the beginnings of mathematics probably were more shaped by curiosity and less subject to vision-narrowing and misinterpretation-producing utilitarianism than were the beginnings of economics. Of course, commercial arithmetic had its origin in ancient commerce much as algebra owed its origin in part to the needs of counting houses in Europe and the Levant in and after the late Middle Ages.[30]

"It is a relatively good approximation to truth," wrote John Von Neumann, "that mathematical ideas originate in empirics, although the genealogy is sometimes long and obscure. But, once they are so conceived, the subject begins to live a peculiar life of its own and is better compared to a creative one, governed by almost entirely aesthetical motivations, than to anything else and, in particular, to an empirical science."[31] Whence mathematics was incorrectly described more than a century ago as "the study which knows nothing of observation, nothing of experi-

[28] Morris Kline, *Mathematics in Western Culture.*

[29] E.g., see Barry Gordon, *Economic Analysis*, chs. 6–9; R. A. DeRoover, "Scholastic Economics: Survival and Lasting Influences from the Sixteenth Century to Adam Smith," *Quarterly Journal of Economics* 69:161–90. See also S. T. Worland, *Scholasticism and Welfare Economics.* William Letwin puts the origin of scientific economics in England in the seventeenth century. See his *Origins of Scientific Economics.*

[30] E.g., see R. D. Carmichael, "Motives for the Cultivation of Mathematics," *Scientific Monthly*, September 1950, pp. 179–88; Wallace K. Ferguson, *The Renaissance.*

[31] "The Mathematician," in *The World of Mathematics*, ed. J. R. Newman, 4: 2053–63, esp. p. 2063.

ment."[32] Such an interpretation, however inaccurate, could not have been warranted in respect of economics in ancient or in modern times. For the vision(s) ancient writers had of pieces of the economic world, or of the model a contemporary economist might map upon that world, would reflect parameters of the economic world in question,[33] among them a greater proneness to disaster (especially in early Mesopotamia where urban support depended on an uncertain rural surplus). For example, given low crop yields and margins above requirements in good years, variability in yields due to drought, severe cold, pests, etc., together with poor transportation and interlocality relations, food shortage and famine were everpresent threats outside the tropics and regions with adequate and secure irrigation—threats against which storage of grain constituted a safeguard, albeit sometimes an uncertain one, until modern times.[34] Whence storage remained a political and economic concern as did the need to provide irrigation, important in both ancient India and Middle Asia. Indeed, meeting this need eventually became the basis for K. A. Wittfogel's conception of a hydraulic order of life.[35]

While mathematics may have a greater internal propensity than economics[36] to develop and while economics is less liable to an autistic existence, neither can flourish under the conditions constituting such an existence. Thus mathematics, according to von Neumann, needs to be periodically rejuvenated by injections "of more or less directly empirical ideas" lest it separate into a "disorganized mass of details and complexities,"[37] a fate to which economics with its more empirically oriented concerns probably is less liable than mathematics.

---

[32] J. J. Sylvester refuted this view in 1869. See his "The Study that Knows Nothing of Observation," in Newman, 3:1758–66.

[33] E.g., see my *Indian Economics*, ch. 1; also Thorkild Jacobsen, "Ancient Mesopotamian Religion," pp. 473–84.

[34] E.g., see Jacobsen, "Ancient Mesopotamian Religion," pp. 474–79; Frank A. Southard, "Famine," *Encyclopedia of the Social Sciences* 6:85–90; and H. A. Haring, "Warehousing," ibid., 15:354–58; L. M. Hacker, "Food Supply," ibid., 6: 332–38; Derk Bodde, "Henry A. Wallace and the Ever-Normal Granary," *Far Eastern Quarterly* 5:411–26. See also Sahlins, *Stone Age Economics*. On the minimal need for national grain reserves in modern times see D. Gale Johnson, *World Food Problems and Prospects*, ch. 6.

[35] See A. J. Ahmad, "Irrigation in Relation to State Power in Middle Asia," *International Studies* 1: 388–413.

[36] E.g., Maupertius was inspired to discover the principle of least action by an erroneous premise of Descartes. See Jerome Fee, "Maupertius and the Principle of Least Action," *Scientific Monthly* 52: 1–8.

[37] John Von Neumann, "The Mathematician," in *The World of Mathematics*, ed. James R. Newman, 4: 2053–2063, esp. p. 2063.

Turning now to origins of mathematics, not to elementary[38] or primordial culture origins,[39] or to the climate of ideological opinion,[40] but to pragmatic mathematical expressions, we find that much in ancient mathematics originated as a means of facilitating computation connected with solving practical problems, many if not most of which were economic in character. Emphasis therefore was upon practical arithmetic and mensuration.[41] "Nowhere in all Oriental mathematics do we find any attempt at what we call a demonstration. No argumentation was presented, but only the prescription of certain rules: 'Do such, do so.' We are ignorant of the way in which the theories were found."[42] Chinese mathematicians "ap-

[38]Children apparently "first become aware of numbers in terms of ordered sequences and only later in terms of quantities." See Charles J. Brainerd, "The Origins of Number Concepts," *Scientific American* 233:101–13. Cf. O. Koehler, "The Ability of Birds to 'Count'," in Newman, 1:489–96.

[39]"Mathematics is a development of thought that had its beginning with the origin of man and culture," much as economics had its origin in man's concrete economic behavior. See Leslie A. White, "The Locus of Mathematical Reality: An Anthropological Footnote," in Newman, 4:2348–64. See also Raymond L. Wilder, *Evolution of Mathematical Concepts* ; Donald Smeltzer, *Man and Number*. O. Neugebauer found no number mysticism in Babylonian mathematical texts. See "The Survival of Babylonian Methods in the Exact Sciences of Antiquity and Middle Ages," *Proceedings of the American Philosophical Society* 107: 528–35, esp. p. 528. See also Karl Menninger, pp. 152–70.

[40]Needham suggests the possibility that interaction of Chinese and Indian ideas stimulated the discovery of zero, the symbol for nothingness. He notes also that "the absence of the idea of a creator deity, and hence of a supreme lawgiver, together with a firm conviction . . . that the whole universe was an organized, self-sufficient system, led to an all-embracing Order in which there was no room for Laws of Nature and hence few regularities to which it would be profitable to apply mathematics in the mundane sphere." Joseph Needham, *Science and Civilisation in China* 3:148, 152–53; also 2, sec. 18. On pp. 156–57 Needham indicates that for the view, traditional in medieval Europe, the Gallilean revolution substituted, "a world-view essentially mechanistic" and replaced "the world of quality" by "a world of quantity." The basic idea of "Hindu (Arabic) numerals" is Babylonian in origin according to Neugebauer, p. 530.

[41]E.g., see D. J. Struik, *A Concise History of Mathematics* 1, chs. 1–3; Lancelot Hogben, *The Wonderful World of Mathematics*; Newman, 1:10–11, 170–79, 442–64. See also Needham, n. 43, below. Japanese mathematics was greatly influenced in the 2nd century B.C. by a Chinese text (authored by Chang T'sang) that included a number of commercial, partnership, and mensuration problems. See D. E. Smith and Yoshio Mikami, *A History of Japanese Mathematics*, pp. 12–13, 15, 17. On Uruk texts on fractions see M. E. L. Mallowan, *Early Mesopotamia and Iran*, p. 68.

[42]Struik, 1:32. See also Newman, "The Rhind Papyrus" in Newman, 1: 169–78; C. B. Boyer, *A History of Mathematics*, pp. 44–45; Neugebauer, p. 530.

plied their methods to all kinds of practical problems, and no doubt demands for solutions arising from taxation, irrigation and fortification . . . often stimulated their work."[43]

In time mathematics became more general and abstract, especially at the hands of the Greeks. For while the content of Greek mathematics was not so original (according to Neugebauer) it "was doubtless on a higher level" than that of other ancient peoples, "if only on account of its more abstract and systematic character, as seen in Euclid; but . . . it was weak or tardy just where the mathematics of India and China (more faithfully based, perhaps, on those of the Babylonians) were strong, namely in algebra."[44] Greek students of mathematics were philosophically oriented, interested in the "why," the "how" and general mathematical proof—in "the understanding of man's place in the universe according to a rational scheme," in finding "order in Chaos,"[45] a finding that later contributed to the development of economic theory.

Given the slowness with which mathematics became general and abstract, it is not surprising that pieces of concrete economic knowledge were not architectonically combined and made to yield explanatory propositions in ancient times or even until after the Middle Ages. After all, economic relations were more deeply embedded in empirics than those whence mathematics issued, but yet more generalizable than legal principles, also of empirical origin.

C. Early Exchange

As has been suggested, the development of exchange on sufficient scale must have contributed to the growth of economic ideas if not economic science in the ancient world. Exchange in the ancient world was facilitated by the early development of the use of money, banking instruments, and deposit banking[46] as well as by enlargement of the areas within which trade could be carried on. At the same time exchange en-

---

[43] Joseph Needham, 3, ch. 19, p. 48; also pp. 23–26, 151–54, esp. p. 152, on emphasis upon "concrete" rather than "abstract" numbers.

[44] Ibid., pp. 150–51, but see pp. 91–97.

[45] Struik, 1: 41; Boyer, pp. 52, 70–71. It was Greek belief in a nondivine First Cause that probably accounts for their development of a concept of causality unknown in Asia. See Georgescu-Roegen, *Analytical Economics*, pp. 9–11.

[46] M. A. Copeland, "Concerning the Origin of a Money Economy," *The American Journal of Economics and Sociology* 33:1–18; W. H. Leemans, *The Old-Babylonian Merchant*, ch. 2; Upendra Thakur, "Early-Indian Mints," pp. 266–95, and "A Study in Barter and Exchange in Ancient India," *Journal of the Economic and Social History of the Orient* 15 (1972): 297–315; Limet; H. G. Creel, *The Origins of Statecraft in China* 1:55, 125, ch. 7; Raymond Bogaert, *Les origins antiques de la banque de depot; Une mise au point accompagnée d'une esquisse*

countered institutional constraints which made so-called ancient economies much less free than modern exchange economies which rest much
more completely upon mobile rather than immobile capital. As a result
a potential economist in any ancient land would not see about him a set
of operations that might evoke anything like a Walrasian or even a Mar-
shallian model of what was going on.

Although theaters of trade often were small, international trade in
some products was carried on at great distance. Thus if, as Thapar suggests, India and Western Asia were trading partners even in Harappan
times,[47] this region in turn could trade with the Far East and the Mediterranean world.

The empirics of a relatively free and flexible economy, such as the
Greek and the Roman, were more conducive to economic discussion than
were those of earlier archaic economies wherein transactions took place
within and among local communities and between a political center and
other such centers as well as with foreigners, perhaps somewhat in keeping with an August Lösch model.[48] The Graeco-Roman world, observes
Finley, was "essentially and precisely one of private ownership" whereas
"the near Eastern Economies were dominated by large palace- or temple-
complexes, who owned the greater part of the arable, virtually monopolized anything that can be called 'industrial production' as well as foreign
trade (which includes inter-city trade, not merely trade with foreign
ports), and organized the economic, military, political and religious life of
the society through a single complicated, bureaucratic, record-keeping
operation for which the word 'rationing,' taken very broadly, is . . . [a]
one-word description."[49]

de banque en Mesopotamie, esp. pp. 126–29, 174; A. P. Usher, Early History of
Deposit Banking in Mediterranean Europe.

[47] Romila Thapar, "A Possible Identification of Meluhha, Dilmun and Makan,"
Journal of the Economics and Social History of the Orient 18:1–44; M. P. Charlesworth, "Roman Trade with India: A Resurvey," in Studies in Roman Economic
and Social History, ed. P. R. Coleman-Norton, ch. 10; Philip L. Kohl.

[48] E.g., see George Dalton, "Theoretical Issues in Economic Anthropology,"
Current Anthropology 10: 63–102, esp. pp. 66–74; also Leemans, "Landlease";
A. J. Jawad, The Advent of the Era of Townships in Northern Mesopotamia. On
primitive trade see M. D. Sahlins, Stone Age Economics.

[49] M. I. Finley, The Ancient Economy, pp. 28–29, also 22–23 on the "exchang-
ing process." The word "freedom" Finley adds, had no equivalent in any ancient
"Near Eastern language," including Hebrew or any "Far Eastern language" (p. 28
and p. 182 n. 38). Temple economic activities sometimes were extensive and
varied. E.g., see A. T. Olmsted, History of the Persian Empire, pp. 75, 80–83;
T. R. S. Broughton, "New Evidence on Temple-Estates in Asia Minor," in P. R.
Coleman-Norton, ch. 16. See also R. Ghirshman, Iran, pp. 181–88, 240; Hawkes,
pp. 34–36, 41–42, 120–23, 147–50, 157–60.

Protoeconomics evolved with the transmutation of experience and discussion into capsulated practical "wisdom" (e.g., legal dicta, proverbs, administrative rules, etc.) and sometimes in response to developments in other sciences with which economic views interacted.[50] Rational consideration of capsulated wisdom and evolving administrative practice may have suggested means of analysis suited to generalizing it, together with its implications for decision-makers of divers sorts.[51]

The failure of protoeconomics to develop into economics in ancient times is attributable not wholly to a lack of observable economic behavior or to incapacity to size up economic situations. Failure was due in part to the slowness with which thought was emancipated from myth[52] or its equivalents. For, given both a philosophical orientation with interest in the abstraction of demonstrable principles and a *disposition* to focus this interest upon the market and its forms and mechanisms of exchange, common knowledge about the behavior of prices and supplies might have been translated into demonstrable principles. It was the lack of this *disposition* that prevented the early development of economics, given that much was known of economic behavior.

The development of political stability in strength as well as in area subject thereto tended to contribute to economic progress and thereby make for improvement in economic analysis. As it was fear of political instability[53] dominated the thought of many ancient writers who viewed the world in Hobbesian terms and who, while recognizing the dependence of the state on exchange, believed exchange needed to be "just" in order that political instability might be averted. One might, as did some law makers (e.g., Hammurabi),[54] prohibit individual types of injustice, or

[50] E.g., economic administration, being dependent upon mathematics, stimulated improvement in mathematics which in turn improved administrative economics. See Hawkes, pp. 218–19, 223–25. See also Bernardelli.

[51] Somewhat illustrative in Cato's agricultural treatise written from both an ethical and a managerial point of view about a 62–acre farm employing slave and seasonal free labor and specializing in the production of wine and olive oil. He disapproved of lending at interest, found agriculture much less subject to risk than sea trade, discussed storing grain in anticipation of rising prices, and described the determinants (among them plenty of employable labor to meet seasonal needs) of the value of farm property and its good management. See Cato the Censor, *On Farming*, pp. 1–8. Cf. an early "The First 'Farmer's Almanac'" in Kramer, *History Begins at Sumer*, ch. 11. See also on later agricultural investment and profits Richard Duncan-Jones, *The Economy of the Roman Empire*, ch. 2.

[52] Frankfort, ch. 8.

[53] E.g., on Aristotle s concern as contrasted with the views of "liberal" Greeks, see Havelock, chs. 11–13.

[54] In the prologue to his code Hammurabi described its purpose to be "to cause

set down preconditions of justice as Plato, Aristotle, Cicero, and others attempted, or derive rules from a supposed Natural Order, or (as Greek "liberals" preferred) arrive at rules experimentally, or count upon a competitive price system to keep exchange "just." In time, as noted earlier, justice came to be viewed as giving to each his due or what belonged to him and thereby contributing to political stability.[55]

Interpersonal and intergroup stability early became great enough to make credit and interest possible. Indeed, as Sidney Homer found, in historic times credit preceded "the coming of money by over two thousand years" and credit based on documented loans (sometimes at interest) of "grain by volume and loans of metal by weight" date from around 3000 B.C., and these loans were preceded by undocumented instances of credit. While the development of credit was associated with that of exchange, loans in kind or secured by land could and did emerge both with the opportunity to make profitable use of borrowed "capital" and with the need to meet temporary shortages of "capital." Moreover, while there is no early evidence of what might be called capital theory, there did come into being views regarding appropriate lending terms.[56]

Our review of the problem of getting at the content of early economic thought suggests that if modern anthropologists improved their theoretical formulation of early economies it would be easier to infer the nature and degree of economic generalization characteristic of these economies. Essential in particular is more complete knowledge of ancient trade systems, of the degree to which networks of markets were present, and of the role and behavior of price. Then one would be better prepared to conjecture what sort of vision philosophers might or did form of ongoing economic activity and the kinds of exchange involved. Indeed, Lamberg-Karlovsky argues that in Mesopotamia "already in the third millennium exchange was on a considerable scale—enough one might infer to allow a philosopher to conceptualize a model of the mechanisms involved were he so minded."[57]

---

justice to prevail in the land, to prevent the strong from oppressing the weak, . . . to further the welfare of the people" while in the code itself specific regulations were set down. See R. F. Harper, *The Code of Hammurabi, King of Babylon*, p. 3. This code partially substituted lex talionis for prescribed monetary payments for bodily injuries. Lambert, pp. 12–13; Harper, pp. 7–83; Driver and Miles, vol. 1.

[55] Rudolph Sohm, *The Institutes*, pp. 22–25.

[56] Sidney Homer, *A History of Interest Rates*, chs. 1–2; Driver and Miles, vol. 1, passim.

[57] On the state of relevant anthropological theory see Sabloff and Lamberg-Karlovsky, especially the latter's contribution on "Third Millennium Exchange and Production."

D. Mesopotamia

The Near East including Mesopotamia was made up of relatively small linguistically differentiated units. "Mesopotamian civilization" then was analogous to "European civilization" in that each may be viewed as the product of a number of peoples who, while diverse, shared an inherent unity though not one conducive to the emergence of an overriding territorial state. While one finds sophisticated economic relationships in Mesopotamia, local conditions—e.g., those conducive to the development of a storage economy—did not conduce to a free-enterprise economy nor, as mentioned earlier, did the philosophical orientation of the scribes and philosophers conduce to their seeing an economic system beneath ongoing economic life. Yet the units composing the region had a common system of law as well as a common civilization.[58]

Economic considerations underlay the conduct of affairs among the people of Mesopotamia. For example, there is evidence of proverbs connecting life expectancy with thriftiness, of the existence of private property, of a well developed credit system, and of a wide-ranging network of economic decision-making. Because we lack treatises such as Aristotle's when dealing with extended periods we are limited in our understanding of the changes in economic thinking and practice that may have accompanied political and cultural change—information we have respecting Athens and Greece.[59]

We may, with Oppenheim, accept "the essential unity of Mesopotamian civilization" and the inference of Driver and Miles from their study of Akkadian, Babylonian, and Assyrian laws and related matter of an "irresistable" conclusion that "there was a common customary law

[58] This and several of the following paragraphs are based upon A. Leo Oppenheim, *Letters from Mesopotamia*, and *Ancient Mesopotamia*; K. R. Veenhof, *Aspects of Old Assyrian Trade and its Terminology*; C. H. W. Johns, *Babylonian and Assyrian Laws, Contracts, and Letters*; S. N. Kramer, *History Begins at Sumer*; W. H. Leemans, *The Old-Babylonian Merchant*; Joseph H. Vlaemmick, *Histoire et doctrines de la comptabilité*. For a brief account of continuing changes in the distribution of power among the potential entities composing the Near East see E. R. Bevan, *Ancient Mesopotamia*; John A. Wilson, *The Burden of Egypt*; W. G. DeBurgh, *The Legacy of the Ancient World*, vol. 1.

[59] The economic observations of Hesiod and Herodotus approximate Mesopotamian ideas more closely than do Aristotle's or (centuries later) Islamic ideas. E.g., see Barry Gordon, "Aristotle and Hesiod: The Economic Problem in Greek Thought," *Review of Social Economy* 21: 147–56. See also my "Herodotus on the Subject Matter of Economics," *Scientific Monthly* 81: 276–85, and "Aristotle on Economic Imputation and Related Matters," *Southern Economic Journal* 21: 371–89, and "Economic Thought in Islam: Ibn Khaldun," *Comparative Studies in Society and History* 6: 269–306.

throughout the Fertile Crescent" and that "this common law was to a considerable extent written law."[60] This civilization was the product of several thousands of years of evolution, together with shifts in the center of power and changes in economic organization and trading interests.[61]

We do not find anything like an analytical treatise on economic phenomena in any of these regions. This lack may be due in part to underlying patterns of the culture and its apparent relative uncongeniality to a rational body of integrating theory that rises above the particular and facilitates inference, deduction, and generalization. For example, the Sumerians did not undergird their mathematics, science, history, legal codes, etc., with theory;[62] yet we do find the author of a "Farmer's Almanac" expressing himself in marginal terms[63] and proverbs connecting

---

[60] See Oppenheim, *Letters from Mesopotamia*, 1, esp. p. 16, and *Ancient Mesopotamia*, esp. pp. 83–95 on "economic facts"; also Driver and Miles, 1: 9, 56 (vol. 2 consists of the texts and their translation). See also C. H. W. Johns, *Babylonian and Assyrian Laws, Contracts and Letters*; A. S. Cook, *The Laws of Moses and the Code of Hammurabi*; Morris Jastrow, Jr., *The Civilization of Babylonia and Assyria*, ch. 6; I. M. Diakonoff, ed., *Ancient Mesopotamia*. On selections from codes and collections of laws relating to economic and personal relations and crime in Mesopotamia see James B. Pritchard, *Ancient Near Eastern Texts Relating to the Old Testament*, 2nd ed., pp. 159–223.

[61] E.g., see Bevan, and Kohl, pp. 463–92.

[62] In his *History Begins at Sumer* (p. 36), S. N. Kramer writes:

Thus, in the linguistic field, we have quite a number of Sumerian grammatical lists that imply an awareness of numerous grammatical classifications, but nowhere do we find a single explicit grammatical definition or rule. In mathematics we find many tables, problems, and solutions, but no statement of general principles, axioms, and theorems. In what might be termed the "natural sciences," the Sumerian teachers compiled long lists of trees, plants, animals, and stones. The reason for the particular ordering of the objects listed is still obscure, but certainly it does not stem from a fundamental understanding of, or approach to, botanical, zoological, or mineralogical principles and laws. The Sumerians compiled numerous law codes, which no doubt contained, in their original complete state, hundreds of individual laws, but nowhere is there a statement of legal theory. In the field of history, the Sumerian temple and palace archivists noted and wrote down a varied assortment of significant events of a political, military religious character. But this did not lead to the writing of connected and meaningful history.

Oppenheim notes the "absence of polemic in cuneiform literature," in "The Intellectual in Mesopotamian Society," *Daedalus* 104: 38; however, compare Oppenheim, *Ancient Mesopotamia*, pp. 248–50, on the scribes. Informative in respect to the problem under discussion is Thorlief Boman, *Hebrew Thought Compared with Greek*, pp. 200–208. See also M. C. Astour, *Hellenosemetica*.

[63] Kramer, *History Begins*, p. 67. That Sumerian agriculture yielded a wage

savings with life expectancy and thriftiness.[64] Moreover, economic motivation seems to have been pronounced.[65]

Although "the civilization of ancient Mesopotamia was the most advanced of its day and was unrivalled for centuries,"[66] "neither in Mesopotamia nor in Israel does one see the birth of genuine rationalism, nor was it through logical reflection that the Hebrews eliminated polytheism. It could not have been otherwise when one considers that the Orient did not know, as Greece did, political institutions with equalitarian tendencies that encouraged free discussion. On the contrary, the constant strengthening of monarchical despotism developed a hierarchical system of subordination."[67] "There is no doubt," observes Eric Weil, "that the Greeks, particularly those of the sixth, fifth, and fourth centuries, discovered the principle of reasonable and therefore universally valid thought. Practically everything that follows from this creative discovery is due to them, including the reaching of decisions by means of dialogue, without recourse to violence and without mythical or historical authority."[68]

Whereas one encounters little speculative thought and search for rational explanation in Egypt, Assyria, and Babylonia, for example,[69] one finds the Greek thinker seeking "rational explanation for every fact and rational grounds for every judgment."[70] The Hebrew, unlike the Greek, "did not think things out" and allow reason a voice.[71] Even among the Greeks "it was not till well in the fifth century that men's thinking and conduct claimed equal attention with the problems of physical nature" and gave rise not only to a moral and political philosophy, but to a new and enlarged conception of the nature of reality, and of man's place and destiny in the universe."[72] With the Greeks, therefore, "reason" became the "highest arbiter" and made Greek philosophy independent of "the prescriptive sanctities of religion,"[73] of identification of the state with the

---

adequate for an unskilled worker's family and one higher than that in India in 1960 is suggested by data in T. B. Jones and J. W. Snyder in *Sumerian Economic Texts from the Third Ur Dynasty*, p. 252. Cf. Clark and Haswell, pp. 58, 61–62.

[64] Kramer, *History Begins*, pp. 121–25.

[65] Oppenheim, *Ancient Mesopotamia*, pp. 87–89.

[66] Shin T. Kang, *Sumerian Economic Texts From the Drehem Archive*, 2: 428.

[67] Paul Garelli, "The Changing Facets of Conservative Mesopotamian Thought," *Daedalus* 104: 47–56, esp. p. 55.

[68] Eric Weil, "What Is a Breakthrough in History," *Daedalus* 104: 21–36, esp. pp. 28–29.

[69] W. E. De Burgh, *The Legacy of the Ancient World* 1: 21, 30–31.

[70] Ibid., pp. 50–51, 60.

[71] Ibid., p. 89.

[72] Ibid., pp. 127, 159–61.

[73] Henri Frankfort and H. A. Frankfort in Frankfort, et al., pp. 261–62. See also Wilson, *The Burden*, pp. 2–3, 172–73, 313.

god-King, and of the whims and demands of deities—perhaps in response to the growth of society in complexity and mobility.[74]

Contributive also to failure of anything like economic science to develop in the Middle East was the absence both of a competitive economy requiring explanation and specialists whose concern it was to develop explanations of economic behavior. In Mesopotamia and Egypt this task might have been assumed by the scribes who, however, conceived their function to be not analysis but record keeping, especially for temple and palace.[75] "The very invention of writing owes its existence and its characteristic features to the needs of the bureaucracy. Writing served not only to record the designations of staples, materials, animals, etc.—that could have been done in conventional symbols (logograms)—but also to render personal names, which often had to be written phonetically. The resultant mixture of phonetic and logographic writing made the schooling of the scribe a lengthy and complex process which, in turn, severely curtailed literacy."[76] Eventually the scribe was sometimes charged to prepare not only records but also pronouncements and literary creations, and was occasionally enabled to become an independent expert;[77] but he did not direct his "creative effort" to what amounted to economic analysis.[78]

E. Mesopotamian Law

Turning next to law and regulation we find that in Mesopotamia as elsewhere the object of law and presumably of the law-supporting apparatus of state corresponded to that declared by Hammurabi in the prologue to his code, namely, "to cause justice to prevail in the land, to prevent the strong from oppressing the weak, . . . to further the welfare of the people,"[79]—an object supposedly attainable, however, only insofar as the state remained *both* strong (e.g., as a result of suppression of antisocial elements, or as a result of compliance with ethical principles, such as

[74]"What we call rational discourse is not a cultural specialty of the West but a necessity for any complex and mobile society." See S. C. Humphreys, "'Transcendence' and Intellectual Roles: The Ancient Greek Case," *Daedalus* 104: 91–118, esp. p. 91; also Louis Dumont, "On the Comparative Understanding of Non-Modern Civilizations," ibid., pp. 153–72.

[75]Oppenheim, *Ancient Mesopotamia*, pp. 248–78, 298, 331, and "The Intellectual in Mesopotamian Society," *Daedalus* 104:43–46.

[76]Ibid., p. 39.

[77]Ibid., pp. 43–44.

[78]Oppenheim, *Ancient Mesopotamia*, pp. 250–55, 277.

[79]R. F. Harper, p. 3. Today Hammurabi's date is put in the twentieth century B.C. See also Driver and Miles, 1: xxiv–xxv. See also on earlier Sumerian codes, Kramer, *History Begins*, chs. 8–9, 14, 27.

Confucius's principles of *li* and *hsing*) and dedicated to preservation of the welfare and happiness of the people.[80]

Emphasis upon collective welfare therefore implied collective economic intervention insofar as the future of competition and the market was not well comprehended and the degree of competition itself was found inadequate, with some actual prices likely to exceed "just" prices.[81] Presumably competition tended to flourish in proportion as the state relied upon "moral suasion" rather than upon force (other than was considered necessary to curb antisocial activities)[82] and as dynamic forces became ascendant over static forces.[83]

Codes such as the "Laws of Hammurabi," together with contemporary documents, "are a unique source for the history of civilization, as of the life, manners and society of an ancient people." The Laws, together with the rulers' letters to governors of provinces and other officers, tell how property, succession, sale of physical property, pasturing, corveé and taxation, farming, irrigation, work and wages, temple roles, medical fees, loans, weights and measures, foreign trade, slaves, etc., were viewed and regulated, the degree to which land tenure resembled a feudal system, and the extent to which the weak and helpless were cared for.[84] Such codes do not, however, adequately record the degree to which ancient economies were dominated by "state- or temple-administered redistribution systems" as Polanyi and others have held,[85] or by the price system

[80] E.g., see Hermelindo Banico, "Kauṭilya and the Legalist Concept of State and Government: A Comparative Study," *Asian Studies* 9:107ff., esp. pp. 107–10; also Jean Escarra, *Le droit Chinois*, pp. 7–30, 69–84, 435–36.

[81] E.g., see K. R. Veenhof, p. 353; A. L. Oppenheim, "The Seafaring Merchants of Ur," *Journal of American Oriental Studies* 74: 8. W. F. Leemans reports no evidence of "restrictive" guilds in Babylonia in *The Old-Babylonian Merchant*, pp. 67–68. But compare Oppenheim, *Ancient Mesopotamia*, pp. 79–81.

[82] E.g., see Leemans, *Old-Babylonian Merchant*; Johns, ch. 25; L. S. Ledisma, "The Concept of Sovereignty in Pre-Modern Asia," *Asian Studies* 9: 89ff., esp. p. 100; Liang Ch'i-ch'ao, *La conception de la loi et les théories des Legistes à la veille des Tsin*, pp. 43–45, 66; Derk Bodde and Clarence Morris, *Law in Imperial China*, ch. 1.

[83] E.g., see R. C. Blitz and Millard Long, "The Economics of Usury Regulation," *Journal of Political Economy* 83: 608–19, esp. pp. 618–19.

[84] Driver and Miles, 1: 57–58. See also Johns, chs. 4, 20, 27, and divers Middle East codes included in Pritchard. Compare Bodde and Morris, ch. 1. Codes could not, however, prevent the emergence of such problems as silting and salinization concomitant with irrigation (e.g., in Mesopotamia) and with decline in crop yields between 2700 B.C. and 1700 B.C. See Oppenheim, *Ancient Mesopotamia*, pp. 40–41, 84–85; Kang, 2:421–28; Thorkild Jacobsen and R. M. Adams, "Salt and Silt in Ancient Mesopotamian Agriculture," *Science* 128:1251–58.

[85] See Karl Polanyi's *Primitive, Archaic, and Modern Economies*, esp. chs. 1, 6,

and the market.[86] There is evidence, however, that at times in the Mesopotamian region and tangential areas economically motivated and relatively uncircumscribed trade could and did flourish,[87] with fluctuating prices generating risk and entrepreneurial opportunities, with some provisions for finance, and with the content of Mesopotamian law itself responding to commercial development and to "insistence upon private property and individual rights."[88] Veenhof therefore finds untenable the thesis that Mesopotamian economies were "marketless," but he cannot determine the degree to which they became "free enterprise" in character.[89]

F. The Mesopotamian Economy

The Mesopotamian economy, unlike that in Canaan, was predominantly agricultural, though trade in raw materials, luxuries, and textiles played an important role, both at the international level and between city and

---

7, 9, 13, and Dalton's introduction; I. M. Diakonoff; also Robert M. Adams, "Anthropological Perspectives on Ancient Trade," *Current Anthropology* 15: 239–58, esp. pp. 246–48, 252–53, 255–56. Kohl, p. 468, rejects Polanyi's argument, saying that "it is now certain that Polanyi was incorrect in insisting that true market exchange never developed in Mesopotamia." On the relations between a self-supporting storage economy administered by the palace or the temple and performance of the same functions by a private economy see Oppenheim, *Ancient Mesopotamia*, pp. 88–95. R. M. Adams and H. J. Nissen discuss the nonapplicability of the so-called hydraulic theory to early Mesopotamian urban development, in *The Uruk Countryside*.

[86] Even in the absence of a code competition was likely to be variously restrained. For example, while "there was nothing in Egypt corresponding to the Mesopotamian codes" and "detailed written law, publicly displayed as the symbol of impersonal justice," there was law "personally derived from the god-king . . . tailored as justice and equity to the individual appellant." However, pharaonic law as dispensed by viziers usually was customary law. See John A. Wilson, *The Burden of Egypt*, pp. 172–73. Moreover, goods probably "moved locally and within a circumscribed range of village and neighboring village without specific authorization" (pp. 81–83, also pp. 293–94).

[87] Veenhoff, pp. 86–88, 348, 399–400.

[88] E.g., see E. A. Speiser, "Early Law and Civilization," pp. 863–77; Oppenheim, *Letters*, pp. 5–6, 21–23 on temples and storage economy, and pp. 39–46 on the use of money, finance, etc. Cf. Bodde and Morris, p. 10.

[89] Veenhof, pp. 86–88, 266–302, 334–456; also Kohl, p. 468. See also on the role of merchants W. F. Leemans, *The Old-Babylonian Merchant*, and his *Foreign Trade in the Old-Babylonian Period*. M. E. L. Mallowan (ch. 3, also p. 8) infers that in Uruk private business was carried on alongside state business.

country.[90] This economy, a storage economy in character, rested upon an agrarian foundation consisting of an irrigated and intensively cultivated land base, together with complementary herds of cattle.[91] This foundation was unstable, however, given its vulnerability to salinization, a process that reduced yield per acre about 65 per cent between 2400 B.C. and 1700 B.C.[92] Responsibility for decisions bearing upon production and exchange rested in varying degree with state, temple, and the private sector.

Oppenheim stresses the crucial importance of "the use of silver as a means of payment and as currency on all levels of transactions" in the first half of the first millennium all over the Near East and to the West. "Formerly, silver was used nearly exclusively—especially in private transactions—as a standard in relation to staples, other metals, and customary services." The use of silver gave rise to "economic freedom" and to "fluidity in the distribution of wealth and its well-known consequences" such as the accumulation of capital and lending.[93]

A variety of interest rates had long existed, with the rate possibly varying according to locality and the durable commodity in terms of which the rate (i.e., what Keynes called the "own-rate") was expressed, but with the "normal" rate corresponding to the rate fixed by authorities and often reflecting current practice. Apparently the "own-rate" on grain was higher than that on money.[94] "Amongst the Sumerians the idea of interest was originally derived from loans of beasts, not of grain or money; but the extension of the practice to seed-corn and then to money for the purchase of seed-corn must have taken place at an early date." The Babylonian term used for "interest," was a general term for "increment" and thus described interest "as a growth or increase on the commodity lent,

[90] E.g., see Oppenheim, *Ancient Mesopotamia*, pp. 84, 89–95, 112, 129. See also Kohl, pp. 463–92; Robert M. Adams, "Strategies of Maximization, Stability, and Resilience in Mesopotamian Society, Settlement and Agriculture," *Proceedings of the American Philosophical Society* 122: 329–35.

[91] Ibid., p. 330. On storage economy see Oppenheim, *Ancient Mesopotamia*, pp. 89–90.

[92] Thorkild Jacobsen and Robert M. Adams, "Salt and Silt in Ancient Mesopotamian Agriculture"; Adams, "Strategies"; pp. 330–31; Oppenheim, *Ancient Mesopotamia*, pp. 83–85.

[93] *Letters from Mesopotamia*, p. 46.

[94] Driver and Miles, 1:173–74, 176; Oppenheim, *Ancient Mesopotamia*, pp. 107–8. J. M. Keynes, however, pointed to reasons why the monetary own-rate tended to be highest in *The General Theory of Employment, Interest, and Money*, ch. 17. According to Sidney Homer, the normal interest rates on grain were higher than those on silver until in the first millennium B.C. *A History of Interest Rates*, p. 31.

whether cattle, grain or money."[95] This conception thus bore resemblance to the organic theories of interest, such as those put forward by Henry George and Alexander del Mar.[96]

The charging of interest was not prohibited as later in Moslem law or restricted to loans to foreigners and to nonpoor as in Hebrew Law.[97] Interest rates in Mesopotamian lands seem to have ranged from 5 to 50 percent, usually around 20–35 percent.[98] Hammurabi's code prohibited compound interest, permissible at an earlier date.[99]

The rudiments of a free enterprise system seem to have emerged in Mesopotamia, though not as the dominant system. Individuals, partnerships, and agencies made economic decisions, together with temples and the state bureaucracy. Along with collective property there was individual property, alienable as well as leasable. Wages of some nonslave craftsmen and manual labor as well as some rents were subject to regulation, but others were not. Some, but not all fees were fixed by authorities. In what appears often to have been a scribe's paradise, violation of financial and other contractual obligations was subject to penalty. While economic rationality and behavior were evident, manuals had not been developed to guide merchants. Moreover, nothing like manuals were written to explain how either a relatively free or a bureaucratic economy functions.[100]

Considerable information has been assembled by Sidney Homer respecting the use of credit in Sumer, Babylonia, and Assyria. Prior to the development of coined money in the first millennium the use of grain and silver as media in cities made necessary state intervention "to provide rules for exchange and repayment" when the relative values of grain and silver varied.[101] In Sumer transfers and loans of property were already being carefully recorded and subject to regulation, as were interest rates, prices, and commercial transactions. However, credit customs remained relatively stable over much of the three millennia B.C. Even so, given the large amount of commercial activity and private undertakings,

[95] Driver and Miles, 1: 174.

[96] See Irving Fisher, *The Theory of Interest*, pp. 164–65.

[97] Driver and Miles, 1: 175–77; Oppenheim, *Ancient Mesopotamia*, pp. 88–89.

[98] Driver and Miles, 1: 175–77. Penalty and exceptional rates of over 100 percent are reported. Ibid., p. 176, also p. 192 n., on a loan resembling a maritime loan. See also Oppenheim, *Ancient Mesopotamia*, pp. 88–90, 102; Homer, ch. 2.

[99] Leemans, *Old-Babylonian Merchant*, p. 15. Several problems in mathematical texts explained the computation of compound interest. See also Oppenheim, *Ancient Mesopotamia*, pp. 306–7.

[100] Compare Johns, chs. 4, 16–18, 20, 22–23, 25–29; Driver and Miles, 1, pt. 3, chs. 2–3, 5, 9–11.

[101] Homer, ch. 2, esp. pp. 25–26.

interest rate fluctuations must have existed.[102] Rules for the conduct of business were not incorporated in manuals, nor was the economy as such described or analyzed. The economy was not yet perceived as a system. Nor had laissez faire a voice, as in China.

Given the conditions described and the recognition of some economic relationships, such as that between plenty and price, it might be anticipated that texts expounding economic principles or relationships would have been developed. Several conditions militated against such development, however. The existence of an underlying economic system of a mixed sort seems not to have been recognized. There existed no body or class with an interest in or a responsibility for formulating explanations of behavioral systems such as an economy; such interest lay outside the concern even of scribes. A spirit of inquiry untrammeled by the "ever-present activity of gods and spirits," such as animated the Greeks, had not developed in Mesopotamia or in Egypt to make apparent the economic system that underlay a people's economic behavior.[103] Their interest and approaches remained essentially ad hoc and immediate in character and neglectful of underlying systems and principles. Hence, although their empirical world was developed enough to reveal at least the rudiments of an economic system, neither in Mesopotamia nor in Egypt was the system perceived and used as a basis for policy.

Ethical problems were recognized, however, along with the need to keep law in line "with changed social, economic or political conditions," although merchant ethical standards were high.[104] "The very presence" of great organizations in the Mesopotamian city seems to have created an "equilibrium of forces and an over-all harmony that endowed the city with longevity which the Greek *polis* could not achieve."[105] The establishment of a system of weights and measures and regulatory codes reinforced the ethical content of custom[106] perhaps as balance among the classes composing Mesopotamian society.[107]

[102] Ibid., ch. 2.

[103] E.g., see Wilson, *The Burden of Egypt*, pp. 313, 116; Henri Frankfort and H. A. Frankfort, ch. 8; also Margueron, p. 178. On the scribes see Oppenheim, *Ancient Mesopotamia*, pp. 126, 248–82, 298.

[104] Oppenheim, *Ancient Mesopotamia*, pp. 231, also pp. 89–90, 92 on ethical standards.

[105] Ibid., p. 114.

[106] Ibid., pp. 107, 158.

[107] On the class structure see, e.g., Diakonoff.

3

Early Indian Economic Thought

Chanakya (i.e., Kauṭilya): "So! Who dares
to challenge Chandragupta—while I live."
Vishakadatta, *The Signet Ring of Rakshasa*

Most representative of economic thought in ancient India is the
Arthaśāstra attributed to Kauṭilya, minister to Chandragupta, founder of
the Maurya Empire, a work reenforced by the *Dharmaśāstra* attributed
to Manu that assumed final form after the second century B.C.[1] Attention
will be devoted mainly to the work associated with Kauṭilya's name rather
than to Manu's which deals with "dharma," a comprehensive term embracing a variety of conduct-determining factors issuing out of dharma
with emphasis upon duties rather than upon administration. Kauṭilya was
the first to assign a higher place to artha (i.e., to wealth, etc.) than to
dharma.[2]

While the precise identity of Kauṭilya and the state about which he
wrote, together with other details of the work attributed to him, are
somewhat enveloped in uncertainty, the economic content of the
Arthaśāstra is quite informative respecting economic practice and thought
in Northern India in the last third of the last millennium B.C.[3] This work
"marks the culmination of a long period of speculation on matters which

[1] See my *Indian Economic Thought*, chs. 3–4, and my "Arthaśāstra Economics"
in *Administration and Economic Development in India*, ed. Ralph Braibanti and
Joseph J. Spengler, ch. 8. For convenience I shall write Kauṭilya instead of other
spellings of his name.

[2] See my *Indian Economic Thought*, pp. 55–59; also A. B. Keith, *A History of
Sanskrit Literature*.

[3] I rely upon R. P. Kangle, *The Kauṭilīya Arthaśāstra*. Pt. 2 consists of Kangle's
English translation of the Sanskrit original (i.e., pt. 1); my references to books,
sections, paragraphs, and pages are generally to pt. 2. Pt. 3 constitutes Kangle's
introduction to the study of the *Arthaśāstra*, its origin, date, sources, style,
meaning, along with the many critical studies made of the *Arthaśāstra* since its
first publication in 1909.

form the subject-matter of this śāstra, not its starting point."[4] The text "has principally conditions in Northern India in view."[5] Kangle concludes that "there is no convincing reason why this work should not be regarded as the work of Kauṭilya, who helped Chandragupta to come to power in Magadha,"[6] but he did not write it to instruct Chandragupta or "to describe the constitutional and legal setup obtaining in his Empire."[7] The attribution of the *Arthaśāstra* to Kauṭilya, the traditional master of Indian statecraft, has been compared with the attribution of comparable materials to Moses, Confucius, and others in keeping with the ancient practice of attributing a body of material of multiauthorship to a charismatic author.[8] The *Arthaśāstra* contains the work of at least three hands, among them Kauṭilya. It is "representative of the best of generations of thinkers" and sums up "ancient Indian beliefs about the state with an authority which no individual creation could possess."[9] While its economic content overlaps in some measure that of *Dharmaśāstra* and related literature, the *Arthaśāstra* appears to represent well a bureaucratic vision of the economy between say 300 B.C. and A.D. 300, with emphasis upon administration rather than theory and analysis.[10]

The *Arthaśāstra*, often included in the category of political works of which Machiavelli's *The Prince* is the best known representative, was designed to guide the rulers and overcome centrifugal forces, a task requiring (inter alia) that as a young man the future ruler study "economics" under the guidance of government department heads (1.5.8). For "economics," together with the "science of politics" and philosophy and the three Vedas, constituted *all* the sciences (1.2.1, 2; also 1.2.4, 11).[11] The content of the *Arthaśāstra* therefore is very comprehensive. Most of it has to do with administrative and related problems, with the duties of

[4]Ibid., pt. 3, p. 10. See also ibid., pp. 55, 57–58, 114, 207, 273.

[5]Ibid., p. 115.

[6]Ibid., p. 106.

[7]Ibid., p. 108.

[8]See A. L. Basham's introduction to T. R. Trautmann, *Kauṭilīya and the Arthaśāstra*, pp. x–xi.

[9]Trautmann, *Kauṭilīya*, p. 187.

[10]See ibid.; also my *Indian Economic Thought*, and Radhakrishna Choudhary, *Kauṭilya's Political Ideas and Institutions*, esp. chs. 1–2, 6, 8–9. See also Kangle, 3: 12–16.

[11]There was no term in Sanskrit for "economics" as such. In the *Arthaśāstra*, śāstra, "the science" of *artha* or "wealth" deals with what pertains to the sustenance of men, especially agriculture, cattle-rearing, and trade (1.2.1–4; 15.1.1). In 1.2.11 there is reference to "investigations, by means of reasoning . . . [of] material gain and loss in economics." According to 1.4.1 "agriculture, cattle-rearing and trade . . . constitute economics" and are "beneficial, as they yield grains, cattle, money, forest produce and labour." "Through them, the (king) brings un-

heads of governmental departments, with rules for the guidance of the king and the bureaucracy, with the conduct of legal transactions (e.g., law suits, inheritance, nonpayment of debts, employer-employee relations, deposits, sales, transfer of ownership, etc.), with technical aspects of many public enterprises, with military affairs and foreign relations, and with taxation. Here and there, however, economic topics are touched upon, though not in terms of explicit systematic theory, but on the assumption that material wealth constituted the basis for "spiritual good and sensual pleasures" and the main pillar of the state (1.7.6–7). Precisely what Kautilya meant is not always clear, with the result that a translator of the *Arthaśāstra* as of Chinese, Mesopotamian, and other ancient works or documents may, if under the sway of modern economic nomenclature, find more precise economic sense in ancient works than is really there. One may need, therefore, to study the works of ancient grammarians, of whom the Indian grammarian Panini (mid-fifth century B.C.) was outstanding, in order to avoid misinterpretation.

Of the 15 books constituting the *Arthaśāstra*, Books 2 and 5 deal most fully with the functioning and regulation of the economy—Book 2 with the activities of the heads of the many departments of government and the modes of their operation, and Book 5 (see 5.2) with replenishment of the treasury (dealt with also in 2.6–8 and touched upon in 8.4.49) and the salaries of state servants (5.3). Much attention is devoted to administrative, regulative, and other details such as weights, measures, and coinage (2.12; 2.19–20; 4.4.20), animal slaughter (2.26), animal rations (2.15 and 2.29–31), and food allowances for males, lower classes, women, children, slaves (2.15), legal transactions (Bk.3), and the conduct of military operations (Bks. 9–14).

A vision underlay the concept of *arthaśāstra* (i.e., science of wealth), one of the four "sciences" on which the business of government rested, a science closely related to "political science." This vision embraced a predominantly rural, bureaucratic, and centralized state, albeit one with a great deal of local autonomy (though less temple-economy than developed later on), with a population whose class structure was based on the four varnas, each of which was almost exclusively responsible for certain economic, political, and social functions. Underlying this state was a quite complicated economy resting on both a bureaucracy and private enterprise, much of it under guild rule. It is to this economy, examined below, that Kautilya's economic views relate.

Kautilya defined what amounts to the characteristics of an optimum state or region.

---

der his sway his own party as well as the party of the enemies, by the (use of the) treasury and the army." (1.4.2). See also my *Indian Economic Thought*, p. 63.

Possessed of strong positions in the centre and at the frontiers, capable of sustaining itself and others in times of distress, easy to protect, providing excellent (means of) livelihood, malevolent towards enemies, uneven land, thorns, bands, wild animals, deer and forest tribes, charming, endowed with agricultural land, mines, material forests and elephant forests, beneficial to cattle, beneficial to men, with protected pastures, rich to animals, not depending on rain for water, provided with water-routes and land-routes, with valuable, manifold and plenty of commodities, capable of bearing fines and taxes, with farmers devoted to work, with a wise master, inhabited mostly by the lower *varnas*, with men loyal and honest,—these are excellences of a country (6.1.8).

His vision of the national economy as portrayed in the *Arthaśāstra*—a vision complementary to his vision of the national polity and its development—reenforced his interest in the orderly planning of settlements in the countryside (2.1.1–39; 7.11), of the layouts of cities (2.4.1–32), and the physical ordering of the economy.

Since the *Arthaśāstra* is concerned with the effective performance of a country's polity and economy, many rules and counsels are laid down. Among those by which the King needed to be guided if a state and its economy were to serve a people well Kauṭilya included the following.

In the happiness of the subjects lies the happiness of the King and in what is beneficial to the subjects his own benefit. What is dear to himself is not beneficial to the King, but what is dear to the subjects is beneficial (to him).

Therefore, being ever active, the King should carry out the management of material well-being. The root of material well-being is activity, of material disaster its reverse.

In the absence of activity, there is certain destruction of what is obtained and of what is not yet received. By activity reward is obtained, and one also secures abundance of riches.[12]

The economy described and prescribed for by Kauṭilya was essentially a state-operated and/or regulated economy, but with some scope for guild control (4.1) and private ownership[13]—a mixture the complexity of whose problems was limited by the fact that the principal sources of livelihood were agriculture, cattletending, and trade, with arts and crafts playing a secondary role (1.4.1, 2; 1.3.8).[14] The conduct of economic operations by the state is described in detail in Book 2 devoted to the "activity of the

[12]*Arthaśāstra*, 1.19.34–36.
[13]Ibid., 3:185.
[14]The duties prescribed for the four varnas and four stages of life are described in 1.3.1–17.

heads of departments" and constituting one-fourth of the *Arthaśāstra*. While there was only limited scope for private enterprise in industry, crafts apparently were operated under guild auspices (e.g., see 4.1; also 2.14).[15] Private ownership of land and other property was more common (e.g., cf. 2.1.7–10; 3.1; 3.5–10) but not immune to regulation and to encroachment by the state.[16] Nor were the larger properties owned by temples immune to state interests.[17]

Kauṭilya emphasized the dependence of a state's strength upon the extent of its population and manpower (7.11.23–25), its activity (1.19.35–36), and the effectiveness with which a state's population was used. "From the capacity for doing work is the ability of a person judged. And in accordance with their ability" (1.8.28–29). He believed productive activity to be correlated both with reward and with the absence of diversions from such activity. For example, wages and salaries were somewhat correlated with the productivity and quality of the work done (e.g., see 2.23; 2.28; 2.29; 2.1.22; 3.13; 5.3). He indicated, however, that members of the lower castes or varnas might be more useful for some purposes than members of higher varnas (6.1.8; 7.11.21).

Kauṭilya lay down rules for the distribution of remuneration when work was done jointly or in cooperative undertakings, as when several priests cooperated in a sacrifice (3.14).[18] He indicated that while the simple pleasures of country people reduced the fatigue caused by their work, parks and halls for recreation obstructed work and the flow of goods and taxes (2.1.33.–34; 8.4.23).

Kauṭilya devoted considerable attention to taxation and a state's financial support, identifying over 60 sources of revenue—mainly crown property, land tolls, imports, and fines—and eleven categories of expenditure, much of it in kind. He distinguished between ordinary and emergency taxation but adhered to traditional doctrine—that taxing power is limited, should not be used to excess, and should be graduated in impact—endorsed economy in public expenditure and revenue collection, and stressed the importance of what amounts to social overhead capital and material reserves against public calamities (e.g., war, famine).[19]

[15] Kangle, pt 3, p. 185.

[16] Ibid., pp. 168–73, 226–28.

[17] Ibid., pp. 157–58.

[18] Law respecting joint enterprise is described as growing out of such cooperative sharing. Rules for the distribution of joint remuneration found expression in commercial arithmetic as did interest problems. Indian commercial arithmetic dates back to Kauṭilya's time and earlier. Kauṭilya declared that after tonsure the prince "should learn the use of the alphabet and arithmetic" (1.5.7). See my *Indian Economic Thought*, pp. 77, 79.

[19] *Arthaśāstra*, 2.6, 2.8, 5.2; my *Indian Economic Thought*, pp. 72–73. Kauṭilya identified 40 modes of embezzlement (2.8.20).

Kauṭilya was alert to the significance of man's economic self-interest, his sensitivity to differences in rewards and penalties as well as to his awareness of differences in risk, uncertainty, and other circumstances surrounding loans, modes of trade, etc. He was alert as well to the association of productivity and reward.

Kauṭilya approved lending at interest other than in the form of grain loans, approved interest maxima which reflected differences in risk, uncertainty, and circumstances surrounding loans; they ranged from 1.25 percent monthly to 20 or more percent monthly on loans connected with high-risk trade.[20] Six types of interest were identified. Kauṭilya related the salaries of state employees to the significance of what they did and the wages of workers in industry roughly to their productivity. Rules for the distribution of remuneration when work was done jointly were laid down and expressed in commercial arithmetic. In short, we find in the *Arthaśāstra* a more sophisticated and all-inclusive vision of the national economy than is found in comparable writings in China or Mesopotamia—a vision, moreover, that is complementary to his vision of the national polity, its development, and its problems.[21]

Kauṭilya's views on man's economic behavior, on his response to economic penalties and rewards, are found mainly in his discussion of pricing, resource use (e.g., 2.24 on agricultural practice), and price and wage regulation. He either did not grasp fully the functions of competition, or he feared that it would not be unconstrained enough to settle prices at cost plus what amounts to reasonable profit in keeping with the conditions surrounding an activity (e.g., see 2.12, 2.16–18; 2.21; 2.23–25; 2.28; 4.2). Or he may have supposed that, given the state of supply in relation to demand, competition might increase price unduly (3.9.5). The rationing role of price is not discussed.

He dealt with the fixation of wages in particular industries as well as with penalties for poor performance (2.24, 28–29; 3.1.22; 3.12.27–28; 3.13–27; 3.14.1, 8; 4.1.5, 7). In his account of the bureaucratic salary structure Kauṭilya indicated great variation in the salary structure and in the degree to which bureaucratic salaries exceeded the annual wages of ordinary workers (5.3). He also indicated that the aggregate wage and salary bill of a state should not exceed one-fourth of its revenue (5.3.1).

Money-lending was a lawful occupation in India even before Kauṭilya wrote, as in nearly all of the ancient world.[22] However, opprobrium at-

---

[20] Ibid., 2.1.13–15; 3.11–12; 5.3.42–44; 7.11–12.

[21] See my *Indian Economic Thought*, esp. ch. 3. Kauṭilya *Arthaśāstra*, esp. bks. 1–3.

[22] None of the legal codes of the ancient world outside of the *Bible* contains laws proscribing lending at interest, although in some cases the rate was fixed. See Hillel Gonioran, "The Biblical Law Against Loans on Interest," *Journal of Near*

tached to the charging of excessive or usurious interest. The allowable rates varied widely in keeping with the commonly understood variables in risk, a condition to be considered by judges when determining if a rate was excessive (3.11.3).

3.11.1 "One *pana* and a quarter is the lawful rate of interest per month on one hundred *panas*,[23] five *panas* for purposes of trade, ten *panas* for those going through forests, twenty *panas* for those going by sea (3.11.2). For one charging or making another charge a rate beyond that, the punishment shall be the lowest fine for violence, for witnesses, each one of them half the fine (3.11.3). If, however, the king is unable to ensure protection, the (judge) shall take into consideration the usual practice among creditors and debtors."

This paragraph appears in section 63 dealing with the "nonpayment of debts." The paragraph that follows deals with interest somewhat in the guise of profit and profit-sharing in agriculture (3.11.4–5). The precise meaning of Kautilya's statements are not always beyond dispute.[24]

Kautilya's approach and concerns in his *Arthasāstra* precluded his envisioning an economy dominated by competition and a resulting economic flexibility. His concern was the instruction of the ruler of a quite small kingdom lying within the borders of India, with emphasis upon its governance.[25] His economic opinions usually must have reflected what had become settled practice or had won the approval of earlier authors or authorities on whom Kautilya had drawn. His work, though prepared for a hypothetical ruler and often marked by exceptions on his part to what earlier authorities had said, probably includes only a limited amount of economic matter original with Kautilya.

B. Manu's Dharmaśāstra

Most important of the *dharmaśāstras* is the Manusmriti, ascribed to Manu and put into final form between 200 B.C. and A.D. 200; it is the first to come down to us in entirety. It probably was influenced by Kautilya's work as well as by authors upon whom Kautilya drew.[26] The

Eastern Studies 30:127–34. According to Neal M. Soss, freeing the individual from pressing economic concerns and competitive consumption freed energy for noneconomic uses and made energy available for "serving the divine will," the "primary function of the Hebrew nation in the world." See "Old Testament Law and Economic Society," *Journal of the History of Ideas* 34:343–44.

[23] Presumably this rate is on secured loans. On variability in risk on loans ranging from the secured loan to those connected with high-risk trade see *Arthasāstra*, 2.1.13–15; 3.11–12; 5.3.42–44; 7.11–12.

[24] See Kangle's note to his translation, pt. 2, p. 261 n.

[25] See Kangle, pt. 3, pp. 63–65, 120–22, 278–79.

[26] See my *Indian Economic Thought*, ch. 4, on Manu's work.

Dharmaśāstra is distinct in origin and scope from the *Arthaśāstra* which "is primarily concerned with rulership, which involves questions of administration, including the administration of law and the punishment of criminals"—subjects with which the "Dharmaśāstra" in its origin had nothing to do."[27] The latter had to do with expounding "duties or practices sanctified by custom" from the standpoint, not of a lawgiver but of "a moral preceptor who lays down duties and regards deviations from them as sins to be expiated by the individual himself rather than as crimes to be punished by the state."[28] "The fact is that the essence of the difference lies in the circumstance that Dharmaśāstra is in its origin addressed to the ordinary individual and concerned with strict observance of duties by him, while Arthaśāstra is primarily concerned with the administration of a state by its ruler." The "few rules on law and administration which we find in the early Dharmaśāstra works were derived by them from some other source" than the Vedic schools "in which the Dharmasmastra works arose."[29] This source "was quite obviously the works on Nitiśāstra or Arthaśāstra."[30]

In his *Dharmaśāstra* Manu drew upon the extant arthaśāstra and dharmasutra literature and incorporated into his work much of what was found therein and had been tested by experience. Like his forerunners, Manu did not engage in explicit economic analysis, though he did include considerable legal and related matter which treated of economic transactions.[31] His rules, however, epitomized as well as helped to shape Hindu economic regulatory thought bearing upon the occupations, privileges, and duties of the four classes or varnas as well as upon lending at interest, price and wage fixing, and the collection of revenue. Security of property was assured to others than the wicked and the Shudra (i.e. members of the lowest varna).[32]

Manu was much less favorable to economic activity than Kauṭilya. Un-

---

[27] Kangle, pt. 3, p. 13.

[28] Ibid., p. 13.

[29] Ibid., p. 14, *artha* or "king's laws" are distinguished from "dharma laws." Ibid., p. 224.

[30] Ibid., p. 15. On Nitiśāstra, "the science laying down conduct proper for the ruler" and the overcoming of anarchy resulting when "men were overcome by delusion, greed, love of pleasures and other base passions," see pp. 3–6, esp. p. 5. See also pp. 269–70 on the similarity of Kauṭilya's theory of human behavior to that of Machiavelli, Hobbes, and Thucydides.

[31] See my *Indian Economic Thought*, pp. 82–89. I have used G. Bühler's translation, *The Laws of Manu*, in *Sacred Books of the East*, vol. 25. Of the sixteen types of legal transactions or relationships dealt with by Kauṭilya at least eleven had to do with economic issues. See *Arthaśāstra*, bk. 3.

[32] See my *Indian Economic Thought*, p. 89.

like Kautilya, Manu made piety superior to wealth and wealth to pleasure and ruled that wealth was not to be attained at the expense of "virtue" (IV, 176; VII, 151–52). Agriculture is sometimes denigrated, as are trade and money lending (IV, 5–6, 28–29, 91–94; IX, 257). "Superintending mines (or factories) of any sort" or "executing great mechanical works" (XI, 64) is described as an offense. The major economic roles—agriculture, cattletending, trade, moneylending and common labor and service—were assigned to the two lowest varnas. (I, 88–91; IV 2–6).[33] The varna rules blunted incentive and greatly reduced interoccupational mobility.

Receipt of interest was subject to constraints though sanctioned. Maximum monthly rates of 2, 3, 4, and 5 percent, respectively, were allowed on unpledged loans to Brahmans, Kshatriyas, Vaishyas, and Shudras (V, 141–43). Higher rates were permitted on sea-voyage loans and risky land-voyage loans (VIII, 157). While higher rates were permitted, this was only under exceptional conditions. Debtors were subjected to a 5 percent penalty for nonpayment when due (VIII, 139).[34]

In practice only a Vaishya was permitted to lend (VIII, 410). However, a Brahman or Kshatriya might lend if he were in distress and needed money "for sacred purposes" but even then only "to a very sinful man at a small interest" (X, 117). Indian interest rates did not differ greatly from those reported in Mesopotamia and the Mediterranean world.[35]

Manu laid down conditions respecting the rights and obligations of workmen and officers employed by the king and others. The daily maintenance and pay presented was in proportion to a position and the importance of the work done and ranged from something like a base minimum to an amount six times as high (VII, 126–27; also X, 124). Local officers were allotted income-yielding land or revenue (VII, 119). Workmen who failed to perform their assigned tasks were subject to penalities (VIII, 215, 235, 240–41, 243, 396–97). Unlike Kautilya (3.13.33), Manu did not subject an employer to a fine for nonpayment of wages.

Manu subjected the activities of traders to regulations. They were required to behave honestly, not cheat on prices, or charge excessive prices, adulterate products, or give short measure (VIII, 203, 403; IX, 257, 286–87). The king fixed the rates for the purchase or sale of all marketable goods, often with the help of experts along with weights and measures (VIII, 401–2; VII, 157, 403–9). Completed transactions found unsatisfactory were subject to recision (VIII, 222–23, 228).[36]

---

[33] See my *Indian Economic Thought*, pp. 90–92.
[34] See ibid., pp. 92–93.
[35] Sidney Homer, *A History of Interest Rates*, pp. 29–32, 40–43, 64.
[36] Cf. Kautilya on valid and invalid transactions (3.1.2–16).

Manu allowed the king his due for protecting his subjects as he would a worker's, but he attached less importance to revenue and the treasury than Kauṭilya did (VII, 128, 156–57; VIII, 170–72; IX, 294–97). Moreover, he indicated that the king should hold his imposition within prescribed limits.[37] Manu attached less importance to capital formation, state development, and population growth, and more to charity, than did Kauṭilya. Presumably, given good government and security of life and property, development would take place automatically. He described as an optimum country in which to settle one "which is chiefly (inhabited) by Aryans, not subject to epidemic diseases (or similar troubles), and pleasant, when the Vassals are obedient" and the people easily find their livelihood (VII, 69). Given such a kingdom and good government a king easily prospered (VII, 110–24).

Manu had in view an essentially static and quasiascriptive society in which only quite limited scope was allowed economically creative individuals and in which the augmentation of output was assigned only secondary importance. Manu warned that whereas oppressive kings were in danger of their lives, a king who governed his kingdom well easily prospered (VII, 97–104, 110–24).

Manu's discussion was less systematic than Kauṭilya's. He was less concerned with economic matters and economic development. Manu put greater store upon hierarchy than Kauṭilya did and failed to appreciate as did Kauṭilya the value of the contributions of the Shudra, that is, the lowest Varna. Kauṭilya was more alert to economic values, incentive, more practical, less bound by religious belief.

[37] See my *Indian Economic Thought*, pp. 95–96.

4

Beginnings in China

*Economically, the Chinese have been practically
free. Except for a few laws regulating consumption
the people have been able to do as they pleased. . . .
While the Confucian school has been in favor of
social rules and legislation, the Confucianists . . .
have not been extremists either for or against regulation. According to the classical teachings restrictions should not be put on trade. . . .*
E. D. Thomas, *Chinese Political Thought*

A. Introduction

While Confucius was preceded "by long centuries of religious and ethical
development," the archaeological record of China has been much less
rich in written materials than that of (say) Mesopotamia. Presumably the
early written literature in China has not survived. The materials on which
it was written could not survive as did those in use in Mesopotamia and
Egypt.[1] Even so, the proto-Confucian literature seems "inimical to the
mythic, the fantastic, and the ecstatic," reflecting an "image of an all-embracing, sociopolitical and cultural order in which men relate to each
other in terms of a structured system of roles—familial and political."[2]

While concern respecting economic behavior and its regulation found
some expression in Chinese schools of philosophy, the Confucian and Legalist schools were dominant during much of the pre-Christian millennium, although the Confucian was destined to become ascendant. These

[1] Benjamin I. Schwartz, "The Age of Transcendence," *Daedalus* 104: 57–68. On
China before 1000 B.C. see Ho Ping-ti, *The Cradle of the East*.

[2] Schwartz, "Transcendence," p. 58. On thought antedating Confucius see
Liang Ch'i-ch'ao, *History of Chinese Political Thought*. "All the great thinkers of
China lived during the three hundred years between 530 and 230 B.C., the
Golden Age of Chinese Philosophy," which ranged from the Taoists on the extreme left to the Legalists on the extreme right (pp. 23–31, 34–37). On pre-Con-
fucian thought see also Wu Kuo-cheng, *Ancient Chinese Political Theories*, chs.
1–3, 9; E. D. Thomas, *Chinese Political Thought*; Liang Ch'i-ch'ao, *History of
Chinese Political Thought*, ch. 1; H. A. Giles, *Confucianism and Its Rivals*, chs.
1–2.

two schools, along with the minor philosophical schools, were less formal than the Greeks, and stressed man's moral qualities, together with human affairs, rather than knowledge as such, methodology, epistemology, logic, or model states;[3] yet they manifested an understanding of the response of price to variations in supply and demand though not in a systematic sense. Moreover, if Creel's finding is correct, the Chinese schools flourished in an area larger and more extensive than that of other ancient civilizations, a condition reflected in Confucius's idealization of the early part of the Chou period (1122?–256 B.C.)[4] as well as in the Confucian conception of *li* as designating "all the institutions and relationships, both political and social, which made for harmonious living in a Confucian Society"—a conception quite different from the Legalist's *fa* or law.[5] The greater emphasis of the Legalists upon utilitarianism—in the form of satisficing rather than of maximizing as the behavioral target—sharply distinguished this school both from the quite realist Confucian school[6] and the Taoist and lesser philosophical schools.

Chinese economic thought during the period covered found expression not in treatises on economic relations and behavior as such but mainly in general discussions of human behavior and in policy recommendations and policies themselves. Much more of what may be called economic thought is to be found in the writings of policy-oriented Legalists than in the broader visions of a social order found in Confucian teachings. Inasmuch as most of what may be called early Chinese economic thought is to be found in Confucian and Legalist writings, particularly in the latter, attention will be confined essentially to the views of these two schools.

The Confucian and the Legalist schools were almost diametrically opposed in their conceptions of human nature and the essentials of social and economic organization. Han Fei Tzŭ (c. 280 B.C.–233 B.C.), initially a student of Taoism and Confucianism (under Hsün Tzŭ) and subsequently "perfecter" and expositor of the ideas and policies of the Legalist

---

[3] Fung Yu-lan, *A History of Chinese Philosophy*, 1: 1–6.

[4] Herrlee G. Creel, *The Origins of Statecraft in China*; also Schwartz, "Transcendence"; Lin Yutang, *The Wisdom of Confucius*; Chen Huan-chang, *The Economic Principles of Confucius and His School*.

[5] Derk Bodde and Clarence Morris, *Law in Imperial China*, pp. 19–27; Lin Yutang, *Wisdom of Confucius*, ch. 8.

[6] "Food and drink and sex are the great desires of mankind, and death and poverty and suffering are the great fears or aversions of mankind. Therefore, desires and fear (or greed and hatred) are the great motive forces of the human heart." As translated by Lin Yutang, *Wisdom of Confucius*, p. 235. Confucius's main orthodox continuator was more optimistic, believing human nature good if not disordered by a bad environment. Ibid., ch. 11. See also Chen Huan-chang, pp. 135–58.

school,[7] describes human nature as evil and "punishment and favor" as the "two handles" with which "the enlightened ruler controls his ministers."[8] For morality, religion, and ceremony the Legalist school had little or no use, nor was it interested in the lives of private individuals except as they affected the interests of the ruling class and the functioning of a strong, awe-inspiring, bureaucratic, and centralized state.[9] The Confucians rejected a political order neglectful of the role of "heaven" and based on sanctions of physical coercion instead of on spiritual-moral authority. Schwartz summarizes Confucian teaching as follows:[10]

> In an ideal Confucian society, where the behavior of the ruling class is based on an internalized *li*, neither offensive military undertakings nor sanctions or penal law will be necessary. This does not, as some say, mean that government becomes wholly an affair of moral influence and moral example. There is in Confucius and Mencius a concept of state policy. The state policy consists, however, mainly of negative injunctions. A ruling class governed by an internalized *li* will refrain from imposing heavy burdens of taxation and levees of corvée labor. It will not indulge in excessive public works projects for purposes of display and will avoid wars wherever possible. It will practice light government and thus leave the agricultural population free to produce its own livelihood. The socially conditioned masses, in their turn, can be expected to respond to the moral example of those above only when their livelihood is assured. Here again we see that, while Confucianism by no means precludes the possibility that worthy individuals from below may enter the ranks of superior men, the assumption remains that the great mass of peasants will not be able to acquire the cultivation required. Given proper social conditions, however, they can be led to practice those rules of social life that should govern their own existence.

In sum, Confucianism introduced and sustained a spirit of laissez faire in Chinese social thought—a spirit that both militated against the permanent ascendancy of Legalist controls and Confucianized law and the

[7] Fung Yu-lan, chs. 12–13; Joseph Needham, *Science and Civilisation in China*, 2, ch. 12.

[8] Lin Yutang, *Wisdom of Confucius*, p. 31.

[9] Ibid., pp. 6–8. Han Fei Tzŭ drew on the Legalist *Book of Lord Shang*, also concerned with politics and with the nature and use of power. See also Fung Yu-lan, 1, ch. 13; *The Complete Works of Han Fei Tzŭ*; Liang Ch'i-ch'ao, *La conception*, ch. 7. See also Liang En-yuan, "The Legalist School Was the Product of Great Social Change in the Spring and Autumn and Warring States Periods," *Chinese Studies in Philosophy* 8:4–20.

[10] Schwartz, "Transcendence," esp. p. 64.

prevailing ideology. The Confucianism that triumphed did so in part, however, through its borrowing from its philosophic rivals and becoming eclectic in contrast with the less eclectic Confucianism of the founder or that of his continuator, Mencius. Taoism also contributed to the acceptance of laissez faire.[11]

We shall first review developments of Confucian and minor-school thought, then examine the Legalist views which were much more economic in character, and finally note the essential ascendancy of the Confucian school toward the end of the first millennium B.C. However, before turning to the views expressed by members of non-Legalist schools, note may be taken of the composition of the Chinese economy and its predominantly agricultural character. Fung Yu-lan even identifies an "Agricultural School" which advocated a kind of agricultural egalitarianism.[12] Moreover, of the eight objects of government, "food" (especially grain) was ranked first, and "media of exchange" (e.g., textiles and metals), essential to markets and the distribution of products, was ranked second, according to the authors of *Han Shu*, a work rivaled only by its great predecessor and model, the illustrious "Historical Record," the *Shih-chi* of Ch'ien Ssù-ma (and his father).[13] In *Han Shu*, moreover, are reported the quantitative and related findings of Li K'uei (ca. 400 B.C.), China's first "statistical economist," who developed a policy for increasing the yield of land, together with a system of grain storage and price stabiliza-

[11] On the triumph of Confucianism see Bodde and Morris, pp. 27–29, 498–500; Homer H. Dubs's commentaries in his 3-volume translation of Pan Ku's *Han Shu*, as *The History of the Former Han Dynasty*. See also Chen Huan-chang, pp. 168–82. On the Taoist defense of complete liberty and the goodness of nature, together with Taoist criticism of Confucian and other schools, see especially the works of Lao Tzŭ and Chuang Tzŭ, discussed in Fung Yu-lan, 1, chs. 8, 10. After 207 B.C. the aristocracy lost power and the Confucian conception that imperial authority was limited by custom became ascendant. See Dubs in his translation of Pan Ku's work, 1:13, 15. See also "Outline of Lectures on the History of Chinese Philosophy," in *Chinese Studies in Philosophy* 8: 93.

[12] Fung Yu-lan, 1:144–245. On the development of agriculture in China with representative discussions, see Mabel Ping-Hua Lee, *The Economic History of China with Special Reference to Agriculture*. On the role of agriculture in production see Chen Huan-chang, chs. 20–21.

[13] See Nancy Lee Swann's annotated translation of sections of Pan Ku's *Han Shu* 24, under the title *Food & Money in Ancient China*, pp. 110–12. The *Han Shu* was produced in the first century, A.D. (p. 3). It includes much information on grain, grain storage, money, trade and markets, measures, occupations, land use and ownership, pricing and prices, monetary phenomena, economic regulations, etc. See also Homer H. Dubs's 3-volume translation of the chapters from *Han Shu* dealing with the former Han Dynasty and the Memoir of Wang Mang, cited in n. 11, above.

tion, in the little feudatory of Wei (403–387 B.C.).[14] This system will be dealt with below in conjunction with the Legalists who were particularly interested in storage and price stabilization.

B. Confucianism and Minor Schools

Although commerce, agriculture, and economic administration were of importance in and before Confucius's time,[15] Confucius himself was not inclined to single them out for praise. Indeed, while favorable to laissez faire and while not wholly neglectful of concern with economic topics, the Confucian school did not emphasize economic questions.[16] Confucius's real concern was with social organization, together with ethics, politics, and societal harmony, rather than with such subjects as the dominance of Chinese history by the agricultural conquest of China and the business of periodically overcoming local land scarcity.[17] However, Chinese institutions, metaphor, and societal organization, together with its long persisting feudal character, reflected China's agricultural base.[18]

---

[14] Swann, pp. 136–44 from *Han Shu*, and her notes and comments, pp. 21, 25, 54–58, 67 n., 428. Liang Ch'i-ch'ao (*Chinese Political Thought*, pp. 185–87) describes these findings—the statistical analysis of yield and net return, together with the price equalization and stabilization program—as the first Chinese economic policy to be based on "a careful and systematic study of actual conditions." In his commentaries on Wang Mang's reforms Dubs indicates that while the equalization policy may have worked in the small state of Wei in 424–387 B.C., it did not work in the first century B.C. See Dubs's translation of Pan Ku's work, 3: 530–34.

[15] Swann, passim; Fung Yu-lan, 1: 50; J. M. Treistman, *The Pre-history of China*; Chen Huan-chang, ch. 1.

[16] See Chen Huan-chang, pt. 1; Lewis Maverick, ed., *Economic Dialogues in Ancient China: The Kuan Tzŭ* (hereafter referred to as *The Kuan Tzŭ*), pp. 389–400; Needham, 2, ch. 9. According to Liang Ch'i-ch'ao *History of Chinese Political Thought*, pp. 185–92, whereas the Taoists played down material wants, the Legalists emphasized production while the Confucian school was more concerned with distribution. See also Chen Huan-chang, bks. 4, 7.

[17] Bodde and Morris, pt. 1, ch. 1. The "agricultural conquest of China took nearly four thousand years" writes René Grousset, *The Rise and Splendour of the Chinese Empire*, p. 21. See also T. R. Tregear, *A Geography of China*, chs. 2–3; John K. Fairbank, *The United States and China*. In traditional China agriculturalists were considered the only true producers and supporters of the rulers who, "freed from material wants, devoted themselves to the elevation of men." "Each segment thus performed the role best suited to it." See Y. Chu Wang, "Ideas and Men in Traditional China," *Journal of Oriental Studies*. Monumenta Serica, 19: 210–75, esp. p. 216.

[18] Feudalism antedated Confucius, flourishing under the Chou dynasty after 1100 B.C. until the sixth century B.C., after which social, political, economic, and

This feudal structure was congenial to chivalry in war[19] as well as to Confucian principles, so much so that Confucians advocated restoration of the original feudalism of Chou as a solution for the chaos and evils of the Warring States period. Confucianism, however, transcended feudalism,[20] envisaging a society of intellectually unequal members, a "hierarchy of intelligence over ignorance," in which stress was put upon moral cultivation rather than upon material abundance—a society in which man-to-man relationships were governed by a body of elaborate rules designed to promote "harmony by means of self-abnegation and consideration for others,"[21] and in which man's behavior was conditioned by social institutions rather than by his own innate qualities.

The concept of man, together with the factors differentiating men, their improvability, perfectability, and entitlement, varied over time and with schools.[22] Insofar as man's behavior tended to reflect the impact of his social environment upon his training, education, and current behavior, his behavior was subject to improvement through education and the emulation of appropriate models. Hence good example as well as good

---

technological forces began to undermine the old order and eventuate in the Warring States period (403–221 B.C.) and the subsequent unification of the country under the Ch'in and Han rulers (220 B.C.–A.D. 220). On factors affecting feudalism in China see E. S. Kirby, *Economic History of China*, pp. 54–55, 61, 72, 77, 111; also Bodde and Morris, pp. 15–17; Mabel Ping-Hua Lee. On agricultural metaphor see Wright, "The Chinese Language and Foreign Ideas," in *Studies in Chinese Thought*, p. 301.

[19] Grousset, ch. 3. See also S. B. Griffith's introduction to his translation of Sun Tzŭ, *The Art of War*, esp. pp. 30–38 on the conduct of war prior to the fifth century compared with its conduct in the fifth and fourth centuries, the period of "Warring States" separating the dissolution of feudal society from the initial unification of China under the Legalist-dominated Ch'in dynasty (255–207 B.C.). See also W. Allyn Rickett, *Kuan Tzŭ*, pp. 220–31.

[20] Kirby, p. 72, also ch. 9. On this period see also Griffith, on Sun Tzŭ, pp. 20–29, and Derk Bodde, *China's First Unifier: A Study of the Ch'in Dynasty as Seen in the Life of Li Ssŭ (280?–208)*.

[21] Y. Chu Wang, pp. 211, 214; Ho Ping-ti, *The Ladder of Success in Imperial China*, pp. 1–6, 162; Ch'u Chai and Winberg Chai, eds., *The Sacred Books of Confucius and other Confucian Classics*, pp. 12–19. See also Hsu Cho-yun, *Ancient China in Transition*; Derk Bodde, "Harmony and Conflict in Chinese Philosophy," in Arthur F. Wright, ed., *Studies in Chinese Thought*, pp. 19–80. One may trace awareness of concern respecting the extent to which man's behavior is conditioned by social institutions rather than by his own innate qualities from Confucius through Mencius to and beyond the eleventh century A.D. Neo-Confucians.

[22] E.g., see Donald J. Munro, *The Concept of Man in Early China*.

instruction and government gave expression and support to man's benevolence and fundamental virtues.[23]

According to Lionel Giles, "jên, 'benevolence,' forms the centre and pivot of Confucian ethics."[24] Illustrative of the salutary influence of man's social environment, was that of the elementary cultural cell, the family (of which the state was in extension, and with which only monarchical government was compatible), for it was within the family that filial piety, cult of ancestors, and reverence could flourish.[25] This environment, in turn, conduced, along with populationist measures (e.g., penalty taxes, control of migration, nontyrannical government), to the growth and spread of population, a persistent governmental objective.[26]

It is to be noted that the forces which undermined feudalism also helped to undermine the so-called well-field system, a generally impractical system though very dear to Mencius (principal continuator of Confucius) who said "that this system had been practiced by virtuous rulers of former times."[27] Under this system—the Tsing Tien System—a tsing or square of land was divided into nine plots, of which the eight exterior plots were assigned to eight families, and the center plot was reserved to be worked in common, with its product destined mainly as "rent" to the proprietor or government and capable of yielding in three years a supply for one year.[28]

---

[23] Sylvie Goy-Sterboul, "Confucius, ses disciples et la population," *Population* 29 (1974) 771–94, esp. p. 774; also Lin Yutang, *Wisdom of Confucius*, ch. 9, on Confucius's views on education.

[24] See Giles's introduction to his *The Book of Mencius* (abridged), p. 14, also pp. 47, 125.

[25] Goy-Sterboul, "Confucius," p. 774; also Chu-Wang, pp. 214–15; Liang Ch'i-ch'ao, *La conception*, pp. 153–55; Chen Huan-chang, pp. 18–20, 70–72, 145–67, 328–31.

[26] Goy-Sterboul, "Confucius," pp. 776–86. On the course of Chinese population growth see pp. 775–77; John Durand, "The Population Statistics of China, A.D. 2–1953," *Population Studies* 13: 209–56; Ho Ping–ti, *Studies on the Population of China, 1368–1911*.

[27] Creel, H. G., *Chinese Thought from Confucius to Mao Tsê-tung*, p. 82; Kirby, p. 61. Taxation in keeping with Confucian principles consisted in taxation of land at a rate not exceeding one-tenth of the product. See Homer H. Dubs, *Hsüntze, The Moulder of Ancient Confucianism*, pp. 262–63; Chen Huan-chang, bk. 9. T'ang Hsiao-wen, "Why Is Hsün Tzŭ Called a Legalist?" *Chinese Studies in Philosophy* 8:21–35.

[28] E.g., see Lee, *Economic History*, pp. 33–35; Swann, *Food and Money*, pp. 25, 57, 361–63, also pp. 60, 66 on later efforts to restore the system after it had been terminated by Lord Shang. Dubs describes the *ching* system as "a dream of idealistic scholars; it had probably been tried only in a restricted area" and simple

Along with the development of weights and measures under Huang-ti after 2698 B.C., the Tsing Tien System had its beginning, thereafter undergoing elaboration and extension, together with soil classification, fallowing, and drainage improvements; it supposedly achieved maturity along with ancient Chinese civilization under the Chou dynasty, 1122–256 B.C., and developed into a family land allotment system that allowed for differences in quality of land and family size.[29] The system could not persist, however, and eventually succumbed to increasing land taxation and soil exhaustion, together with decay of imperial government, struggle for supremacy among feudal states, and rising governmental costs.[30] With conditions essential to the functioning of the Tsing Tien System no longer present, it was abolished by Shang Yang in Chin State in 350 B.C., being replaced by private ownership of land, a system that was used extensively throughout China.[31]

Of the philosophical schools, some stressed liberty and attached only limited importance to utilitarian objectives, while others stressed utilitarian objectives and assigned an important economic role to the state. Illustrative of the former, as has been shown, are Confucianism and Taoism, and of the latter, Legalism. In contrast with the Legalists who discussed government and economic activity from the viewpoint of the ruler of the state, Confucians, along with Mohists and Taoists, discussed these issues mainly "from the point of view of the people."[32] Laissez faire had virtually unqualified support at the hands of the Taoists who, however, were less concerned with economic issues than were other major schools. For example, according to Lao Tzŭ, author of the treatise on Taoism bearing his name and probably dating from the Warring States period, man "required certain social institutions in order to maintain existence" but he must control these "so that they will not go to an extreme and thus produce opposite reactions." Care must be exercised lest restric-

---

times; "if applied quite literally" as in Han China it "would have been quite impractical." The system had, however, the merit of doing away with tenancy and large land-holdings. See vol. 3 of Dubs's translation, *The History of the Former Han Dynasty*, pp. 519–21, also pp. 521–26 on Wang Mang's attempt to restore the *ching* system. See also Chen Huan-chang, ch. 26.

[29] Lee, pp. 35–45. Chen Huan-chang, ch. 26. On measurements see also Swann, pp. 360–65.

[30] Lee, pp. 45–49 on the growing number of agricultural treatises.

[31] Ibid., pp. 49–61. See also J. L. Duyvendak, *The Book of Lord Shang*, ch. 2. See also Ch'ien Ssŭ-ma, *Records of the Grand Historian of China*, translated by Burton Watson; Swann, *Food and Money*, pp. 25, 57, 60, 66, 69, 117n, 162, 361–63.

[32] Fung Yu-lan, 2: 313.

tions and laws become excessive and self-defeating. "The more restrictions and prohibitions there are in the world, the poorer the people will be. . . . The more laws are promulgated, the more thieves and bandits there will be."[33]

Lao Tzŭ also pointed to the desirability of frugality and the need to curb the desire for acquisition.[34] On Confucianism, Taoism, and laissez faire, Chuang Tzŭ (369–286? B.C.), continuator of Lao Tzŭ's work and critic even of regulatory institutions favored by Confucians, believed that political and social institutions imposed suffering on men inasmuch as institutions could not allow adequately for variation in men's tastes. Good order results spontaneously when things are let alone.[35] Whence letting mankind alone—complete liberty—was indicated.[36] "To the Taoist, Nature is absolute beauty and absolute good."[37]

A laissez faire state of economic affairs was endorsed by Ch'ien Ssŭ-ma (145–c.90 B.C.), distinguished historian, partly on the basis of his historical study (e.g., of "the biographies of the Money-makers") and the influence of Confucianism.[38] He described the distribution of natural resources in parts of China and sought to explain the ways in which money-makers had become wealthy, usually because they were apt in anticipating "what course conditions were going to take and acted accordingly," keeping "a sharp eye out for the opportunities of the times." "They gained their wealth in the secondary occupations and held on to it by investing in agriculture; they seized hold of it in times of crisis and maintained it in times of stability."[39]

---

[33] Fung Yu-lan, 1:170, 186, 187. On the individualistic philosophy of Taoism see E. R. Hughes, Chinese Philosophy in Classical Times, pt. 5. According to Lao Tzŭ, "When one is compelled to do something, the world is already beyond conquering." See Lin Yutang's translation of Lao Tzŭ's Book of Tao, bk. 2, pars. 48, 59, 57–58, in Lin Yutang, ed., The Wisdom of China and India, pp. 608, 611–14.

[34] Fung Yu-lan, Chinese Philosophy 1: 188–91.

[35] Ibid., pp. 228–29; Chen Huan-chang, pp. 42, 111, 115–16, 190–91, 722.

[36] Fung Yu-lan, pp. 229, 230. See also E. R. Hughes, chs. 13–14. Of the Chinese schools only the Taoist "abandoned the idea of hierarchical society entirely." See Ho Ping-ti, The Ladder of Success, p. 4.

[37] Liang Ch'i-ch'ao, History of Chinese Political Thought, p. 72; see also Swann, pp. 419–24.

[38] Ch'ien Ssŭ-ma, Records, pp. 333–56. The occupational pursuits of wealthy persons are also described in the Han Shu (chs. 24 and 91). See Swann, pp. 405–62, also pp. 63, 69–70, 275, 414–15, 437, 461 on resources. See also Joseph J. Spengler, "Ch'ien Ssŭ-ma, Unsuccessful Exponent of Laissez Faire," Southern Economic Journal 30: 223–43.

[39] Ch'ien Ssŭ-ma, Records, pp. 355–56, also pp. 337–41.

While an exponent of the stabilization of the price of grain and commodities through storage and distribution in times of shortage,[40] he found little use for government intervention into a people's economic affairs. Needed were farmers to produce food, artisans to supply manufactures, merchants to circulate goods, and "foresters, fishermen, miners, etc.," to exploit natural resources.

> Society obviously must have farmers before it can eat; foresters, fishermen, miners, etc., before it can make use of natural resources; craftsmen before it can have manufactured goods; and merchants before they can be distributed. But once these exist, what need is there for government directives, mobilizations of labor, or periodic assemblies? Each man has only to be left to utilize his own abilities and exert his strength to obtain what he wishes. Thus, when a commodity is very cheap, it invites a rise in price; when it is very expensive, it invites a reduction. When each person works away at his own occupation and delights in his own business then, like water flowing downward, goods will naturally flow forth ceaselessly day and night without having been summoned, and the people will produce commodities without having been asked. Does this not tally with reason? Is it not a natural result?"[41]

As noted earlier, Confucianism eventually became the paramount philosophy in ruling circles even though Confucius looked upon himself as a teacher and transmitter rather than as an originator of views and teachings designed both to make his students and followers useful to the state and to develop teachers and potential public officials.[42] Confucianism became ascendant over other schools as the political unification of China progressed and made evident the need for civil servants and for "a single system of morality and one social code," such as had been advocated in keeping with Confucian doctrine and was compatible with traditionalism and the absence of technical progress.[43] Moreover, the Confucians were better informed than others respecting old records and regulations and the task of drawing up new institutions for use in government and society. Furthermore, while Confucianism did not eliminate other schools, it did

---

[40] Ibid., p. 337. He cites the *Kuan Tzŭ* to the effect that "only when the granaries are full can people appreciate rites and obligations" (p. 336).

[41] Ibid., p. 344, also p. 345.

[42] On the relations of Confucius (551–479 B.C.) to earlier times and opinions see Fung Yu-lan, 1, chs. 2–4; also Schwartz, "Transcendence." On the institutionalization of Confucian "truth" by state authority see Julia Ching, "Truth and Ideology: The Confucian Way (Tao) and Its Transmission," *Journal of the History of Ideas* 35: 371–80.

[43] Fung Yu-lan, 1: 403–5; Kirby, ch. 8.

absorb supposedly useful elements of thought from the philosophies of other schools.[44]

One factor contributed to the final and persisting ascendancy of Confucianism as both a philosophy and an institutionalized apparatus. That was the incorporation of Confucianism in the competitive examination system developed for the selection of civil servants after China became unified under Han rule of law (essential in a large state), reenforced by Confucian moral principles and advocacy of a hierarchical society "suited to an imperial government." "On account of its common sense, humanism, catholicity, flexibility, and ability to assimilate useful teaching of other schools, Confucianism gradually overshadowed all its ancient rivals" and, during the autocracy of Han Wu-ti (140–87 B.C.), "finally received imperial patronage and established its primacy over other schools." Accordingly, methods of selecting civil servants by examination or otherwise tended to reflect the Confucian view that "rule by the wise and virtuous" is the "very foundation of good government."[45] As a result merit, as evidenced by "knowledge of classics, sterotyped theories of administration and literary attainments," became dominant under Han rule and especially in later centuries, and Confucian principles served as guides for policy.[46]

Confucian economic ideas are associated with the Confucian school rather than with individual members of this school even as alternative sets of ideas are associated with alternative schools rather than with individual members of these schools.[47] In Confucius's day the idea of causation, of "because," was coming into some use though not fully developed until somewhat later (e.g., by Mo Ti, who was born about the time of Confucius's death in 479 B.C.).[48]

[44] Fung Yu-lan, 1: 405–7, also 2, passim; also Bodde and Morris, ch. 1.

[45] Ho Ping-ti, *The Ladder*, pp. 8–10, 5.

[46] Ibid., pp. 11–17 on how this development came about. See also Fung Yu-lan, 1: xviii, 10, 19; Charles O. Hucker, *China's Imperial Past*, ch. 8. For detailed accounts see comments of Homer H. Dubs in his translation of Pan Ku, *The History of the Former Han Dynasty*, 1: 15–22, 215–17; 2: 20–24, 196–98, 285–89, 291–94, 298, 341–53, 365; 3: 10–14, 506–36. Confucian principles could, of course, be misinterpreted and made to lend support to policies basically at variance with these principles. Ibid., 3: 506–7. Chen Huan-chang, ch. 36, defends Confucianism against criticisms of its supposed influence.

[47] Fung Yu-lan, 1: 19–20, 400–407.

[48] E. R. Hughes, *Chinese Philosophy in Classical Times*, pp. xxvii–xxviii, also ch. 3. Later Mencius wrote that "all statements about the nature of things must be based on phenomena, and the essence of phenomena is regularity," and added that "we may determine the date of a solstice a thousand years hence without rising from our seats." See Lionel Giles, *The Book of Mencius* (abridged), pp. 77–78. Underlying this saying, says Giles, is "the idea of universal causality" (p. 78 n).

While Confucius emphasized individual independence and freedom, thus leaning toward "laissez faire," he also stressed the importance of *li*, or rules of propriety, and the "restraint placed by the rules of society upon the individual."[49] For regulation by *li*, unlike regulation by threat of punishment, imbued people with a "sense of honor and respect."[50] Confucius therefore emphasized not the utility or profitability of economic activities but the righteousness of these activities, presumably because their proper purpose would then be served.[51] Undoubtedly his approach was closely associated with the then feudal and hence custom-dominated character of the economy and the absence of that competition which developed with the collapse of feudalism.[52]

Among the earlier continuators of the teachings of Confucius, whose life span witnessed the rise of the "Legalists," the demise of Feudalism, and beginnings of the emergence of a unified China was Mencius (372?–289? B.C.). Though not a utilitarian, he was idealistic and tender-minded in comparison with the later Confucian Hsün Tzŭ (c.298–c.238 B.C.);[53] yet he conceived of man as a political and somewhat economic animal and devoted considerable attention to economic issues. His approach, however, was descriptive and policy-oriented rather than analytical. He stressed individual liberty as did Confucius but, unlike the latter, described the traditional rules as not binding if men found them inapplicable; this qualification was in keeping with Mencius's faith in man's in-born goodness, righteousness, propriety, and wisdom, characteristics that tended to persist in good environments.[54] Mencius therefore

[49] Fung Yu-lan, 1: 59–68, 73–74, 377. On *li*, or "the principle of social order," a social order both "rationalized" and including folkways, customs, ceremonial and related practices, see Lin Yutang, *The Wisdom of Confucius*, pp. 224–26. See also Goy-Sterboul, *Confucius*, and Giles, *Confucianism*.

[50] Giles, *Confucianism*, pp. 198–200. On Confucian stress upon "rightness" see Swann, p. 30 and the many references in the text. Among the writers who stressed utilitarianism some (e.g., Mo Ti) had been stimulated by Confucianism. See Hughes, ch. 3. Mo Ti (or Mo-tseu) asserted the prosperity of a nation to depend in part upon its population being large. See Sylvie Goy-Sterboul, "Mo-Tseu: les idées d'un non Confucien sur la population," *Population* 33: 216–23.

[51] Fung Yu-lan, 1: 74–75, also pp. 84–85; also Hughes, ch. 2.

[52] Fung Yu-lan, 1: 11–13, 316; Griffith, pp. 20–29. Confucius disapproved of "competition for profit." See Lin Yutang, *The Wisdom of Confucius*, p. 149.

[53] Fung Yu-lan, 1: 127–28, 280–81; also H. H. Dubs, *Hsüntze, The Moulder of Ancient Confucianism*, esp. pp. 80, 241–54. That Mencius was quite utilitarian in philosophy, however, is asserted by H. G. Creel who also remarks that "few philosophers have laid more stress than Mencius did on economics." See Creel, *Chinese Thought from Confucius to Mao Tsê-Tung*, pp. 82–83, 86–88. See also Giles, *The Book of Mencius*.

[54] Fung Yu-lan, 1: 117–29; Mencius as translated by Chai and Chai, in *The*

considered people the most "important element (in a state)" and described the function of the ruler to be that of serving the needs of these people, including provision for their education.

Mencius stressed the importance of division of labor and exchange, especially when man's wants and occupational needs were varied, and people differed in ability and skill, but did not call attention to the dynamic effects of specialization as later described by Adam Smith.[55] Mencius pointed out that taxation discouraged taxed activities and that income structures were hierarchical. He pointed to advantages associated with man's limiting his desires, and to the association of lawful behavior with adequacy and stability of income or standard of living.[56] A conservationist who urged economy in man's use of his natural dowry, Mencius stressed the overriding importance of land and grains, emphasized diversified farming and careful cultivation (e.g., deep ploughing), and cautioned against waste of natural resources (e.g., fisheries). As a result population growth would be favored.[57] He did not, however, put forward principles intended for generalization beyond noting correlations.

Mencius was essentially collectivist in orientation. Writing of the Tsing Tien System (i.e., well-field system) at a time when the system was crumbling,[58] he treated the yield of the ninth plot as a collective tax rather than as the forced contribution of a serf to his overlord. It was essential, he insisted, that field boundaries be accurately drawn lest members of a well-field system be overcharged and communal security and the character of the system thereby be undermined.[59] He also deplored the co-existence of food surpluses and shortages.[60]

Confucians were not in full agreement on all issues. Hsün Tzŭ, or Hsüntze, believing man's nature to be "evil," pointed to the disorder that would ensue in the absence of authority—and depicted conditions similar

---

Sacred Books, pp. 92–220, esp. pp. 108–31, and Mencius (trans. by Leonard A. Lyall), Creel, Chinese Thought, pp. 87–92.

[55] Mencius, bk. 5, ch. 4, bk. 6, ch. 4, bk. 7, ch. 7, bk. 10, ch. 2; Fung Yu-lan, 1: 113–17; Giles, The Book, pp. 58–67. See n. 54, above.

[56] Mencius, bk. 3, ch. 5, bk. 5, ch. 3, bk. 10, ch. 2, bk. 14, ch. 35. Giles, The Book of Mencius, pp. 25, 48–49, 110, 112.

[57] Fung Yu-lan, 1: 113–19; Mencius, bk. 5, ch. 4, bk. 6, ch. 4, bk. 7, ch. 7; Giles, The Book of Mencius, pp. 25, 32; Creel, Chinese Thought, ch. 5.

[58] Lee, p. 49.

[59] Mencius, bk. 5, ch. 3; Fung Yu-lan, 1: 117–20. Mencius implies the presence in men of a feeling somewhat similar to Adam Smith's "sympathy" (pp. 120–21); Giles, The Book, pp. 49–50. According to Hsün Tzŭ, like Mencius a disciple of Confucius, the origin of the state lay in man's gregariousness and his capability of recognizing the rights of other men. See Wu Kuo-cheng, Ancient Chinese Political Theories, p. 326.

[60] Swann, pp. 357–58.

to those encountered in Thomas Hobbes's State of Nature.[61] His philosophy was utilitarian in that he believed men avoided what they disliked (e.g., work) and engaged in what they found gainful and profitable.[62] Men's desires exceeded their capacity to satisfy these desires, but with individuals differing in both their desires and in their ability to satisfy them. As a result control was essential, and man's society needed to be structured in terms of the unequal expectations of its members and in keeping with human differences in ability to satisfy these expectations. Even if not innate, inequality was essential to social organization and the peace of society.[63] Hsün Tzŭ counted upon *li*, "the rules of proper conduct, a system of authoritarian ethics promulgated from above," to secure the subservience of the individual to the common good.[64]

Hsün Tzŭ may be said to have found a partial solution for man's problems flowing from scarcity and multiplicity of desires in cultural change and adaptation through education and the creation of appropriate institutions; for while man's nature was evil, training could inculcate goodness. Society and the state had their origin in utilitarian concerns even as did division of labor, together with freedom of exchange and conservation of resources, all essential to man's welfare.[65]

Hsün Tzŭ's defense of authoritarianism partially shunted the development of Confucianism toward Legalism, for he stressed the role of leadership together with decrees, proclamations, and restraints.[66] As Creel observes, "Hsün Tzŭ forms a kind of bridge between Confucianism and Legalism;"[67] he thereby strengthened Legalist-oriented elements present in Confucianism and thus contributed to the triumph of the Confucianist school over other schools.

Unlike Hsün Tzŭ later Confucians put more emphasis upon *li* as a so-

[61] H. H. Dubs, pp. 80, 246–48, 250.

[62] Fung Yu-lan, 1: 228, 294–98; Creel, *Chinese Thought*, pp. 19–22; Dubs, pp. 250–51.

[63] Dubs, pp. 246–52, also pp. 155–58.

[64] Ibid., pp. 253–54. As Dubs points out, Hsüntze did not justify inequality as did Aristotle when discussing slavery. Ibid., pp. 253–54. As Bodde indicates in "Harmony and Conflict in Chinese Philosophy," pp. 47–48, the view of a well functioning society "as an ordered inequality" was "taken for granted by all later Confucians." See also Fung Yu-lan, 1: 295–97.

[65] Fung Yu-lan, 1: 286–88, 290, 295–96, 298, 300–301; Bodde, "Harmony and Conflict," pp. 38, 47–48; Creel, *Chinese Thought*, pp. 120–22, on man's evil nature. See also Liang Ch'i-ch'ao, *History of Chinese Political Thought*, pp. 63–72. He describes "ethics" as "that code which gives direction to human emotions, and restraint on human activities" (p. 66).

[66] Fung Yu-lan, 1: 300, 310–11; Creel, *Chinese Thought*, ch. 7.

[67] Creel, *Chinese Thought*, p. 139.

cietal moulding force.[68] Thus Tung Chung-shu (179?–104? B.C.) sought to harmonize the theories of Confucius, Mencius, and Hsün Tzŭ, and to stress love, righteousness, and wisdom as well as the essentiality of order and institutions, together with rewards and punishments, to hold man's desires in check.[69] Tung Chung-shu stressed the need for "equalizing riches and poverty and closing paths to private aggrandizement" and recommended revival of the "well-field" system as a means of restoring greater equality in land distribution and checking an increase in inequality.[70]

Among the early non-Legalist supporters of utilitarianism Mo Tzŭ (c. 479–c. 381 B.C.) and his school stand out with their emphasis upon the profitableness of activities together with stress on economy and the importance of wealth and populousness.[71] His followers supplied his utilitarianism with a psychological basis.[72] In contrast with the Mohists the "Legalists" treated government and economic activity essentially from the viewpoint of the state.[73] Mo Tzŭ favored population growth, condemned luxury along with useless and excessive expenditure and unprofitable war, and advocated toil and frugality.[74] He also anticipated Thomas Hobbes in stressing the need for a Supreme Ruler amongst men on grounds similar to Hobbes's.[75] The later Mohist school (300 B.C. and later) continued the founder's defense of utilitarianism on grounds similar to Bentham's.[76]

C. Legalists

Representative of so-called Legalist thought are the works of Lord Shang and Han Fei Tzŭ and in considerable measure the *Kuan Tzŭ*. Whereas the Confucian and especially the Taoist school were favorable to a laissez faire economic philosophy and to minimization of the role of the state,[77]

---

[68] Fung Yu-lan, 1: 339–41, 364–65, 375–78.

[69] Ibid., 2: 32–33, 35–40, 42–55, 57, 83, 85.

[70] Ibid., pp. 53–55. On the actual conditions see Lee; Swann.

[71] Fung Yu-lan, 1: 84–94. Mo Tzŭ expressed a kind of marginalism, saying that basic needs should be satisfied before nonessentials are considered (pp. 104–5).

[72] Ibid., pp. 246–51, also p. 375 on Mohists and Confucians.

[73] Ibid., ch. 13; also Duyvendak, ch. 3, on "the school of law."

[74] Fung Yu-lan, 1: 83–91, 95, 104–5; Hughes, pp. 58–62; Goy-Sterboul, "Mo-Tseu."

[75] Fung Yu-lan, 1: 100–103.

[76] Ibid., pp. 248–50; Hughes, ch. 11.

[77] Laissez faire had considerable support in ancient China. See Maverick, ed., *Kuan Tzŭ*, pp. 21, 271ff.; Chen Huan-chang, pp. 369–71, 596, also p. 722 where he states that after "the Han dynasty the Chinese government" . . . "adopted the doctrine of Lao Tzŭ, the *laissez-faire* policy." On the Taoist doctrines, described

the Legalists stressed the importance of the state. The Legalist school "originated from men who were professional politicians, dedicated to the creating of a strong and centralized machinery of state for the rulers they served." They therefore tended to favor agriculture or primary activities at the expense of commerce and "secondary" activities. They looked upon the law as one of several instruments to achieve their purpose and make the state serve the ruler rather than the people (as Agriculturalists, Confucians, Mohists, and Taoists intended),[78] for men were evil, responding to reward, averting punishment, and seeking utility (e.g., favoring the birth of boys at the expense of girls). Legalists, seeking to encourage production, favored distribution based on work-stimulating free competition rather than egalitarian division of output. The ruler had rewards and punishments at his disposal to guide the apparatus of state, to give proper direction to the activities of the people, and to make the state strong.[79]

The views of the Legalists are illustrated in extreme form in *The Book of Lord Shang*, the reputed author of which is connected with the ascendance in the fourth century B.C. of the state of Ch'in over neighboring states, an outcome that resulted in the following century in the unification of China under Li Ssŭ[80] and the emergence of an empire under which Confucianism finally triumphed over other schools.[81]

The economic views of Lord Shang[82] (i.e., Shang Yang) are manifest in his reforms. These included the expansion of agriculture through encouragement of immigration; the replacement of the feudal well-system by private ownership, competition, moderate taxes, and incentive to cultivate fallow land; and the proscribing of nonagricultural occupations so that manpower would flow into agriculture and military undertakings and make the state powerful. He indicated a need to avoid localized overpopulation and underpopulation by encouraging migration from crowded

---

as "hardly worth attention" by Huang Han (see Maverick, ed., *Kuan Tzŭ*, pp. 400–401), see Fung Yu-lan, 1, ch. 8, 10; Needham, 2, ch. 19, esp. pp. 47, 59–61, 71–72, 80, 92, 100–101, 113, 125, 128, 132, 139, 161–63.

[78] Fung Yu-lan, 1: xxxiii, 144–45, 312–13. The Mohists were of a military background while the Confucians and Taoists were scholars (pp. xxxii–xxxiv). See Burton Watson's introduction to his translation of *Han Fei Tzŭ: Basic Writings*.

[79] Fung Yu-lan, *Chinese Philosophy*, 1, ch. 13. On commerce and secondary activities, see Chen Huan-chang, ch. 21–24; also Maverick, ed., *Kuan Tzŭ*.

[80] Derk Bodde, *China's First Unifier*, chs. 1, 6–7, 11, pp. 86–87; also ch. 19 on Li Ssŭ's philosophic background.

[81] Fung Yu-lan, vol. 1, ch. 16, vol. 2, chs. 2, 15; also Chen Huan-chang, ch. 4.

[82] On the text and authorship of these views and their bearing upon the Legalist school see Duyvendak, esp. pp. 131–61.

to underpeopled land. He indicated further that hampering trade, along with the use of money and the maintenance of a right or normal price for grain, would favor agriculture and make for national power. He sought to establish domestic espionage and a system of penalties and rewards designed to preserve political stability.[83] While it is uncertain how much the views attributed to Lord Shang contributed to the development of the Legalist school, the spirit of a number of his ideas was in keeping with those of that school and Shang's continuator, Li Ssŭ.[84]

It may be noted that the well-field system was much less productive and idyllic than Mencius's description of it. According to "economist" Li K'uei, c. 400 B.C., a man with five mouths to feed and 100 *mou* of land to cultivate and paying a 10 percent land tax would produce and retain only about two-thirds as much as he and his family required.[85] Li K'uei also estimated that the yield of grain on cultivable land could be increased and indicated that if the price of grain were stabilized the ill effects of price fluctuation and abnormally high and low prices would be avoided.[86] Lord Shang favored the avoidance of speculation associated with fluctuation in grain yields.[87]

Most informative of pre-Han Chinese writings on economic matters is the *Kuan Tzŭ*, a philosophically materialist work supposedly written between 330 and 200 B.C. by a group of scholars and reflecting both Confucian and Legalist views but dominated by the latter and nationalist in emphasis.[88] The authors had initially in view an essentially agricultural state as had earlier authors, with grain of critical importance as the basis of power and as a means of exchange. Security of the state, military, fiscal, and otherwise, depended upon the accumulation of grain "in inexhaustible granaries," the cultivation of all land, and keeping the population

[83] Duyvendak, introduction, ch. 3, and translation, passim.

[84] For a summary of his economic proposals and reforms see ibid., pp. 41–65; on Li Ssŭ, see Bodde, *China's First Unifier*, chs. 7, 9–11. On Shang's encouragement of agricultural pursuits see Swann, p. 33.

[85] Duyvendak, pp. 42, 47; Swann, pp. 58, 139–44. Shang Yang may have known of Li K'uei's estimates; see Duyvendak, p. 51.

[86] Ibid., pp. 51–53. See also Swann, pp. 54–57, 60–65.

[87] Duyvendak, pp. 49, 86–87, 177–78, 204–5.

[88] Maverick, ed., *The Kuan Tzŭ*, introduction and pp. 219–62, 437–38. According to Huang Han, the translator, the *Kuan Tzŭ* "is so rich in economic ideas that few ancient books of China can match it." Its author(s) founded it upon a materialist base; the need first to establish a national economy and thereafter noneconomic measures (p. 222). On price equalization, grain, and Li K'uei and *The Kuan Tzŭ* see Swann, pp. 24–26, 54–57, 60–68, 153, 222, 358–59, 422–23. See also Fung Yu-lan, 1:19, 417; also Rickett.

engaged in "suitable" (mainly agricultural) tasks, rather than in "second-ary" or nonagricultural activities. Security depended also upon the effective use of rewards and punishments as instruments of motivation.[89] Among the sovereign's duties are included prevention of threats to the food supply, diversion of the labor force from nonessential occupations, and the maintenance of military power.[90] "Gold is the measure of values" (which depend mainly upon "circumstances") and the "market is the regulator of prices" and the guide to economic action and the proper use of resources. The profit motive was a part of human nature. "A good administrator will make use of the desire for profits to guide the people."[91] The state was best suited, however, to perform the essential grain-storage function equitably by taxing, purchasing, and selling grain in such measure as to stabilize the price of grain, the demand for which was inelastic.[92] It was essential to increase the production of metallic coins and their use by the state as an instrument of stabilization—of prices, of the control, storage, and flow of grain, and hence of political control.[93] For, with the government in possession of sufficient stores of grain and metallic money, the state could fix the exchange ratio between money and grain by paying out that which was "heavy" (i.e., relatively high in value) and purchasing that which was "light" (i.e., relatively low in value) and thereby modify the exchange ratio between grain (which was a subsidiary measure of value) and other commodities. "It matters little whether the land is extensive or limited; a state is not rich or poor for that reason." Its economic condition depends on whether the sovereign has carefully mastered the policy of "the light" and "the heavy."[94] "All things in the empire may be controlled and the production of the staple commodities regulated."[95]

Respecting the financial support of the state, the authors viewed exces-

---

[89] *The Kuan Tzŭ*, pp. 31–37, 83–86, 131, 358–77. It is noted that the economic position of the agriculturalist is inferior to that of persons following "secondary pursuits," (pp. 94–99, 131–32). On agriculture and other pursuits see also Chen Huan-chang, chs. 21–23.

[90] Maverick, ed., *The Kuan Tzŭ*, pp. 47, 73–74, 93–96.

[91] Ibid., pp. 48–52, 54, 101–3, 130, 134–44.

[92] Ibid., pp. 84–85, 93–94, 108–10, 112, 115–25, 128–30.

[93] Ibid., pp. 113–15, also p. 126 on control of salt and iron production.

[94] Ibid., pp. 136–43. "The relative values of money and goods are reflected in prices. When money is heavy, then all commodities seem light, conversely, when money is light, then all commodities seem heavy. By working to control grain by means of the metal money, the state may attain stability. This is the method to establish one's rule in the empire" (p. 143). On "the light and the heavy," see pp. 136–212. On Kuan Tzŭ's theory of money see Chen Huan-chang, pp. 435–45.

[95] Maverick, ed., *Kuan Tzŭ*, p. 135.

sive taxation as unfavorable to the productive power of the state and political stability. Accordingly, they favored government operation of certain enterprises as sources of revenue, especially the salt and iron industries and also some of the primary industries, such as fishing, mining, and forestry.[96] It was the responsibility of the state to encourage the production of essential implements and tools, especially military equipment,[97] as well as to facilitate agriculture and domestic and foreign trade.[98] The authors appreciated the selective role of competition,[99] and the contribution that commerce and industry would make, given a good agricultural base, but they condemned those merchants who charged usurious interest or engaged in antisocial behavior.[100] Although the authors of the *Kuan Tzŭ* were critical of the distribution of wealth and income, they did not discuss functional distribution;[101] they did, however, discuss interest, profit, and rent and[102] saw clearly the dependence of the level of wages on the state of demand.[103]

While Han Fei Tzŭ (d. 233) was essentially a Legalist, he coordinated the views of earlier Legalists and drew on Taoist and Confucian thought as well.[104] Much of what he said respecting control of the masses and the ruler's ministers was directed, as noted earlier, to the control of the latter. "The enlightened ruler controls his ministers by means of two handles alone. The two handles are punishment and favor."[105] Control of the ministers provided leverage in a society dominated by the search for what is profitable and beneficial and the avoidance of what is harmful.

His conception of man's behavioral propensities was similar to that of other Legalists, as was his conception of law and its role. Inasmuch as human nature was evil, recourse to rewards and punishments, together with motives of profit and harm, was essential to the assurance of proper behavior. Individuals engaged in what they believed to be to their advan-

---

[96] Ibid., pp. 176, 282. Then presumably the confidence that had given rise to trade would facilitate the trade that "renders goods cheap and readily available for our use" (p. 175). On the authors' treatment of money as a measure of value as well as their rudimentary quantity theory of money and its application in the stabilization of the price of grain see pp. 135–212, 280–93.

[97] Ibid., pp. 293–321, also pp. 113–34, 151–61.

[98] Ibid., pp. 332–34.

[99] Ibid., pp. 38, 100, 117, 144, 425, 426.

[100] Ibid., pp. 94, 144, 191–96, 300–343.

[101] Ibid., pp. 377–86.

[102] Ibid., pp. 101–63, 142–43, 101–96, 230, 237.

[103] Ibid., p. 260.

[104] Fung Yu-lan, vol. 1, ch. 13.

[105] Ibid., pp. 330–31; Han Fei Tzŭ, *The Complete Works*, translated with introduction by W. K. Liao, bk. 2, esp. ch. 7.

tage, even resorting to female infanticide when a female child was considered inconvenient.[106] Appropriate laws and regulations, together with their suitability to the ruler's ends and their effective enforcement, were essential to the maintenance of an orderly state. There was no room, therefore, for the heterodox doctrines of private individuals or for policies that diverted individuals from war and agriculture into the ranks of the Literati.[107]

Han Fei Tzǔ's conception of economic motivation and its significance for efficiency was corollary to his conception of human nature and motives. Since men acted in their own interests it was better to leave them alone in free competition with one another. Therefore he opposed equal division of land, as recommended by Confucians, as well as other policies that might shift control of resources from "the industrious and the economical" to "the wasteful and lazy" and thereby reduce activity and frugality.[108] This opposition was even more important than it had been in the past, he indicated, because population growth had reduced supplies relative to population and thus increased relative "scarcity."[109] Given the nature of economic motivation, however, the task of Han Fei Tzǔ's supreme ruler may have been no more onerous than Quesnay's despot since individuals responded freely to the handles of reward and punishment, of advantage and disadvantage.[110]

Toward the close of the period with which this chapter deals Legalist and essentially Confucian views were partially contrasted in the *Dis-*

[106] Fung Yu-lan, 1: 327. Han Fei Tzǔ wrote in the manner of Adam Smith:

When a man sells his services as a farm hand, the master will give him good food at the expense of his own family, and pay him money and cloth. This is not because he loves the farm hand, but he says: "In this way, his ploughing of the ground will go deeper and his sowing of seeds will be more active." The farm hand, on the other hand, exerts his strength and works busily at tilling and weeding. He exerts all his skill cultivating the fields. This is not because he loves his master, but he says: "In this way I shall have good soup, and money and cloth will come easily." Thus he expends his strength as if between them there were a bond of love such as that of father and son. Yet their hearts are centered on utility, and they both harbor the idea of serving themselves. Therefore in the conduct of human affairs, if one has a mind to do benefit, it will be easy to remain harmonious, even with a native of Yüeh. But if one has a mind to do harm, even father and son will become separated and feel enmity toward one another (*Chüan* 11, p. 6).

[107] Ibid., pp. 321–33, 325–26.

[108] Ibid., p. 328.

[109] Ibid., pp. 328–29. Increasing scarcity owing to population growth had not altered man's nature but had increased the seriousness of the problem (pp. 328–30).

[110] Ibid., p. 331.

courses on Salt and Iron (said to have taken place sometime in the period 86–81 B.C.), which resulted from what amounted to a recommendation by Confucianists that the government remove its monopoly of salt and iron. These discourses were put in debate form by Huan Kuan and subsequently went through a number of editions which contributed to formation of the Confucian canon.[111] Confucianism generally opposed government monopolies.

Among the points made by the Literati, or spokesmen for the Confucian view and against that of the Legalists, was condemnation of the government's engaging in business in "financial competition with the people, dissipating primordial candor and simplicity and sanctioning propensities to selfishness and greed," thereby discouraging "fundamental pursuits" and encouraging "the nonessential."[112] They recommended "that the salt, iron and liquor monopolies and the system of equitable marketing be abolished so that rural pursuits may be encouraged, people be deterred from entering the secondary occupations, and national agriculture be materially and financially benefitted."[113] They also rejected the argument that the government needed the revenue it derived from its policies to guard the state's frontier against barbarian inroads, as well as argued that underdevelopment of the nation's natural resources was due to neglect of "fundamental occupations" and emphasis upon "luxuries and fancy articles," upon speculative trade and profit.[114] The Confucians condemned monopolies, nonessential pursuits, grain shortage, luxurious living, and the "evil habits of idleness therewith associated—conditions allegedly fostered by state policy."[115]

In defense of state policies it was urged that in their absence private monopoly might become ascendant, presumably because a basis for real competition did not exist, an inference in effect rejected by Confucians.[116] State policy, moreover, it was said, made for improvements, progress,

[111] Discourses on Salt and Iron, translated with introduction and notes by Esson M. Gale. On the six monopolies established by Wang Mang as sources of revenue see Dubs's account in 3:526–30 of his translation of Pan Ku's *The History*. On monopolies and markets, see also Swann; also Chen Huan-chang, ch. 27, pp. 477–78.

[112] Gale, *Discourses*, ch. 1, pp. 2–3, 86–87, 107–9

[113] Ibid., p. 3. Under "equitable marketing," efforts were made by the state to "equalize or balance prices by transporting commodites from such places as they were abundant to where they were scarce" (p. 2 n); also pp. 12–17.

[114] Ibid., pp. 4–11; also pp. 15–17, 40–50, 92–92. On frontier problems see pp. 74–80, 99–105.

[115] E.g., see ibid., pp. 18–24, also pp. 25–33. Spokesmen for the state of course defended the importance of the state monopolies and guarding the frontiers, and condemned the private monopolies that might otherwise result (pp. 34–39).

[116] E.g., see ibid., pp. 54–58, 87–91.

security, and development of wealth and resources. This view was also rejected by Confucians,[117] for they believed that in the absence of governmental interference the economy would develop appropriately, in keeping with the needs of the times,[118] and that population would tend to be evenly distributed.[119] In general, the views expressed in the *Discourses* were illustrative of basic economic philosophies already described rather than those that were essentially novel.

D. Triumph of Confucianism

The Confucian conception that imperial authority is limited, should be exercised for the benefit of the people, and should be founded upon justice became ascendant over the legalistic conception of arbitrary and absolute sovereignty about the beginning of the second century.[120]

Under the Emperor Wu (141 B.C. ff.) the examination system flourished and Confucianism became entrenched, though not to the exclusion of all Legalist practices.[121] In the last century B.C. the gradual ascendancy of Confucianism was completed.[122] Dubs attributes the triumph of Confucianism to four factors: its adaptation to imperial government, its capacity for training for prospective government institutions, its complementarity to government officials, and the belief that the prevalence of a single system of thought conduced to the unification of a country.[123]

While Confucian principles were sometimes distorted, as by Wang Mang,[124] or temporarily lost support, their demise came only in the wake of the advent of modern science.[125]

[117] Ibid., pp. 59–105.

[118] Ibid., pp. 79–80.

[119] Ibid., pp. 82–84, 95–97.

[120] Homer Dubs, in commentary in his translation of *The History of the Former Han Dynasty*, 1:15, 216, 218; Swann, pp. 28–30.

[121] Homer H. Dubs, 2:20–22, 25, 197.

[122] Ibid., pp. 341–53.

[123] Ibid., pp. 351–53; also Fung Yu-lan, 1, ch. 16.

[124] Dubs, comments on Wang Mang, 3: 10–14, and memoir on Wang Mang, pp. 88–124, also pp. 506–36.

[125] Ibid., 2: 351. On Confucian and Chinese influence in early modern Europe see Maverick, *China: A Model For Europe*; it includes a translation of F. Quesnay's *Le Despotisme de la Chine*.

5

Economic Justice, the Classical
Greek Contribution

Except the blind Forces of Nature, nothing that
moves in the world is not Greek in its origin.
Sir Henry Sumner Maine

But to wealth men have set themselves
no clear bound.
Solon

As has been indicated in earlier chapters and remarked by S. T. Lowry, "The theoretical line of Greek thought is primarily a belief in natural order and theory. It therefore consists of an attempt to understand and abstract the true nature of this natural order."[1] Barry Gordon traces the emergence of economic thought in the Hellenic world to about 700 B.C. at which time "an entirely oral tradition began to give way in Greek culture to written communication" and it became easier to reflect in a generalized abstract fashion upon an increasingly sophisticated economic environment.[2] He draws attention to a variety of authors (e.g., dramatists, poets, philosophers) who referred to economic conditions or touched upon economic matters prior to the ascendance of the Socratic conception of economics.[3]

In what follows we focus attention mainly upon the interrelation between ethics and economics in the works of Plato and Aristotle and their followers. For the thought of Greek philosophers "was entirely domi-

---

[1]"The Classical Greek Theory of Resource Economics," *Land Economics* 41: 203–8, esp. p. 203. See also S. C. Humphreys, "'Transcendence' and Intellectual Roles." Polybius (205?–125? B.C.) observed that few events may be referred "to Fortune and chance." The *Histories*, bk. 31, ch. 30.

[2]Barry Gordon, *Economic Analysis Before Adam Smith*, p. 1. On the development of Greek society in the period preceding the emergence of the age of Athenian Democracy, see A. W. Winspear, *The Genesis of Plato's Thought*, chs. 1–2. See also S. Todd Lowry, "Recent Literature on Ancient Greek Economic Thought," *Journal of Economic Literature* 17:65–86.

[3]Gordon, ch. 1.

nated by ethical ideas; there was an absolute separation of the ideas of right and wrong in human conduct from that of economic advantage and disadvantage."[4] Moreover, even though one cannot "read into the writings of the Greek philosophers a conception of economic theory which is recognizable today,"[5] the ideas of Plato and (particularly) Aristotle are important in that they influenced subsequent economic thought, especially in the Middle Ages, through scholastic writers and later through early "modern" writers, mainly through emphasizing economic justice rather than price and market behavior.[6]

A. Occasional Economic Commentators

Diverse economic subjects were dealt with by early Greek writers. For example, Solon (638–559 B.C.) as reported by Plutarch (A.D. 46?–120?),[7] "observing the city to be filled with persons that flocked from all parts into Attica for security of living, and that most of the country was barren and unfruitful, and that traders at sea import nothing to those that could give them nothing in exchange, he turned his citizens to trade, and made a law that no son be obliged to relieve a father who had not bred him up to any calling."[8] He thus brought trades into credit and set the "Solonian Economic Revolution" into motion and made the population of Athens and Attica dependent upon external sources for a portion of its food supply, thus casting doubt upon the concept of a self-sufficient city-state which, however, remained dominant, especially in the systems of Plato and Aristotle.[9]

Division of labor was occasionally discussed, not only by Plato but also by others, though not with full recognition of the effects noted by Adam

[4] H. Michell, *The Economics of Ancient Greece*, p. 34.

[5] Ibid.

[6] E.g., see George W. Wilson, "The Economics of the Just Price," *History of Political Economy*, 7: 56–74; R. A. De Roover, "Scholastic Economics: Survival and Lasting Influences from the Sixteenth Century to Adam Smith," *Quarterly Journal of Economics* 69: 161–90; S. T. Worland, *Scholasticism and Welfare Economics*. See also Eric A. Havelock, *The Liberal Temper in Greek Politics*.

[7] Plutarch, *The Lives of the Noble Grecians and Romans*, pp. 97–116 on Solon.

[8] Ibid., p. 110; also pp. 104, 111.

[9] E.g., see Arnold J. Toynbee, *A Study of History* 4: 200–211, 303–6; Michell, pp. 270–75; Kathleen Freeman, *The Work and Life of Solon*. See also A. French, *The Growth of the Athenian Economy*. On Solon's times see French, "Solon and the Megarian Question," *Journal of Hellenic Studies* 77: pt. 2, pp. 238–46; K. H. Waters, "Solon's 'Price Equalisation'," ibid. 80: 181–90; N. G. L. Hammond, "Land Treasure in Athens and Solon's Seisachteia," ibid. 81: 76–98.

Smith.[10] For example, Xenophon (434?–355? B.C.) describes the division of occupations in army, palace, and city, together with its contribution to "superior excellence" of performance and of product and its dependence upon the size of the market.[11] It is "impossible for a man of many trades to be proficient in all of them," but it is possible for a workman to devote his full time to a single occupation and become very proficient in it in a larger city.[12]

While Xenophon did not discuss economic organization in his critical account of Spartan practices and the "Constitution of the Lacedaemonians,"[13] elsewhere in a work attributed to him he explained how Athens might effectively exploit its very favorable location and natural resources, especially its silver mines, and thus make its revenue ample.[14] He emphasized "the unrivalled amenities and advantages of Athens as a commercial center and the need to reduce business risks and improve conditions surrounding foreigners, merchants, and shipowners. He also advocated facilitation of the availability of capital and investment through what amounted to joint-stock companies. He indicated that the state might develop a fleet of public merchant vessels, for lease to private operators. He pointed in particular to the underexploitation of the country's silver mines, even though expansion of their operations was not subject to diminishing pecuniary returns as was increase in the production of some products, and overexploitation of agricultural land.[15] Since the exploitation of the mines was limited by a shortage of labor, he indicated that the state treasury might acquire slaves and let them to mineowners

---

[10] E.g., see Vernard Foley, "The Division of Labor in Plato and Smith," *History of Political Economy* 6: 220–42; also Paul J. McNulty, "A Note on the Division of Labor in Plato and Smith, ibid. 7: 372–78; and Vernard Foley's reply, "Smith and the Greeks," ibid., pp. 379–89. See also E. A. Havelock, esp. pp. 375, 385, 398; also below, n. 60, on Plato.

[11] Xenophon, *Cyropaedia*, vol. 3, esp. pp. 333–35. He notes the incapacity of the Persians to accumulate wealth and use it productively, owing to prodigal consumption.

[12] Ibid., p. 333. Cf. Plutarch's remarks on division of functions in his "Theseus," in *Lives*, p. 16.

[13] See Xenophon's *Scripta Minora*, pp. 135–87. He refers to Spartan avoidance of business affairs and emphasis upon population quality. See Lee Strauss, "The Spirit of Sparta or the Taste of Xenophon," *Social Research* 6: 502–36.

[14] "On the Ways and Means of Improving the Revenues of the State of Athens," *Scripta Minora*, pp. 193–231.

[15] "To put more [labor] on the land than the requisite number is counted loss" whereas "no one ever yet possessed so much silver as to want no more." Ibid., p. 207.

under arrangements that, while covering the cost of the slaves, would help to pool business risks associated with the extension of mining.[16]

The "rent derived from the slaves," together with revenue derived from the associated expansion of business activity, would be a source of financial relief and improvement of the state, expecially if peace flourished and the gods consented to Xenophon's plan.[17] In another work, *Oeconomicus*,[18] Xenophon dealt with husbandry, management, incentives, children as support in old age, population density as an index of goodness of government, and natural resources, the scarcity of which had been stressed already by the poet Hesiod in the late ninth century B.C.[19] He had noted the importance of competition and work with due attention to risk as the only acceptable means of reducing man's want and misery, mainly through properly conducted agricultural activities and secondarily by trading by sea.[20] Xenophon emphasizes what may be called the economics of production and estate management under the general heading of household management.[21] As Lowry points out, Xenophon dealt with: the adjustment of activities to physical nature so as to realize its highest potential (chap. 20); leadership and management of manpower (chaps. 20–21); and what Lowry describes as "geometric or place arrangement" (e.g., the structure of a Phonenician galley).[22] Later Aristotle (*Pol.*, I.10), Lowry observes, "summed up the problem of man dealing with nature . . . as the essence of the economic problem."[23] Unlike the Stoics, who believed that periodic disasters would destroy parts of man's environment, Xenophon as well as Aristotle apparently assumed that man's natural resources were stable.

Greek writers sometimes discussed economic phenomena, but without

[16] Ibid., pp. 205–23.

[17] Ibid., pp. 223–32.

[18] See translation in Leo Strauss, *Xenophon's Socratic Discourse*.

[19] Hesiod, "Works and Days," *The Homeric Hymns and Homerica*. On economic life in and after Hesiod's day see H. Bolkestein *Economic Life in Greece's Golden Age*, e.g., pp. 27–28 on scarcity of land and deferment of marriage.

[20] Hesiod, passim. See also Barry Gordon's discussion of Hesiod on "the economics of self-sufficiency," *Economic Analysis*, pp. 2–7, and his "Aristotle and Hesiod: The Economic Problem in Greek Thought," *Review of Social Economy* 21: 147–56; also his "Aristotle and the Development of Value Theory," *Quarterly Journal of Economics* 78:115–28, esp. pp. 123–24. On Hesiod's views on competition, justice, etc., see also Winspear, ch. 2.

[21] *Oeconomicus*, ch. 1, chs. 4–6 on the case for farming, chs. 12–14 on training stewards, and chs. 15–21 on the art of farming.

[22] Lowry, "The Classical Greek Theory of Natural Resource Economics," pp. 203–5.

[23] Ibid., p. 206, also p. 208.

engaging in economic analysis. For example, the historian Herodotus (5th century B.C.) wrote extensively on economic conditions in the many countries which he visited, but not on price formation, distribution, monetary behavior, etc., for he had little if any notion of an economic system.[24] Similarly, the historian Thucydides (471?–400 B.C.) referred to economic phenomena (e.g., the resources of Athens, silver, provisions, merchants, shipbuilding, gold mining, helots, taxation, colonization) but undertook no economic analysis. He described the early history of Hellas in Hobbesian terms, related how population pressure had developed in Attica and elsewhere and made necessary the sending out of colonies, and described how, as the power of Hellas had grown, "the acquisition of wealth" had become "more an object" and monarchies had initially given place to tyrannies. But he attributed the Peloponnesian War to Lacedae-monian fear of the growth of the power of Athens rather than to imme-diately economic causes.[25]

Economic behavior could receive attention in the courts when mo-nopolistic arrangements were subject to prosecution. For example, in 355 B.C. Lysias (whose father was a friend of Plato), when discussing what amounts to a violation of a bilateral monopoly arrangement, utilized as evidence the manner in which prices behaved, sometimes in response to rumors.[26]

B. Greek Culture and Economic Justice

Despite the rational approach of the Greeks to the study of social as of natural phenomena, they did not isolate the economy and the price sys-tem, show how the price system enabled specialists to cooperate effec-tively, or otherwise study the behavior of the price system. This neglect may be attributable (as Lowry suggests) to the fact that "in Aristotle's day, when virtually all commercial activity was in the hands of metics, no such natural market process seems to have been recognized, and the common practice among municipal governments was apparently to resort to public regulation, particularly of the flows of staples such as corn upon which the people depended."[27] Moreover, as Lowry points out, free-market con-

[24] See my "Herodotus on the Subject Matter of Economics," *The Scientific Monthly* 81:276–85. This article is based upon his *History*. See also Sir John L. Myres, *Herodotus: Father of History*.

[25] See *The Complete Writings of Thucydides*, esp. bk. 1, ch. 1.

[26] "Lysias: Against the Corn Dealers," in *Greek Economics*, ed. M. L. W. Laist-ner, pp. 4–9.

[27] S. Todd Lowry, "Aristotle's 'Natural Limit' and the Economics of Price Regu-lation," *Greek, Roman, and Byzantine Studies* 15:61.

ditions did not prevail; monopoly, or price regulation often was present, while variation in the quality of goods made for individual bargaining.[28] The Greeks therefore studied a complex of socioeconomic phenomena— politics, ethics, economic behavior and justice, conditions of sociopolitical stability—mainly within the framework of the polis or city-state. In this section we deal with their approach in general, in the two following sections, with the approaches of Plato and Aristotle, the principal formulators of the classic Greek approach to economic and related phenomena, and in the last section with the decline of the classic Greek approach as evidenced mainly in the work of the Roman Cicero.

As has been noted, the novel and distinguishing characteristic of the classic Greek approach was its freedom from the mythopoeic elements which dominated the views of both the Egyptians and the inhabitants of Mesopotamia. The Greeks early freed themselves largely of other-worldliness and of "the prescriptive sanctities" of religion; they came to rely upon reason, and having assumed the world to be an intelligible whole, developed the implications of their various theories concerning it, together with an apparatus of thought for the conduct of their inquiries.[29] These inquiries were directed into the field (among others) of the good, of justice and its economic instrumentalities, and of the place of economic behavior in a polity, especially the polis.[30]

The bridge between ethics and economics in the ancient as in the medieval world consisted largely in concern with "a man's lot or destined portion," a concept implied by the early Greek term *Moira*, and the constraining influence of *diké* in the sense of custom. Notions of this sort, present already in the aristocratic Homeric age and continuing into the seventh and sixth centuries when an "articulate civilization" was growing

---

[28] S. Todd Lowry, "Aristotle's Mathematical Analysis of Exchange," *History of Political Economy* 1:65. See also Thomas J. Lewis, "Acquisition and Anxiety: Aristotle's Case Against the Market," *Canadian Journal of Economics* 11:69–90, esp. pp. 83–87, wherein a distinction is shown between the interhousehold exchange discussed in *Pol.* 1 and the intercommodity exchange, an inferior form, discussed in *Nic. Eth.* 5.

[29] See Henri Frankfort et al., ch. 8; John Burnet, *Early Greek Philosophy*, 4th ed., introduction.

[30] Justice, as noted in early chapters, was not a primary subject of philosophical inquiry at the hands of the Egyptian and the Mesopotamian peoples. However, "the idea that justice was something to which man had a right began slowly to take form, and in the second millennium—appropriately the millennium of the famous code of Hammurabi—justice as right rather than justice as favour seems to have become the general conception." See Frankfort et al., p. 223. With the Egyptians justice long lay "in the impartial administration of law rather than the redress of human injustice," and just dealing consisted in giving correct measure and satisfying need (pp. 100, 120).

in the Greek world, were subsequently intellectualized, in the main by Plato and Aristotle, and explicitly related to economic behavior and welfare.[31] One may accept as granted that no society can persist without consensus regarding a man's "destined portion" and expectations based upon this consensus; that how this portion is defined reflects the distribution of political power within society; that this definition will change as consensus and the political structure change; and that intellectualization of the portion and its role will progress as economic exchange and individual freedom increase.

In the works of Plato and Aristotle the importance of "justice," together with its realization, is formulated in terms of the city-state that had lost its "place of first-rate importance in the political development of European society" by the time of Aristotle's death which marks the break in the continuity of political philosophy. Thereafter, with "the beginning, of the theory of natural law in the Stoic school of Cicero and Seneca, from the latter to the Fathers of the Church, and from them through medieval political philosophy to the modern doctrine of the rights of man, we have a continuous and unbroken development."[32] As Cochrane points out, however, "the Augustan Empire, with its claim to 'eternity' as a final and definitive expression of classical order" was "merely the culmination of an effort begun centuries before in Hellas, the effort to create a world which should be safe for civilization."[33]

Plato and Aristotle looked upon economic activities as instrumental, to be carried on within the framework of the polis (or city-state) and subject to the principles of law and of a justice that had evolved out of an earlier conception of "due share" and compensation in accordance therewith. This conception underwent transformation and idealization even before it was intellectualized by Plato and Aristotle. For both men the object of a citizen's existence in the polis[34] was living the good or virtuous life and

---

[31] On early Greek views see John Ferguson, *Moral Values in the Ancient World*, chs. 1–2; Havelock, chs. 1–2. Also selections from Homer on, in Hilda D. Oakeley, ed., *Greek Ethical Thought*; A. D. Winspear, chs. 2–3.

[32] See *On The Commonwealth*, by Marcus Tullius Cicero, trans. George H. Sabine and Stanley B. Smith, introduction, esp. pp. 7–10.

[33] Charles N. Cochrane, *Christianity and Classical Culture*, preface, p. v.

[34] As Jaeger shows, the extent to which the intellectual and artistic lives of its citizens were dominated by the polis varied, being very great in Sparta and not so great in the commercial Ionian cities where the individual citizen was allowed great scope "for the development of his potentialities" and where "versatility, individual initiative, and wide vision" were early manifested. Athens too exercised much dominance, but allowed the individual to develop; its culture was the first "to strike a balance between the outward-striving energy of the individual and the unifying power of the state." See Werner Jaeger, *Paideia: The Ideals of Greek Culture*, 2nd ed., 1:99–102, 137, 149.

giving expression to the particular virtues, and above all to the sum of virtue to justice. Accordingly, the impact of exchange and distribution upon man's welfare was appraised in terms of their influence upon his living the virtuous life.

The content of *areté* or excellence and the meaning of justice underwent change as the character of Greek society underwent modification. Initially valour and warlike prowess were stressed. Whereas Homer looked upon *areté* as a "combination of proud and courtly morality with warlike valour," the Spartan poet, Tyrtaeus, defined it as courage or warlike prowess; but where Homer believed only individual nobles could manifest *areté*, Tyrtaeus treated it as a civic ideal which Sparta's citizens

---

To Jaeger's view (3:265), that the city-state was "the fundamental fact in Greek history" from the time of Homer to that of Alexander, Ehrenberg takes some exception. According to him, the polis, which he describes as characteristically "a community of citizens" and the "product of long evolution," came into being around 800 B.C., when the walled towns which had replaced the Mycenean type of open town had become sufficiently integrated with the surrounding country. While aristocrats turned demagogues played a part in the development of the polis, justice (*diké*) was described by Hesiod (in "Works and Days") around 700 B.C. as that by which the noble is restrained and for which he is responsible; and individuality is made to bow before the will and the way of the polis. From the sixth century on, attempts of powerful individuals to establish monarchies were checked by "the new controlling idea of *Nomos*" (Law), a yet more powerful instrument than the legal basis of *diké*. The beginning of the "international dissolution of the Polis" is to be found in the Age of Pericles, "the first period of great individuals no more bound to the Polis." From the time of Hesiod on down to the period of the impending dissolution of the polis, Greek authors strove to idealize the polis into a "dream city directed by right and law, by discipline and order, or by equality and concord." See Victor Ehrenberg, "When Did the Polis Rise?" *Journal of Hellenic Studies* 57:147–59; see also R. M. Cook, "Ionia and Greece in the Eighth and Seventh Centuries, B.C.," ibid. 66:87–88.

The polis, of course, was not a very effective instrument for coping with the conflict between rich and poor, given the prevailing low-output techniques of production, or for meeting the demands of international political relations. And so it was on the verge of giving place to other forms when Aristotle, oblivious to the significance of the future career of his most famous pupil, Alexander, based his *Politics* upon the parochial polis even as Plato had done. See Mason Hammond, *City-State and World-State in Greek and Roman Political Theory Until Augustus*; Cochrane, ch. 2; Paul Vinogradoff, *Outlines of Historical Jurisprudence*, vol. 2. See also Kathleen Freeman, *Greek City States*; A. Toynbee, *A Study of History* 4:200ff., 206ff., 303ff.; Victor Ehrenberg, *Alexander and the Greeks*; and Ernest Barker's introduction, notes, and appendixes to his translation of Aristotle's *Politics*. On general economic conditions see H. Michell, and on social and economic conditions in classical Athens, see Victor Ehrenberg, *The People of Aristophanes*.

generally were capable of expressing.[35] The peasant poet, Hesiod, described work as the only means to *areté* which embraced "both personal ability and its products—welfare, success, repute," thereby stressing the potentialities of the peasent class and individuals generally.[36]

Since the administration of justice, whether by the early kings or by their aristocratic successors, frequently resulted in offenders' making compensation to injured parties, the term *diké* or justice (originally signifying "due share") also referred to penalities involved in suits. In time, however, as the polis developed, the significance of the term was derived from the normative element underlying the formulae employed in the settlement of suits, etc., and *diké* came to mean "the due share which each man can rightly claim; and then, the principle guarantees that claim." It also referred to that "equality" which presumably resulted when "justice" was realized. That quality which enabled men to avoid committing offences was named *dikaiosyné*, or righteousness (or justice)."The new *dikaiosyné . . .* became areté *par excellence* as soon as the Greeks believed that they had found, in written law, a reliable criterion for right and wrong. After *nomos*—that is, current legal usage—was codified, the general idea of righteousness acquired a palpable content. It consisted in obedience to the laws of the state."[37] Thereupon "righteousness" or "justice" became the sum of all virtue and "the areté of the perfect citizen embracing and transcending all others" and supplanting previously held ideals.[38]

In accordance with this view, law becomes "the objective expression of the state" and the instrument through which approved ideals are inculcated, achieved, or guaranteed. The polis "imposes its way of life on each

---

[35] Jaeger, 1:5, 7, 90, 93, 173–74. See also pp. 197, 201, 203, 214ff., 220 on the class and familistic conceptions of the aristocrats, Theognis and Pindar. See also Ferguson, *Moral Values*, esp. chs. 1–3.

[36] Jaeger, 1:70–74; also Hesiod, pp. 19, 25–31. F. J. Teggart accredits Hesiod with setting before men the first "idea of human progress: the idea that a good life is attainable" through the "activity of men themselves" when they are actuated "by a common regard for justice." Thucydides supplied the second idea of progress, "that advancement in culture is growth, and will follow a determinate course, if nothing interferes;" and Plato, the third, "that the organization and maintenance of a good life necessitates the creation of a State in which authority will allot to each individual his special task, and will see that he performs it." See Teggart, "The Argument of Hesiod's Works and Days," *Journal of the History of Ideas* 8:45–77, esp. p. 77; also Barry Gordon, *Economic Analysis*.

[37] Jaeger, 1:105, also pp. 103–4.

[38] Ibid., pp. 105–7; cf. Aristotle, *Nic. Eth.*, 1129^b. The citizen of the polis, being bound to do his duty in times of both war and peace, was required to be courageous.

individual, and marks him for its own. From it are derived the norms which govern the life of its citizens. Conduct that injures it is bad, conduct that helps it is good."[39] Within the polis man found his political place and his communal existence, together with such individual liberty and private life as the prevailing codes allowed him.[40] Among the forces bringing about compliance with justice-producing laws Solon (who considered man a responsible moral agent subject to retribution and who supposed cause and effect to hold in the realm of social affairs) included the tendency of injustice to disrupt the life of the community,[41] but he did not translate this observation into terms of homeostasis or maintenance of social equilibrium.[42]

So great was the impression made by the example of the polis, that

[39] Jaeger, 1:108–9, 115, also pp. 110–13. Goodness of character, Aristotle later indicated, could only be acquired through habituation whereas goodness of intellect could be taught to those with capacity and of good character. See John Burnet, *The Ethics of Aristotle*, p. 68.

[40] Jaeger, pp. 111, 115, 128. Pericles emphasized both the amount of freedom allowed citizens in their private relations under the Athenian "democracy" and the fact that "advancement in public life" depended, not upon class considerations, but upon "reputation for capacity." See Thucydides, *The Peloponnesian War* 2:37, 104. This standard, of the sort encountered in societies with a "universalistic-achievement pattern" (see T. Parsons, *The Social System*, pp. 182ff.), was only imperfectly realized in fifth-century Athens, according to F. W. Walbank ("The Causes of Greek Decline," *Journal of Hellenic Studies* 63:12), and less so in other city-states (Toynbee, *History* 4:200–206).

[41] Jaeger, 1:141–44, 159–61; 3:5ff. Solon was convinced (p. 140, also p. 323), as had been Hesiod ("Works and Days"), that "justice is an inseparable part of the divine world-order." See also Kathleen Freeman, *Solon*, esp. pp. 207ff., frg. 2, 12, 14, 22, 30–31. While Solon believed that only righteously gained wealth proves retainable, he noted that wealth can slip through the fingers of its holders whereas *areté* cannot. See Jaeger, 1:144, 146, 201ff., 451. On Solon's contribution generally see also Toynbee, 4:200ff., 303ff. Pericles seems to have found a sanction for law observance in public opinion (Thucydides, *Complete Writings* 2:37).

[42] As we indicate below (see next note) Anaximander and Heraclitus gave expression to a theory of cosmological justice whereunder they referred to the encroachment of elements or "opposites," one upon another, to the consequences of such encroachment, and to the limitations circumscribing it. See John Burnet, *Greek Philosophy*, pt. 1, 22–23, 61–22, 106, and *Early Greek Philosophy*, pp. 144–45, 161–66. Presumably this theory could have been translated into terms of physical equilibration, or, by analogy, social equilibration, but this was not done, and so the opportunity to formulate a fruitful equilibrium theory was forfeited. (Some of Heraclitus's remarks concerning strife can be translated into Hegelian terms.) Anaximander had an idea of "adaptation to environment and survival of the fittest" as did Empedokles, but this idea did not give rise to any sort of equilibrium theory. See Burnet, *Early Greek*, pp. 71, 243–44.

several natural philosophers transferred from political life to the realm of nature the concepts of justice and of a communal order maintained by law. Thus Anaximander reasoned—metaphorically it usually is held—that the cosmos (or the realm of nature) was subject to moral law, while Heraclitus asserted that man is subject to the Logos, the law of the universe, human laws being connected with natural law and "nourished" by "divine" law.[43] As Jaeger states, however, it was generally accepted, prior to the fifth century, that there ruled in heaven and later in nature "the same law and the same justice that revered as the highest moral standard," and that the law of the polis harmonized with the law of the cosmos. But in the course of the fifth century some of the older sophists[44] developed the view that the law of the polis did not coincide with that of nature (the cosmos), being a control imposed from without, which sometimes required men to act contrary to nature or to their advantage, and which they complied with for fear of sanctions; or they asserted that laws are merely convenants men agree upon to prevent the strife that would otherwise ensue; or they claimed that laws do not effectively protect the weak, might often making right.[45] These views were rejected by Aristotle

[43]See Jaeger, 1:110, 159–61, 180–84; also 1:159ff., and 3:293ff., where it is said that "causality in nature was explained, by analogy with legal processes, as retribution;" also Kathleen Freeman, *Ancilla to the Pre-Socratic Philosophers*, pp. 19, 24ff., frgs. 1–2, 28, 30, 44–45, 50, 89, 114. See also Kathleen Freeman, *The Pre-Socratic Philosophers*, pp. 63–64, 110, 112, 115–17, 122, 124, 127; and John Burnet, *Greek Philosophy*, pp. 22–23, 61–62, 106. Burnet suggests (p. 106) that "when the regular course of nature began to be observed, no better name could be found for it than Right or Justice [diké], a word which properly meant the unchanging custom that guided human life." Both the Egyptian and the Mesopotamian people interpreted the cosmos in social terms. See Frankfort, pp. 70, 146–47.

[44]The sophists claimed that political areté should be founded upon knowledge and could be taught. See Jaeger, 1:286–93. On what Socrates thought could be taught respecting virtue see Burnet, *Greek Philosophy*, pp. 170–77. Earlier Solon had indicated that the law-maker was in need of much greater capacity for judgment than the mere law-obeyer. See Jaeger, 1:148–49. On Greek views of nature and natural law see also Havelock, passim, and Collingwood, *The Idea of Nature*, pt. 1.

[45]Jaeger, 1:323, 326–30; Havelock, pp. 231, 349–50; Freeman, *Pre-Socratic Philosophers*, pp. 369, 379–80, 388, 397–98, 419–20, and for opposite view, pp. 391, 415–16; Burnet, *Greek Philosophy*, pp. 105–7, 109, 117, 121, and *Essays and Addresses*, pp. 23–28. The view (especially that of Heraclitus) that strife permeated the cosmos probably contributed to the view that conflict characterized the world of men, at least in the absence of suitable and effectively enforced laws. On might makes right in international affairs, see Thucydides, *Complete Writings*, 5:17.331.

who looked upon law as an instrument by which men were made just, and by Plato who asserted that if Law and Nature were opposed, right would not be distinguished from wrong, and restraint would be abolished.[46] It remained for Plato and Aristotle, especially the latter, to determine the place of justice among the virtues[47] and to make more precise the meaning of justice.

Before turning to Plato we shall touch upon the views of Democritus and Archytas. Democritus apparently esteemed moderation above courage and justice, though he considered the two latter important virtues. He counselled moderation, remarking that "he is fortunate who is happy with moderate means," and noted that friendliness, generosity, and mutual aid made for harmony, well-being, and justice. He did not define justice,[48] except to say that it consisted in doing "what should be done." While he observed that compliance with the requirements of justice pro-

[46] Aristotle *Politics* 1280ᵇ; Plato *Laws* 889–90 and *Republic* 359. For general accounts of the substitution, in fifth-century Greek philosophy, of interest in the distinction between the natural and the conventional for interest in the distinction between the permanent and the manifold, see G. H. Sabine and S. B. Smith, introduction to their translation of Cicero's *De Republica*, pp. 15ff; G. H. Sabine, *A History of Political Theory*, ch. 2; and Ernest Barker, *Greek Political Theory: Plato and His Predecessors*, 2nd ed. Life according to nature was interpreted either to mean pursuit of self-interest (e.g., power, advantage, pleasure, etc., of the individual) or to signify compliance with a higher and more or less cosmic moral code that flowed from man's essential nature (e.g., Stoic cosmopolitanism in keeping with universal and world-wide law). In either case, therefore, life according to nature involved conflict with the rules of traditional morality and with the laws and practices obtaining in existing communities. Conflict was not so marked in the works of Plato and Aristotle because they believed the perfect society realizable within the polis and because (see Burnet, *Early Greek Philosophy*, 2nd ed., p. 13) they also looked upon the natural state of something as its best state and as that which was the goal of its development.

[47] Plato indicated that "the essence of the citizen's highest areté" had been variously found in courage, prudence or temperance, justice, and wisdom, the last having been described as supreme by Xenophanes who found in it the source of justice, law, right order, and welfare. See *Republic* 442–43; Jaeger, 1:173–74, 289; Freeman, *Ancilla*, pp. 20–21. Aristotle, who defined each virtue much more sharply than did Plato, discussed about a dozen moral virtues and several intellectual virtues in his *Nicomachean Ethics* wherein also (1129ᵇ) he referred to the view that justice comprehends every virtue

[48] See Freeman, *Ancilla*, pp. 92ff., frgs. 3, 170–71, 185, 187, 189, 191, 194, 211, 214, 219, 223, 255, 282–87, 291. He described (frg. 279) private property as more conducive to industry and thrift than communal property. Malthusian sentiments are also expressed (frgs. 276–77). Earlier Phaleas had proposed equalization of property (Aristotle *Pol.* 1266ᵇ). On the political theory of Democritus see Havelock, ch. 6.

duced a satisfying state of mind, he indicated that law was essential to the prevention of injustice, the preservation of justice, and the improvement of man.[49] While he emphasized rewarding according to merit, saying that "he has the greatest share of justice who awards the greatest offices (honours?) (*to the most deserving*)," he did not otherwise define justice in distribution or exchange in the extant fragments of his work.[50] He esteemed serenity of spirit highly, as did so many of the ancient philosophers, thus giving expression to a value that was not likely to be conducive to progress in the realm of material things.[51]

Plato's idea of justice must have been influenced by Pythagorean notions of proportion and fairness.[52] According to the Pythagoreans, E. L. Minar, Jr., finds: "The eternal fact of inevitable inequality underlies everything and is the basis for social institutions. Society is made up of individuals differing in virtue and other qualities, some of whom are naturally rulers, some naturally subjects. . . . The perfectly harmonious and truly well-ordered state is achieved by the cooperation of both classes [rulers and ruled], each within its proper sphere. . . . In the aristocratic society equality . . . does prevail. This is the so-called geometrical equality."[53] The Pythagoreans apparently believed that both corrective and distributive justice consisted in every man receiving what is his due.[54] Ar-

---

[49] Freeman, *Ancilla*, frgs. 174, 215, 245, 248, 252, 256–58, 261–62, 282, 287.

[50] Ibid., frg. 263. On his work see also Freeman, *Pre-Socratic Philosophers*, esp. pp. 315–22, and Burnet, *Greek Philosophy*, pp. 199–201.

[51] Gilbert Murray states that the ancients went straight for an appeal to the soul "because, with their very small capacity to improve material conditions, they felt themselves denied recourse to external remedies for unhappiness and wickedness," such as are resorted to by "us moderns" who have "the organization, the knowledge, the power, the necessary instruments, in all of which respects the ancients were utterly deficient." So they often sought personally to "attain an inward peace" through philosophy or saintliness. See "Reactions To The Peloponnesian War," *Journal of Hellenic Studies* 63:8. Hellenistic philosophers generally (e.g., Cynics, Stoics, Epicureans) depreciated or tried to disregard the world, or turned their thought inward. For this reason, among others, effective use was not made of such techniques as existed, they were not significantly improved, and there did not come into being a set of values suited to make possible the rise of modern capitalism.

[52] See Burnet, *Greek Philosophy*, p. 48, and *Early Greek Philosophy*, p. 106; Freeman, *Pre-Socratic Philosophers*, p. 110; also A. D. Winspear, ch. 4 and passim.

[53] *Early Pythagorean Politics*, pp. 108–9, 110, 118.

[54] Ibid., pp. 117–18. See also *Nic. Eth.*, 1132[b], where Aristotle rejects the Pythagorean view that the principle of reciprocity is applicable without qualification in the realm of corrective justice. See also S. Todd Lowry, "Aristotle's Mathematical Analysis of Exchange," pp. 44–66.

chytas, friend of Plato and a mathematician, gave expression to the Pythagorean notion of proportional justice when he wrote:

> Right Reckoning, when discovered, checks civil strife and increases concord; for where it has been achieved, there can be no excess of gain, and equality reigns. It brings us to terms over business contracts, and through it the poor receive from the men of means, and the rich give to the needy, both trusting that through it (*Right Reckoning*) they will be treated fairly. Being the standard and deterrent of wrongdoers, it checks those who are able to reckon (*consequences*) before they do wrong, convincing them that they will not be able to avoid detection when they come against it; but when they are not able (*to reckon*) it shows them that in this lies their wrongdoing, and so prevents them from commiting the wrong deed.[55]

C. Plato's Conception of Economics

Plato's thought is conservative, nonliberal in character,[56] and focused upon life in the polis, or city-state. His conception[57] of what constituted a satisfactory distributive or exchange arrangement flows from his conception of societies—particularly, ideal societies—as made up of functionally differentiated components which are hierarchically organized, and from his associated conception of justice as being expressible in terms of proportionality, terms earlier stressed by Pythagoreans.[58] The city-

[55] Freeman, *Ancilla*, p. 80, frg. 3. For slightly different translations see Minar, p. 91, and Josef Soudek's excellent paper, "Aristotle's Theory of Exchange: An Inquiry Into The Origin of Economic Analysis," *Proceedings Of The American Philosophical Society* 96:57. On Archytas see Freeman, *Pre-Socratic Philosophers*, pp. 234ff., and Minar, esp. pp. 86ff., 111ff. Soudek believes (p. 57) that Aristotle's view—that the establishment of social order in a community consists in the discovery and the application of right proportions—was inspired by Archytas about whose philosophy Aristotle wrote a book (according to Diogenes Laertius *Lives of Eminent Philosophers* 5:25). See also S. Todd Lowry, "Aristotle's Mathematical Analysis of Exchange."

[56] Winspear, pt. 1, esp. ch. 4.

[57] This paragraph and the one that follows are based upon *Rep.* 370–75, and *Laws* 737–38, also 847. In *Timaeus* 24 Plato treats of division of labor in Egypt. On Plato's views concerning the origin of justice in the soul and the resemblance existing between the perfect state and the soul, see Jaeger, 2:200–208, 240–42. The *Republic* was composed before 386 B.C.; the *Laws*, after 357 B.C.; *Gorgias*, before 386 B.C.; the other dialogues cited, much later. I have made use principally of Jowett's translation of the *Dialogues of Plato*.

[58] See *Rep.* 369–70, 433–34, on specialization of function and division of labor. On the Pythagorean conception of justice as geometrical equality, based on indi-

state (polis) had not arisen, as some asserted, out of a convention or pact entered into by men to escape the evils of an essentially Hobbesian world.[59] It had arisen out of the diversity of mankind's needs. For these needs, being various, could not well be satisfied by individuals acting alone. They could best be supplied when to each need there corresponded a category of citizens who specialized in its satisfaction and when each individual did "the thing to which his nature was best adapted" and avoided meddling in the corresponding activities of others.[60] Such an ar-

---

vidual differences, rather than arithmetical equality based on the absence of such differences, see Winspear, ch. 4. K. R. Popper characterizes the *Republic* as "probably the most elaborate monograph on justice ever written," a monograph in which Plato expresses a theory running counter to the humanitarian theory of justice, when he defends natural privilege, holism or collectivism in general, and the principle that it is "the end of the individual to maintain, and to strengthen, the stability of the state." Popper thus finds Plato to be an advocate of a closed or totalitarian society, and the enemy of the "open society" in which "individuals are confronted with personal decisions." See *The Open Society and Its Enemies* 1: 80, 82, 152.

[59] Herodotus (*History* 1:96–97) anticipated the Hobbesian situation when, on the basis of Athenian opinion, he made Median spokesmen declare that, since they had experienced lawlessness and "perpetual war" between "justice and injustice" so long as they had been without a central authority: "We cannot possibly . . . go on living in this country if things continue as they now are; let us therefore set a king over us, so that the land may be well governed, and we ourselves may be able to attend to our own affairs and not be forced to quit our country on account of anarchy." Plato rejected the Hobbesian type of argument which had been anticipated by the Sophists. "And so when men have both done and suffered injuries and have had experience of both, not being able to avoid the one and obtain the other, they think that they had better agree among themselves to have neither; hence there arise laws and mutual convenents; and that which is ordained by law is termed by them lawful and just. This they affirm to be the origin and nature of justice;—it is a mean or compromise, between the best of all, which is to do injustice and not be punished, and the worst of all, which is to suffer injustice without the power of retaliation; and justice, being at a middle point between the two, is tolerated not as a good, but as the lesser evil, and honoured by reason of the inability of men to do injustice. For no man who is worthy to be called a man would ever submit to such an agreement if he were able to resist; he would be mad if he did." See *Rep.* 359; *Theaetetus* 172; also *Laws* 679, where it is said that when numbers are few and subsistence is not lacking, there is no war and strife. See *Rep.* 338ff., for criticism of the might-makes-right theory, and *Gorgias* 487–89, 504–5, on this and related theories.

[60] See *Rep.* 369–74, on the emergence of association and division of labor from the multiplicity of man's wants. Plato recognized a need for the farmer, the builder, the clothier, the cobbler, the instrument-maker, the herdsman, the foreign-trader, the retail trader, and, if the state became larger, for other callings.

rangement was compatible with the view that the good life and hence an individual's happiness consisted in the good performance of his proper function.[61] It entailed that the three (or more) classes "in the State severally [do] their own business" and refrain from interfering in that of others; it required, as will be seen, that the population act in accordance with the rules of justice; and it presupposed a population large enough to permit defense of the polis and suitable division of labor.[62]

It being the primary purpose of the ideal state to enable its members (above all, its citizens) to live morally and develop certain virtues—wisdom, courage, temperance or self-control, (justice), it was necessary that the differentiated individuals composing the state be bound together since the resulting unity was essential to the cultivation of virtue. This bond was supplied by justice, which served to organize the specialized members of the state.[63] Whether, in Plato's opinion, justice, or arrangements designed to produce justice, would by themselves suffice to unify the various groups found in the state, is not always clear. Presumably, as moderns might say, formal arrangements need buttressing by informal ones. He suggests at various points the need for "communion of mind,"

Even so, he asked (*Rep.* 590) "why are mean employments and manual arts a reproach?" and assigned (*Laws* 918–20) retail trade to metics (aliens) since it usually tended to be carried on for gain instead of merely for its proper end, the carrying on of necessary exchange in a society of specialists. The principal advantage of division of labor (*Rep* 370) was that it enabled each man to do the "one thing which is natural to him" and to do "it at the right time," and that (*Laws* 846–48) it recognized that "Hardly any human being is capable of pursuing two professions or two arts rightly, or of practising one art himself, and superintending someone else who is practising another." In the *Laws* (643, 743) both technical education and agriculture designed to furnish subsistence were approved.

[61] See Barker, pp. 158–59, 260–64, and pp. 355–56, on Plato's identification of justice, or right-doing, with happiness. Whereas, in the *Republic* goodness is virtually identified with justice, in the *Laws* it is virtually identified with self-control (ibid., pp. 153–54 n, 297ff.; Burnet, *The Ethics of Aristotle*, pp. 2–3).

[62] An excessive population also was to be avoided. See *Rep.* 372ff., 423; *Laws* 737, 745–47; also *Rep.* 459–60; *Laws* 740, 764, 771–76. Plato apparently looked with somewhat more favor upon economic activities than did Aristotle. Herodotus, when contrasting the Greek and Persian attitudes toward trade, did not express the misgivings about it that one encounters in the works of Plato and Aristotle See *History*, e.g., 1:153, 2:167.

[63] See *Laws* 630–31, 688ff.; *Rep.* 428–45; Barker, pp. 176ff., 296ff. Whereas, in the *Republic* justice differentiates and coordinates functions, in the *Laws* self-control (i.e., the submission of appetite to reason) harmonizes the different elements found in the state, and becomes ascendant even over justice. Plato looked upon virtue as a unity and upon good as a unity. See Burnet, *Ethics of Aristotle*, pp. xlviii, 2–3.

"community of feeling," "common feeling," "common feeling of pleasure and pain," "common interest in the same thing," "friendship and the absence of hatred and division." These conditions of mind and feeling were essential to effective communication within the state and to establishment of a situation in which an injury to any one part would be felt in other parts. It was to establish a situation and to avert "plurality" and "discord" that in the *Republic* Plato advocated "community of property" and "community of women and children" for the guardian class. At most, however, he did little more than anticipate modern theories of social cohesion.[64]

When a society is hierarchically organized, with each individual part of an order and required to fill an appointed place therein, and when a society, being specialized (as was each of Plato's model states), must engage in exchange, a problem necessarily arises, that of integrating the specialists and determining justice in the distribution of privileges and in the exchange of goods and services.[65] In general, justice entailed "the having and doing what is one's own, and belongs to him."[66] Unfortunately,

[64]*Rep.* 462–64; *Laws* 694, 697, 739; *Alcibiades* 1.126; *Gorgias* 481. Cf. Aristophanes's satire of communism in *Ecclesiazusae*. Plato seems to have anticipated the modern view that informal organizations complement formal organizations, for he says that "unwritten customs" fill up the interstices of written laws and so serve, as do written laws, to "bind together" the state. See *Laws* 793; cf. Aristotle's treatment of administrative rulings in *Politics* 3.16. In the *Republic* law plays a small part, the philosopher king representing reason, whereas in the *Laws* the law becomes "the surrogate" for reason which remains "the supreme force in nature" (Sabine, pp. 68–76). However, when the role of law becomes great, attention is likely to be directed to the interests and claims which affect the content of law and are brought into balance through law. It was in the *Laws* that Plato dealt with the "mutual adjustment of claims and interests" and that Aristotle found more realistic points of departure (see ibid., pp. 85–86; Barker, p. 39ff.).

[65]Plato's conception of justice is much more inclusive than a discussion of justice in distribution and exchange suggests; as the organizing principle of society it embraces the performance of his duty by each member of this moral organism, together with the code of ethics that animates each to discharge his function. It differed from the Roman conception of judicial rules, rights, and remedies. See Barker, esp. pp. 176–80, 260–64.

[66]*Rep.* 433. C. B. Welles calls this "the earliest statement of the famous Roman principle, *suum cuique.*" See his "The Economic Background of Plato's Communism," *Journal of Economic History*, Sup. 8:108. See also M.P. Guibal, *De l'influence de la philosophie sur le droit romain et la jurisprudence de l'époque classique* (Paris, 1937); Fritz Schulz, *History of Roman Legal Science*, pp. 135–37. A somewhat similar dictum respecting remuneration, "give every one according to his ways, and according to the fruit of his doings," appears in Jeremiah 32:19, and 17:10, also Psalms 62:12. Jeremiah dates largely from the last quarter of the seventh century B.C.

it is not always easy to determine "what is a man's own, and belongs to him." Nor did Plato contribute much toward this determination, confining most of what he had to say to the *Laws*.

Let us consider first justice in exchange. In the *Laws* (913) he stated that "dealings between man and man require to be suitably regulated. The principle of them is very simple: —Thou shalt not, if thou canst help, touch that which is mine, or remove the least thing which belongs to me without my consent." And he proceeded to declare that, in his model polis, fraudulent sales and adulteration of goods would be subject to penalty; the granting of credit would be prohibited; retail markups would be regulated; breaches of contract would be actionable; and so on.[67] So also would the lending of money at interest be prohibited, together with the hoarding of gold and silver, though interest would be collectable on overdue accounts.[68] These regulations were intended to assure what Aristotle later called justice in exchange and rectificatory justice, together with "arithmetical" equality (that is, equality between individuals who, in respect of the transaction in question, were equals); they involved the "rule of measure, weight, and number."

The correct or just distribution of offices and honors presupposed the application not of arithmetical equality, but of "another equality, of a better and higher kind," namely, proportionate equality. It "is the source of the greatest good to individuals and states. For it gives to the greater more, and to the inferior less and in proportion to the nature of each; and, above all, greater honour always to the greater virtue, and to the less less; and to either in proportion to their respective measure of virtue and education. And this is justice, is ever the true principle of

---

[67] *Laws* 743, 847–50, 914–21. Cf. *Rep.* 556, where, to prevent "scandalous money-making" he proposed that every one shall enter into voluntary contracts at his own risk." In a work sometimes attributed to Aristotle (*Atheniensium Respublica*, 5) he described Athenian price-control measures. Plato distinguished (*Sophist* 219–24) "productive" from "acquisitive" arts. An art is productive when it "brings into existence something that did not exist before" (e.g., agriculture, construction, moulding vessels, tending animals). Acquisitive arts do not bring anything into existence though they may give rise to a monetary or other type of return. They include exchange, which is voluntary, and is effected by gifts, hire, purchase or taking "by force of word or deed," as in hunting, fishing, fighting and conquest. Plato's emphasis on bringing something into being did not imply any stress upon capital accumulation as (e.g.,) did Adam Smith's notion of productive labor. Later Aristotle (*Metaphysics* 2.[or 7] 8) described production in general as the introduction of specific forms into matter, a conception that was to be repeated in substance by Cantillon, Condillac, J. B. Say, and others.

[68] *Laws* 742–43, 921; cf. *Rep.* 556.

states. . . ."[69] In the *Republic* (539–40) the selection of the guardians was based on tested ability and patriotism. In the *Laws* Plato suggests awarding rulership to those "most obedient to the laws of the state" and giving least preference to wealth when ordaining honors; and yet he recommends that, in a newly established colony, "offices and contributions and distributions . . . be proportioned to the value of each person's wealth, and not solely" to his goods of the soul, or to his bodily goods (which while inferior to goods of the soul, are superior to wealth).[70] It was taken for granted by Plato as well as by Aristotle that citizens must know both how to rule and how to obey, that noncitizen free men had legal rights as well as obligations, and that slaves were entitled to just and kind treatment.[71] There seems to have been implicit in this conception of proportionate equality some notion of a network of reciprocal rights and duties; but, particularly in Plato's scheme, it allowed the individual little choice except that of performing his alloted function in the prescribed way. So there was little conception of the state as guarantor of either individual rights or the performance of individual duties, or of the individual duties, or of the individual acting largely from internal motives rather than from external sactions.[72]

The preservation of unity required that the workings of justice and of community of feeling be reenforced by arrangements designed to pre-

[69] *Laws* 757. In *Gorgias* 508, where it is said that "communion and friendship and orderliness and temperance and justice bind together heaven and earth and gods and men," Plato states that "geometrical equality is mighty." Democracy is unfavorable to such equality (*Rep* 562–63). While Plato observes that the practitioner of every art must observe a mean between excess and defect (*Statesman* 283ff., 305–11), he does not make great application of this concept (which originated with the Pythagoreans) to justice as does Aristotle. Plato discusses proportion in *Timaeus* 31ff., and mean, measure, and symmetry in *Philebus*, passim, but does not extend these concepts to justice. From this dialogue Aristotle derived his doctrine of the mean, according to Burnet, *Early Greek Philosophy*, p. 112. See also Winspear, ch. 4.

[70] *Laws* 715, 743–44; also 696 where virtue is esteemed above wealth, and 742–43 where possession of great riches is described as unfavorable to that of goodness. The proportioning of allocations to wealth conforms to justice when the allocations entail burdens rather than income as the above statement suggests. On some of the burdens incident upon wealthy persons see Xenophon *Oeconomicus* 2.4ff.; also Aristotle's comments on liturgies (e.g., fitting out triremes, equipping choruses), most of which he considered useless except insofar as they made oligarchy tolerable. See *Pol.* 5.5.6. On the use of lots in the selection of office-holders, see *Laws* 690, 757, 759; *Rep.* 557.

[71] *Laws* 643, 777–78, 848–50; Aristotle *Politics* 1.6–7, 12–13, 3.1, 7.14.

[72] See Barker, *Greek Political Theory*, pp. 7, 176–79, 196 n., 230ff., 320, 354.

vent dissension, faction, and revolution.[73] While these arrangements included provision both for administration by "men who are the wisest about affairs of State" and who are not covetous of money[74] and for the selection of good examiners for service in the courts, they placed major emphasis upon the averting of want, upon the prevention of the individual's accumulating great wealth through money-making or other activities, and upon the avoidance of excessive economic inequality. "In a state which is desirous of being saved from the greatest of all plagues—not faction, but rather distraction—there should exist among the citizens neither extreme poverty, nor, again, excess of wealth, for both are productive of both these evils."[75]

Plato, therefore, proposed greatly restricting both economic activity and the accumulation and use of property. As has been noted, crafts and trading for profit would be denied to citizens, money-lending at interest and the accumulation of gold and silver would be prohibited, only the importation of luxuries would be allowed, and other restrictions would be put into effect.[76] Citizens engaging to establish a colony were to be divided into four classes based upon wealth, with the amount held by a member of the wealthiest class not to exceed five times that held by a member of the least wealthy class.[77] While Plato specified that the total number of citizens composing his ideal polis was to continue unchanged, together with the magnitude of the average amount of land held by them, he contemplated some interclass movement on the part of individuals.[78] Given this condition and the further condition that the granting of credit

[73]That the Greeks had long theorized about forms of government is suggested by Herodotus's account (*History* 3.80–83) which reflected Athenian opinion (see J. S. Morrison, "The Place of Protagoras in Athenian Public Life," *Classical Quarterly* 35:12–13) of the advantages and weaknesses of democracy, oligarchy, and monarchy. He suggested that both democracy and oligarchy tended to give place to monarchy.

[74]*Rep.* 521, 548–49. Money as such is not evil, being but an instrument which "reduces the inequalities and incommensurabilities of goods to equality and common measure" (*Laws* 918). Elsewhere (ibid., 746–47) Plato declared that "the law ought to order" the units of measure (i.e., ranks, weights, measures, coins, etc.) to be so defined "as to be commensurable and agreeable to one another." On Socratic monetary theory see Gordon, *Economic Analysis*, pp. 43–48.

[75]*Laws* 744.

[76]*Laws* 741–44, 846–50, 914–21. Even dowries would be disallowed (ibid. 742).

[77]*Laws* 741, 744–45. The size of a citizen's minimum holding is not specified, but is was small, with one-third of the produce reserved for citizens (*Laws* 848).

[78]*Laws* 740–41, 744–45, 855–56. In Western Asia prevention of the alienation of land was approved and attempted. See Eli Ginzberg, *Studies In the Economics of The Bible, Jewish Quarterly Review* 22:373–74, 407–8; Edward Chiera, pp. 181ff.

be prohibited, Plato (presumably) inferred, the incurrence of indebtedness by individuals would be averted as would such causes of dissension as redivisions of land, loss of property through foreclosure, and movements to abolish indebtedness.[79] The untoward effects associated with wealth-accumulation and moneymaking[80] would be minimized by restrictions upon the acquisition and use of property and by turning the conduct of retail trade over to aliens.[81] It is not clear whether he intended liberality to reenforce these checks to wealth-accumulation, or to assist the poor for whom, if they were victims of misfortune, poor relief was indicated.[82]

Summarizing Plato's views respecting economic welfare, it may be said that he did not attach great importance to material progress, and that some of the values stressed by him, together with the rigidity of the framework within which they had to find expression, were not conducive to material progress.[83] Neither a satisfactory distribution of wealth nor appropriate prices would result in the absence of legal constraints. Competition was not approved as an end in itself. Moreover, Plato's conception of the individual discharging his allotted function within an orderly societal scheme served both to emphasize complementarity rather than competition and to underscore moral responsibility to society rather than pursuit of individual advantage.[84] The function of competition (as distinguished from ascription) as an allocator of economic tasks, roles, and rewards was not appreciated by Plato, nor was its contribution to the formation of prices. The limits to which economic activity was subject within the polis were relaxed, albeit moderately, when foreign trade served (as it did not in Plato's polis) to enlarge the milieu within which enterprise could be carried on.

[79] *Laws* 736, 849–50, 915 on credit; *Rep.* 555.

[80] *Rep.* 422, 550–51, 562; *Laws* 705, 741, 743, 842, 918ff.

[81] *Rep.* 556; *Laws* 920. It would not be necessary for foreigners to carry on retail trade if the "best" men engaged in it, and extortionate practices were averted (*Laws* 918–19).

[82] *Laws* 936; also *Rep.* 485–86, where covetousness is condemned and liberality is described as a quality of the philosopher. In Athens the poor derived relief from payments for attending the assembly and law courts and from the "theoric" or spectators' fund which allowed the applicant two obols a day to attend the theatre during festivals. See *Nic. Eth.* 2.7; also Barker's comments, in his edition of *Pol.*, pp. lvi, 67, 318, 379. Cripples unable to work and lacking means could qualify to receive two obols a day from the state for their support. See *Atheniensium Respublica* 49.4, of which Aristotle may be the author.

[83] Such values as underlay basing reward upon merit and insisting upon justice in exchange were favorable to material progress.

[84] Cf. Barker, *Greek Political Theory*, pp. 157 n, 176–80.

Plato's contemporary, Isocrates, described justice in part as had Plato and remarked several empirical aspects of Greek economic life. He declared that what had contributed most to the goodness of the Athenians' government "was that of the two recognized kinds of equality—that which makes the same award to all alike and that which gives to each man his due—they did not fail to grasp which was the more serviceable; but, rejecting as unjust that which holds the good and the bad are worthy of the same honours, and preferring rather that which rewards and punishes every man according to his deserts, they governed the city on this principle, not filling the offices by lot from all the citizens, but selecting the best and the ablest for each function of the state."[85] He noted that while laws were essential for the protection of persons, it was "not by legislation, but by morals" that states were well directed and men were disposed to do what was right.[86]

He commented several times on circumstances underlying economic prosperity, but did not connect these comments with his remarks on justice. He observed that men were animated by the prospect of gain and that industry tended to flourish when it could be pursued profitably; and he noted that progress was most likely when men had the "courage constantly to change" that which was in need of change.[87] He remarked that "those of the same order of talent in each profession have incomes which are comparable."[88] He indicated that population pressure made for scarcity of necessities, strife, and efforts at colonization.[89] In part perhaps

[85]*Areopagiticus* 21–22, (written about 355 B.C.). The same idea was expressed in *Nicocles* 14–15 (written about 373 B.C.), wherein, among other things, "the very essence of justice" is described as consisting in rewarding individuals "according to their deserts." Elsewhere he praises "justice" (see *To Demonicus* 15, 38; *Archidamus* 35) and notes that in a democratic state " all enjoy equal rights" (*Against Lochites* 19–21). In his discussion of "arbitration," of the overpayment of athletes, and of contracts, however, he does not make use of a principle of justice. See *Against Callimachus* 10; *Panegyricus* 1–2; *Antidosis* 301–2; *To the Rulers of Mytilene* 4–5; *Trapeziticus* 2. I have used the Loeb Classical Library edition of Isocrate's works.

[86]See *Panegyricus* 38–41; *Areop.* 40–41; *Against Lochites* 1. In *Against the Sophists* 14–15, he described ability as a result of both natural endowment and "practical experience."

[87]See *To Nicocles* 17–18; *Antidosis* 217–18; *Evagoras* 7. He touched several times upon disadvantages associated with wealth, however (*Areop.* 4; *Archidamus* 101–2; *To Demonicus* 6–7, 28).

[88]*Antidosis* 157–58. He seems to have had vaguely in mind a notion of relatively noncompeting groups.

[89]*Pan.* 34–38; *Helen* 67–79. War too could stimulate colonization (*Archidamus* 72–74). Isocrates remarked that insecurity of property, together with frequency of poverty, had increased in Athens, but he did not attribute it to growth of

because he recognized the importance of commerce to the prosperity of Athens, he favored the attraction and fair treatment of foreigners even though he seems to have considered the size of the population of Athens to be in excess of the political optimum.[90]

D. Aristotle's Conception of Economics

In the field of social science Aristotle's work focused more upon political problems than upon economic issues. While he wrote no work devoted specifically to economics, a seven-page work, *Oeconomica*, by "a Peripatetic writer who was a pupil either of Aristotle himself or of a disciple" of Aristotle, suggests how Aristotle may have conceived of "economics."[91] Herein "economics" deals with a household while political science deals with a city, that is, with an aggregate made up of households, land and property. Economic science founds a household and makes use of it while political science constitutes a city and makes "a right use of it." Agriculture, which ranks first among forms of property, made use of by the self-sufficient household, is most just and natural in that it does not take anything away from men "as do retail trading and the mercenary arts." Moreover, the household produces the children who support their parents in old age. Good slaves rank high among a household's possessions and therefore need to be managed with care. What Aristotle called "the economist" ought to be able to acquire wealth, use it well, diversify it, and preserve it appropriately. The author envisaged Attica as consisting primarily of small estates and secondarily of large estates.

Aristotle, in evaluating economic actions, takes into account whether

---

population. See *Areop.* 82–83; *On the Peace* 45–46; *Antidosis* 159–60. He reports both Malthusian and anti-Malthusian sentiments (ibid., 155; *Evagoras* 72).

[90] See *Antidosis* 171–72; *Pan.*, 41–46; *To Nicoles* 22; *To the Rulers of Mytilene* 4. *Panegyricus* was written about 380 B.C. for the purpose of inducing the feuding Greek city-states to unite and conquer Persia. This panhellenic policy had been advocated earlier by Gordias who also found a cure for internal dissension in external diversion. See Freeman, *Pre-Socratic Philosophers*, p. 362; Barker, pp. 267–68.

In *Eryxias*, now attributed to an early third-century (B.C.) member of the Academy (see D. E. Eichholz, "The Pseudo-Platonic Dialogue ERYXIAS," *Classical Quarterly*, 29:129–49) the author ignores justice. He restricts the term wealth to indispensable things which directly satisfy bodily needs, but in the course of the dialogue has speakers say that the value of money is fixed by convention, that recognized usefulness is an attribute of wealth, and that the instruments of production possess derived value (*Eryxias* 400, 401–6).

[91] *Oeconomica*, translated by E. S. Forster, is bound with *Politica*, translated by Benjamin Jowett, in *The Works of Aristotle*, ed. W. D. Ross, vol. 10.

an action is in keeping with the proper function of that action. For example, since the proper function of trade is to serve man's material needs, as is characteristic of barter, trade carried on only for the sake of revenue is unnatural; it is not subject to limits such as tend to rule in the case of barter and when the sole object of trade is the purchase of goods for their natural use—limits that are not operative in commercial trade.[92] With Aristotle as with Plato the primary purpose of the polis[93] was to enable those composing its population to realize, within its physical and moral boundaries, the "highest good" (i.e., felicity, well-being) attainable[94] by them through the pursuit of an active and appropriately virtuous life.[95]

[92] See S. Todd Lowry, "Aristotle's 'Natural Limit'," pp. 57–63. See *Pol.* 1.9–11, 13.

[93] The dimensions of Aristotle's ideal polis however differ somewhat from those of the polis described in Plato's *Laws.* This polis included 5,040 citizen families of four members each, together with about 40,000 slaves and metics, and embraced a territory of 200–800 square miles. The resulting population density, 75–300 per square mile, may therefore have exceeded densely populated Attica's 200 per square mile. See Welles, pp. 113–14, based on *Laws* 704, 737, 740–41, 745, 848. Though Plato had recommended controlling numbers through colonization and regulation of natural increase, Aristotle, who looked upon population pressure as a principal cause of poverty and who mentioned several methods of quantitative and qualitative control of numbers (abortion, child-exposure, colonization), believed that Plato's ideal state would require more land than usually was available to a city and would make too little provision for the control of its numbers (*Pol.* 2.6, 9–11, 6.5, 7.4, 16; cf. Plato *Laws* 707–9, 736, 740–41, 754). Aristotle observed that a state "only begins to exist when it has attained a population sufficient for a good life in the political community: it may indeed, if it somewhat exceeds this number, be a greater state. . . . The best limit of the population of a state is the largest number which suffices for the purposes of life, and can be taken at a single view." (*Pol.* 7.4, also 5). In *Critias* 111–12, Plato indicated that the erosion of Attica's land had not been accompanied by a diminution in her population.

[94] In nature all things are ordered to some end, and ends may be so arranged that one, "the chief good," is sought for itself and not as a means to some other end. See *Metaphysics,* 12.10; *Nic. Eth.* 1.1–2. Since the population embraced citizens, slaves, and others, not all could practice goodness perfectly and realize "the best and highest life possible." In actual life some may share fully while others may share only partially or not at all. See *Pol.* 7.7–10, and Barker's note, p. 300, of his edition, where he interprets Aristotle as suggesting that there may be states in which not only citizens (as in ideal states) but others may be parts of the state.

[95] *Pol.* 1.2, 7.1–3. Aristotle rejected Plato's idea of a universal good, saying there are many kinds of virtue and that rarely can any one excel in all (ibid., 3.4; *Nic. Eth.* 3–5). Man's happiness was to be found in his performing his own proper

While Aristotle admitted that men may be brought together by their common interests, he found the origin of the state in the fact "that the polis belongs to the class of things that exist by nature, and that man is by nature an animal intended to live in a polis."[96] For this reason (presumably) and because of disadvantages associated with community of women and property and with extreme unity, Aristotle looked upon the degree of unity sought by Plato as unnecessary and as inimical to a state's continued existence as a state. Community of women and children ran counter to the experience and good sense of mankind just as did community of property; the former, by dissolving natural affection and regard; the latter, by undermining liberality and benevolence and by producing dispute and diminution of effort through reduction of the necessarily high correlation between effort and reward. A high degree of unity was incompatible with a state's essentially plural make-up, with the degree of differentiation of function naturally inherent in a state,[97] and with such division of labor as the attainment of communal self-sufficiency required.[98] But pluralism and differentiation of function entailed reciprocity and exchange, in accordance with the appropriate principles of justice, which became the bond holding men together in Aristotle's ideal state, a state in which business activity, being unfavorable to moral activity, needed to be confined to essentials.[99]

---

function well; being an "activity of the soul," it depended mainly "upon goodness of character" (which is produced by habituation) and but slightly upon material conditions. See Burnet, *Ethics of Aristotle*, pp. xlviii ff., 1–5, 108.

[96] *Pol.* 1253ᵃ; 1, 3. See also 7.8–10, where among the elements necessary for the existence of the state he includes: farmers to produce food; craftsmen to man the arts and crafts; a military and police force; a propertied class and a certain supply of property, alike for domestic use and for military purposes; priests to conduct public worship; and a system of deliberation and jurisdiction for deciding private dealings. Given these elements, a state is self-sufficient for the purposes of life. Slaves are included with property.

[97] *Pol.* 1.2; 2.1–3. In accordance with the differentiation of function found in nature and with the fact that some individuals lacked a developed deliberative faculty, there existed a natural basis for a mutually beneficial master-slave relationship. Under this relationship, those capable of deliberating and exercising authority guided those capable of obedience but incapable of deliberation. See *Pol.* 1.4–7, 13; *Nic. Eth.* 1161ᵇ. As L. H. Rifkin remarks ("Aristotle on Equality: Criticism of A. J. Carlyle's Theory," *Journal of the History of Ideas* 14:279–81), Aristotle did not sharply distinguish, as did Plato, between slaves and other social classes, and he did not imply the slave to be inferior on grounds of race or status.

[98] *Pol.* 2.1–5.

[99] *Pol* 1.2; 2.2; 3.12; *Nic. Eth.* 5.5. What is "divisible is called a plurality"; what is "indivisible" is called "one" or unity. See *Metaphysics*, 10.3. As noted earlier, Aristotle's use of proportion to represent just relations among unequals probably

Aristotle gave most attention to particular justice, this being a part of general or universal justice[100] which is synonymous with goodness or righteousness. When men, as members of an association, behave appropriately and fairly, they are complying with the rules of particular justice, manifesting (as it was put centuries later in Justinian's *Institutes* and repeated for many centuries thereafter) that "set and constant purpose which gives to every man his due."[101] Particular justice includes *distributive* justice, which "is manifested in distributions of honour or money or other things that fall to be divided among those who have a share in the constitution (for in these it is possible for one man to have a share either unequal or equal to that of another)"; *corrective* (or remedial or rectificatory) justice, which is concerned with both voluntary and involuntary private transactions;[102] and reciprocal or *commutative* justice, which differs somewhat from both corrective and distributive justice, being concerned with economic exchange.[103] Aristotle distinguished between political justice, which exists between members of a self-sufficient political association (e.g., the polis) who are free and (suitably) equal, and nonpolitical justice, which exists between superior and inferior members of lesser associations (e.g., household, family). Political justice thus in-

---

was influenced by the Pythagoreans who stressed interindividual differences in virtue and other qualities and found in the concept of proportion the tool suited to represent just relations in a world of unequals. On Aristotle's attitude toward business activity, see Havelock, esp. chs. 11–12.

[100] Justice was included in the category of moral virtues, but not in that of intellectual virtues, though "practical wisdom" enabled man to choose the right means to the right end whose selection had been inspired by one of the virtues. While nearly every moral virtue represented a mean between an excess and a defect of feeling or action, justice represented a different sort of mean than did the other moral virtues. Aristotle named the virtues stressed by Plato (i.e., courage, wisdom, justice, temperance) but assigned highest place to theoretical wisdom. Aristotle also identified the virtues concerned with money, honor, anger, and social intercourse. Well-being he described as "activity of the soul in accordance with virtue." See *Nic. Eth.* 2–4; W. D. Ross, *Aristotle*, 5th ed., pp. 190, 202–3, 215, 220–21, 232–34; also *Pol.* 3.13, 7.15, and Burnet, *Ethics of Aristotle*, pp. 69–73.

[101] *Institutes*, 1.1.1. Particular justice is, in the phrase of Ulpian and later "in the phrase of Justinian, *constans et perpetua voluntas suum cuique tribuendi*," remarks Barker in his edition of the *Politics*, p. 362. See also R. W. and A. J. Carlyle, *A History of Medieval Political Theory in the West*, 2nd ed., pp. 57–58; Max Hamburger, *Morals and Law*, pp. 50, 110.

[102] *Nic. Eth.* 5.1–4.

[103] *Nic. Eth.* 5.5; also Ross, *Aristotle*, pp. 212–13, and Hamburger, *Morals*, pp. 44–53. For a more detailed account see Josef Soudek, pp. 52–53, who found only two writers (Pufendorf and D. G. Ritchie) who had distinguished reciprocal or commutative justice from distributive and corrective justice.

cluded both general and particular justice as expressed in the moral and legal structure of the polis. The rules of political justice were drawn from two sources, from that which held naturally and so was universally recognized as constituting justice,[104] and from that which was determined by convention and converted into a part of justice by legal enactment.[105] Aristotle distinguished between justice in the sense of what is lawful and equity in the sense of something that is separate from law and justice but corrects law by taking into account the concrete circumstances of particular cases to which a general law is not perfectly applicable.[106]

Corrective or rectificatory justice is concerned with private transactions, both those which are voluntary (e.g., selling, buying, pledging, lending with or without interest, depositing, letting for hire) and those which are involuntary (e.g., theft, adultery, etc.; assault, murder, imprisonment.)[107] This form of justice assured redress when, in voluntary or involuntary transactions in respect of which the participating parties were

[104]The essence of law consists in its being an impersonal rule that proceeds from "moral prudence and understanding" and rational principle, and not in its being conventional or enacted. The legislator merely discovers and declares the impersonal rule of law; he does not enact it. And he can discover and declare it only if he has the necessary legislative wisdom; and even then law, since it is a general rule, must be supplemented by equity. It is the objective of the legislator to make citizens "good by forming their habits." See *Nic. Eth.* 2.1; 5.6, 10.9–10; *Pol.* 3.9, 15, 16, and Barker's discussion in his translation, pp. livff., 366–69. In the *Rhetoric*, 1373[b], "universal law," or "the law of nature," is described as "a natural form of the just and unjust which is common to all men" and is distinguished from the community's declared or "particular" law.

[105]*Nic. Eth.* 5.6–8; *Rhetoric* 1372[a]–1375[b]; Barker, *Pol.* Appendix 2. Aristotle distinguished between political and absolute justice, but did not define the latter. Barker p. 364) infers it to be absolute in that it is justice "between man and man *sub specie humanitatis*" as distinguished from justice "between citizen and citizen *sub specie civitatis*." Cf. *Nic. Eth.* 1134[a].

[106]See *Politics* (Barker edition), pp. liv–lv, 365–69, also 3.16; *Nic. Eth.* 5.10; Vinogradoff, pp. 63ff. Aristotle distinguished between legal or enacted justice and unwritten or customary (expressed in social opinion) justice. See *Rhetoric* 1373[b], 1374[a]. Unwritten law is a part of a community's declared particular law (1373[b])

[107]*Nic. Eth.* 1131[a]. The voluntary transactions correspond to contracts in English and Roman law; the involuntary transactions, to torts or delicts. Description of this form of justice as corrective or rectificatory is held warranted by the fact that the law gives redress only when an individual has suffered a private wrong (tort, delict), or a hurt in the from of a violation of a legally valid contract. See H. D. P. Lee, "The Legal Background of Two Passages in the *Nichomachean Ethics*," *Classical Quarterly* 31:129–40; also Vinogradoff, pp. 46ff. The nature of the act, as distinct from the rank of the victim, was stressed by Demosthenes in *Against Meidias* 46.

arithmetically equal, one or the other party had suffered injustice because the conditions of corrective justice had been violated. Justice was restored when equality, "the intermediate between loss and gain," was restored.

> The law looks only to the distinctive character of the injury and treats the parties as equal. . . . Therefore, this kind of injustice being an inequality, the judge tries to equalize it . . . by means of the penalty, taking away from the gain of the assailant [or beneficiary]. . . . Corrective justice will be the intermediate between loss and gain. . . . The judge restores equality. . . .
>
> In buying and selling and in all other matters in which the law has left people free to make their own terms, . . . when they get neither more nor less but just what belongs to themselves, they say that they have their own and that they neither lose nor gain. . . . The just . . . consists in having an equal amount before and after the transaction.[108]

In sum, remedial justice has to do with the judicial power and the administration of justice whereas reciprocity, as will be seen, has to do largely with economic equilibration, and distributive justice with the legislative and executive task of distributing wealth, honor, rewards, etc.[109]

Reciprocal justice, or justice in exchange, which centuries later came to be called commutative justice, held men together in "associations for exchange" and so was essential to the continuation of that specialization and exchange which underlay the economic life of the polis. This form of justice usually was arithmetical as well as geometrical in character, since it entailed both the exchange of equally valuable products and the reward of each transacting specialist in proportion to his skill. "It is by proportionate requital that the city holds together."[110] It is in consequence of the

---

[108] *Nic. Eth.* 1132^a, 1132^b, also 1132^b on rejection of *lex talionis*. It is not always clear what solution corrective justice requires in a particular case. E.g., see Ross, *Aristotle.*, pp. 211–12; Burnet, *Ethics*, pp. 220–22; whose example corresponds to Burnet's explanation. In general, corrective justice entails restoration of the positions of the affected parties as they existed before the unjust transaction, but it is not always easy to determine what these positions were. So the solution may consist in establishing as the correct value for each party (to a transaction) the mean of their respective claims; or in transferring the gainer's gain to the loser; or in transferring from the gainer to the loser the average of the amount by which the gainer's holding was increased and the amount by which the loser's holding was decreased. When a party to a transaction demands less than he is legally entitled to, he is behaving equitably (*Nic. Eth.* 1138^a).

[109] See Hamburger, pp. 50–52. According to Soudek, corrective justice is essentially natural (pp. 52–53).

[110] *Nic. Eth.* 1132^b. Elsewhere he states that "the well-being of every polis de-

four-fold coincidence underlying barter that men (who usually "choose what is advantageous")[111] enter into barter or exchange transactions. "Now proportionate return is secured by cross-junction. Let A be a builder, B a shoemaker, C a house, D a shoe. The builder, then, must get from the shoemaker the latter's work, and must himself give him in return his own. If, then, first there is proportionate equality of goods and then reciprocal action takes place, the result we mention will be effected."[112]

It is essential first that the transacting parties give up and receive quantities of goods that are equal in value. Since goods in themselves differ greatly physically they cannot be made commensurate per se. But they can be made "sufficiently" commensurate "with reference to demand" or need or want-satisfaction, and this commensurability in terms of need, or demand, or want-satisfying power, or utility, can be translated into terms of a monetary unit by which all things are measured and made equitable.[113] If the goods, upon being translated into monetary units, prove to be equal, exchange can and will take place. "All goods must therefore be measured by some one thing, as we said before. Now this unit is in truth demand,[114] which holds all things together (for if men did not need one another's goods at all, or did not need them equally, there would be no exchange or not the same exchange; but money has become by conven-

---

pends on each of its elements rendering to the others an amount equivalent to what it receives from them" (*Pol.* 2.2). See also *Nic. Eth.* 1165[a], where he says that one should try to assign to every class "what is appropriate, and to compare the claims of each class with respect to nearness of relation and to virtue or usefulness."

[111] *Nic. Eth.* 1162[b]; also *Rhetoric* 1365[b], on self-interest.

[112] *Nic. Eth.* 1133[a]. That reciprocal demand or need "holds things together is shown by the fact that when men do not need one another, i.e., when neither needs the other or one does not need the other, they do not exchange, as we do when someone wants what one has oneself, e.g., when people permit the exportation of corn for wine." ibid., 1133[b], also 1133[a], 1164[a], or barter.

[113] *Nic. Eth.* 1133[b]. "All goods must have a price set on them; for then there will always be exchange, and if so, association of man with man." "Let A be a house, B ten minae, C a bed. A is half of B, if the house is worth five minae or equal to them; the bed, C, is a tenth of B; it is plain, then, how many beds are equal to a house, viz. five. That exchange took place thus before there was money is plain; for it makes no difference whether it is five beds that exchange for a house, or the money value of five beds." It is not clear whether these money values obtain in the market as well as in the minds of the transacting parties, for Aristotle treats of individual transactions in his ethical writings.

[114] Soudek (p. 60) suggests that in place of the word "demand" the term "need," in the double sense of an individual's want of a good and the capacity of that good to give want-satisfaction, should be used to represent Aristotle's meaning.

tion a sort of representative of demand."[115]Presumably, therefore, equality in exchange requires that when A gives up C to B in exchange for D, the money values of C and D are equal, and each exchanger expects to derive more want-satisfaction from that which he acquires than from that which he surrenders in exchange for it. That any one of a number of exchange ratios between the units composing C and D, respectively, might meet this test Aristotle apparently recognized, for he several times stated that the potential receiver's appraisal (in terms of utility) of the value of a thing was superior to the supplier's appraisal, since the supplier could engage to furnish the thing on the basis of the receiver's appraisal and the expectation of an equivalent in return.[116] Had Aristotle expressed himself in terms of a contract locus he would have defined the middle region of exchange ratios as being more just than those at either extreme, given that the middle ratios were compatible with the requirement that reward be proportional to skill. Aristotle does not employ the concept of cost or that of marginal utility; his analysis runs rather in terms of the utilities of the things exchanged and their monetary equivalents.

It is essential secondly that each exchanger be rewarded according to his relative skill, though skill and its measure are not defined well if at all. "There is nothing to prevent the work of the one being better than that of the other; they must therefore be equated." In fact, this is usually the case. "For it is not two doctors that associate for exchange, but a doctor and a farmer, or in general people who are different and unequal; but these must be equated." The use of money facilitates this equation. "It measures all things, and therefore the excess and defect—how many shoes are equal to a house." In order that there may be exchange and intercourse, "the number of shoes exchanged for a house must therefore correspond to the ratio of builder to shoemaker. . . . There will, then, be

[115]*Nic. Eth.* 1133ª. Money is thus "an intermediate," having "been introduced" to make goods commensurate and facilitate exchange or barter; its function as a unit of comparison is subordinate, as is its function as a store of value, to its function as a facilitator of such barter and exchange as are essential to the realization of a society's end. Thus, respecting money's function as a store of value, he states that if, at the time of the transaction, a seller does not yet require the thing supplied by the other party to the transaction, he may accept money instead, as "surety," and subsequently exchange it for the goods he wants, since its "worth" tends to be "steadier" than that of goods. Aristotle has hard money in mind, though when he describes money as existing by convention and not by nature, he states that "it is in our power to change it and make it useless." See *Nic. Eth.* 1133ª, 1133ᵇ; also *Pol.* 1.9. Elsewhere (*Nic. Eth.* 1156ª) he says that "the useful . . . is always changing," thus implying that men's wants change.

[116]*Nic. Eth.* 1163ª, also 1164ª. He does not here refer to monopoly which he elsewhere describes as making for higher prices and profits (*Pol.* 1.11).

reciprocity when the terms have been equated so that as farmer is to shoemaker, the amount of the shoemaker's work is to that of the farmer's work for which it exchanges.[117] In all friendships between dissimilars it is, as we have said, proportion that equalizes the parties and preserves the friendship; e.g., in the political form of friendship the shoemaker gets a return for his shoes in proportion to his worth, and the weaver and all other craftsmen do the same."[118]

Lowry concludes that Aristotle "was unable to formulate a conceptual relationship with sufficient clarity in abstract mathematical terms to guarantee its perpetuation." Furthermore, his "theories of mutuality and reciprocal demand" were not appreciated though comparative advantage was implied therein.[119]

Aristotle's exposition with its exclusive emphasis upon utility and its neglect of cost is in the Austrian tradition, rather than in that of the English classical school. The value of a means or an instrument is a derivative of the value of its product, just as the value of everything except that which is desired for itself is a derivative of something that is desired for itself.[120] Accordingly, both external goods and goods of the body are instrumental to goods of the soul (i.e., the virtues, which are internal goods as are those of the body) which are good in themselves, and hence not subject to limitations respecting use and accumulation as are the others.

Aristotle's economic analysis, of course, had to do almost entirely with external goods. While he associated the value of goods and services with their utility, or want-satisfying power, which he considered subject to change,[121] he did not define production in terms of utility. Instead he

[117] Nic Eth. 1133^a, 10–23, 33ff.

[118] Nic. Eth. 1163^b. If A and B are the exchangers and C and D are their products, then proportionate reciprocity obtains, with equal values being exchanged and each exchanger being rewarded in accordance with his skill. See Soudek, pp. 61–62, 74.

[119] "Aristotle's Analysis of Exchange," pp. 64–65.

[120] See Nic. Eth. 1.1–2, 5–6; Pol. 1; Rhetoric 1.6–7; Topica, 3, passim. Aristotle has been represented as anticipating the Austrian imputation theory. See Oskar Kraus, "Die Aristotelische Werttheorie in ihren Beziehungen zu den Lehren der modernen Psychologenschule," Zeitschrift für die gesamte Staatswissenschaft 61:573–92, esp. pp. 584ff., and Die Werttheorien (Brünn, 1938), ch. 3, 40. While Aristotle may be called a forerunner of the Austrian school, he can hardly be accredited with anticipating imputation theory except in the loose sense that the value of means reflects the value of the ends they serve. See my "Aristotle On Economic Imputation and Related Matters," Southern Economic Journal 21:371–89. See also Soudek, pp. 65–67, 73–75.

[121] Nic. Eth. 1156^a, 1163^a, 5.5. He encountered but was unable to resolve the paradox of value (Rhetoric 1365^a) because he reasoned in terms of absolute utility instead of marginal utility.

described as instruments of production those which aimed at a result beyond the immediate doing and as instruments of action those (e.g., slaves, household property) which aimed at rendering an immediate service.[122]

Aristotle described as most skilled that member of an occupation or profession who best performed the function therewith associated, but he did not lay down very clear rules for ranking occupations, professions, etc., or for comparing the respective skills of individual members of differently ranked occupations.[123] Accordingly it is not possible for one to determine the relative rates at which skills are required to be remunerated. Suppose A produces C and B produces D, and that C exchanges for D both within the transaction and in the market.[124] Then if C is three pairs of shoes and D two tables, we are given the exchange ratio in real terms. If, furthermore, C represents an outlay of one week of work-time and D an outlay of three weeks, C may be described as three times as skilled as D. However, since Aristotle did not express himself in terms of labor cost, or other input, it is questionable if he would accept this answer, whose validity otherwise depends upon whether the given ratio of exchange between shoes and tables is approximately equal. He does not clearly indicate under what circumstances one may assume that an exchange ratio arrived at in bargaining or found in the market is just. It is not possible, given his assumptions and information, to proceed from the comparative value of the skill of A and B to a correct ratio of exchange

[122] *Pol.* 1.4, and Barker's note in his translation. "Making has an end other than itself, action cannot; for good action itself is an end." See *Nic. Eth.* 6.5; also 6.4, where he says "All art is concerned with coming into being, i.e., with contriving and considering how something may come into being which is capable of either being or not being, and whose origin is in the maker and not in the thing made." See also *Metaphysics* 7.8, for his treatment of production in terms of the introduction of form into matter.

[123] Presumably a member of a higher occupation was superior to one of a lower occupation. See *Pol.* 7.4, also 1.11 where he says: "Suffice it to say that the occupations which require most skill are those in which there is least room for chance: the meanest are those in which most damage is done to physique: the most servile are those in which most use is made of physical strength: the least noble are those in which there is least need for the exercise of goodness." See also *Pol.* 4.4., 12–18, 7.15; also his discussion of requirements for citizenship (*Pol.* 3.1–5) and his observation (*Pol.* 7.4) that goodness of products is associated with goodness of materials. Presumably the quality of products depends also on the instruments of production used, but he does not explicitly say this.

[124] While Aristotle apparently supposed that bargaining between two prospective exchangers would result in a more just exchange ratio, he did not explicitly find in market values a key to what constituted justice in exchange. See *Nic. Eth.* 1133^b, 1163^a, also 9.1; also Soudek, pp. 63–64.

between C and D, for skill and productivity are inadequately defined, and the contribution of complementary nonhuman agents or production is not taken into account.

Justice is a mean in a somewhat different sense than the other moral virtues, in that it is an amount intermediate between receiving and giving up too much or too little. "Justice is that in virtue of which the just man is said to be a doer, by choice, of that which is just, and one who will distribute either between himself and another or between two others not so as to give more of what is desirable to himself and less to his neighbour (and conversely with what is harmful), but so as to give what is equal in accordance with proportion; and similarly in distributing between two other persons."[125]

Distributive justice had to do with the distribution of honor, rewards, offices, wealth, etc. It was agreed by all men "that what is just in distribution must be according to merit in some sense," but they were not agreed respecting what constituted appropriate indices of merit, and the degree to which diverse merits and rewards were commensurable. Respecting how unequal should be the portions of that which was distributed, it being granted that prospective recipients differed in merit, Aristotle declared that complete distributive justice would have been attained only if the ratio of reward received to merit warranting reward was the same for all recipients of rewards. "This, then, is what the just is, the proportional; the unjust is what violates the proportion."[126] And elsewhere: "But that equals should be given and men on a footing of parity

---

[125]*Nic. Eth.* 1133[b], 1134[a]. On voluntary acceptance of less than one's due see ibid., 5.9–11. In *Magna Moralia* 1194[a] (written by a Peripatetic after Aristotle's death in 322 B.C., according to W. Jaeger, *Aristotle*, 2nd ed., pp. 228, 440ff.), it is said that exchange of products must be carried on in accordance with proportional justice if the commonwealth is to be held together.

[126]*Nic. Eth.* 1131[a], 1131[b]; also *Pol*, 3.12, 17; 5.1. Let A and B represent two persons together with their respective claims based upon merit; and C and D, their respective rewards or portions. Then justice obtains when A:B::C:D. No problem of determining a just distribution was involved when the common funds of a partnership were distributed, since the distribution would "be according to the same ratio which the funds put into the business by the partners bear to one another." See *Nic. Eth.* 1131[b]. In *Pol.* (3.9) he said "it is not just for a man who has contributed one pound to share equally in a sum of a hundred pounds (or, for that matter, in the interest accruing upon that sum) with the man who has contributed all the rest." Elsewhere (*Nic. Eth.* 1163[b], 1136[b]) he observed that "no one puts up with the smaller share in *all* things"; if a man contributes wealth to the common stock he expects to be compensated in honor, honor and wealth being intersubstitutable. Arithmetical and proportional equality are contrasted in *Pol.* 5.1.12.

treated on a basis of disparity, is a thing which is contrary to nature; and nothing contrary to nature is right."[127]

Aristotle concerned himself principally with the distribution of offices, honors, rewards, wealth, etc., in the polis, with the criteria underlying the distribution of offices and rewards in states with different types of institutions, and with the determination of what constituted the best or most just system of political distribution; but he did not treat of the distribution of wealth in general. He observed that under democratic constitutions men were treated as more or less arithmetically equal in merit and political rights whereas under nondemocratic constitutions men were held to differ considerably in respect of their justified claims to power, rewards, and offices;[128] and that as these criteria changed, the character of a state's constitution changed.[129] Both the democratic and the oligarchic conceptions of justice were only partial, however. It was not possible to determine on what basis offices and honors ought to be distributed until the true purpose of the state had been ascertained, since those who contributed more to the realization of this purpose—"good action"—should "receive greater recognition from it" than those who were their equals in important respects (e.g., free birth, wealth, culture, good descent) other than "civic excellence" or virtue.[130]

Among the circumstances which, along with the principles of justice already described, contributed to well-being, or to the prospect that well-being would be realized, were the maintenance of political stability and the avoidance of excessive economic inequality. Among the conditions primarily responsible for political disorder he included excessive inequality, want of subsistence, and mistreatment of the underprivileged.[131] He favored the restriction of economic activities essentially to

[127]*Pol.* 7.3.6–7. "It is right to follow, and just to obey" a person superior to others in "goodness" and "capacity for actually doing the best."

[128]"The democratic conception of justice is the enjoyment of arithmetical equality, and not the enjoyment of proportionate equality on the basis of desert." See Barker, *Pol.* 6.2.2; also 4.12 on relation between civic body and constitution. See also 3.8–9, 13, 5.1. While he observed that property qualifications played an important role in oligarchies 4.5–6, 7.2, 6, he indicated that even in democracies political right could be based upon both property and personality 6.3; 4.4. He described as the best form of democracy one based on a farming populace (6.4; also 4.4).

[129]*Pol.* 5.6.

[130]*Pol.* 3.9, 12, 4.12, 5.9, 7.3; also 7.1–3, on the polis and the "highest good." He inferred that since neither arithmetical nor proportionate equality alone insured a lasting form of government, a form incorporating "both kinds of equality" should be selected. See 4.

[131]*Pol.* 4.7; V. For condemnation of use of political power for economic advantage see 5.8 and Barker's note on p. 230 of his translation.

the provision of requisites for the household (together with their use), characterizing both the lending of money at interest and working and trading for profit (as distinguished from work within the household and the exchange necessary to the acquisition of its requisites) as unnatural on the ground that the proper function of money was the facilitation of exchange and the proper function of exchange was the facilitation of necessary barter.[132] While he believed that a moderate amount of external goods was essential to the good life, a greater amount being unfavorable,[133] he looked upon the abolition of private property as conducive to dissension rather than preventive of it, and upon the complete equalization of holdings as violative of man's conception of justice.[134]

He favored ownership by the state of enough land to support the expense of public worship and common tables[135] and restriction of the private ownership and use of land to those eligible for citizenship in order

---

[132]*Pol.* 1.8–11. Acquisition in its natural form aimed at the accumulation of only as much true wealth (i.e., "objects, necessary for life and useful to the association of the polis or household, which are capable of being stored") as was required to serve the moral purpose of the household and the polis. Acquisition in its unnatural form aimed at the accumulation of currency in an amount unlimited and far in excess of what was needed by the household for the service of its purpose. When discussing acquisition as it was carried on, Aristotle noted that some forms were more profitable than others and that the establishment of a monopoly, by a state or by a private person, was followed by higher prices and much greater profits.

[133] "Felicity—no matter whether men find it in pleasure, or goodness, or both of the two—belongs more to those who have cultivated their character and mind to the uttermost, and kept the acquisition of external goods within moderate limits, than it does to those who have acquired more external goods than they possibly can use, and are lacking in the goods of the soul." For only the utility of goods of the soul (i.e., the virtues) continued to increase as their amount grew; one could have too many instruments and even too much of goods of the body (e.g., health, strength). See Barker *Pol.* 7.6 and 9, where he adds that "it is for the sake of the soul that these other things [property, and health of the body] are desirable, and should accordingly be desired by every man of good sense." See also *Pol.* bk.2.7 where he states the wealth of a state should suffice for its defence, but not be so great as to stimulate attack by the covetous; and bk.2.6 where he states that the amount of property should be "sufficient for a life of temperance and liberality" (i.e., for a life intermediate between one of luxury and one of penury). "By 'wealth' we mean all things whose value is measured by money." (*Nic. Eth.*, 1119^b, 26ff.).

[134]*Pol.* 2.5, 7. 10, 18–20.

[135]*Pol.* 7.10. Dining at the common tables being a right of all citizens, provision by the state of the expenses involved guarded poor citizens (but not their families) against want. Aristotle supposed that both the public and the private lands would be tilled by non-Greek slaves or, lacking these, by serfs.

that they might have leisure for goodness and political activities.[136] In general, political stability was most likely to be realized when no individual or class was allowed to become too powerful, and this condition was most likely of attainment in the world of reality when there existed a middle class sufficiently numerous, strong, educated, and rational to mediate between the poor and the rich and to counterbalance their respective demands.[137]

As has been implied, restraint of economic inequality within bounds was advocated by Aristotle on political and moral grounds, and not on the premise that total satisfaction or some analogous magnitude enjoyed by the citizens or by the inhabitants of the polis would be increased. For Aristotle did not think in these terms, resting even his partial recognition of diminishing utility upon the supposition that the satisfaction of given moral ends requires only so much of instrumental and/or bodily goods rather than upon the assumption that utility is expressible in terms of continuous magnitude. He therefore was content to urge that the amount of wealth required was limited by the purpose it served, that property not become too unequally distributed, and that poverty be alleviated principally through measures designed to make the poor self-supporting.[138]

Life in accordance with the virtues concerned with money, namely, liberality and magnificence, would somewhat cushion the impact of inequality. The liberal man avoided both prodigality and meanness, giving "for the sake of the noble" and "to the right people, at the right time, and where it is noble to do so," and refraining from giving "to the wrong people" "at the wrong time."[139] Liberality, of course, presupposed that property is privately owned, but is put to "common" and "proper use;" it could not be manifested under a communist regime.[140] The magnificent man avoided vulgarity and niggardliness, contributing on large scale to the support of "honorable" objects connected with religious worship

---

[136] Day-laborers, artisans, and traders, all of whom pursued a way of life that was "ignoble and inimical to goodness," and husbandmen, who lacked the necessary leisure, were unqualified to become citizens in an ideal state. Those who performed the services of defence, public worship, deliberation and jurisdiction constituted the citizenry. See *Pol.* 7.9.

[137] *Pol.* 4.11–12; also 5.

[138] *Pol.* 1.8–11; 2.1–5; 4.12; 6.5; also 2.6–12, on Plato's and other hypothetical or planned states.

[139] *Nic. Eth.* 4.1–2.

[140] *Pol.* 2.5; also 7.5, where it is said that the territory of a state should suffice to enable the citizens to live "a life of leisure which combines liberality with temperence."

(e.g., votive offerings, building, sacrifices) and other proper objects of public-spirited expenditure.[141]

Aristotle's approach to economic issues, while not neglectful of price behavior and conditions affecting it, diverted his attention from concentrating on price formation and the allocative and stimulative roles of the price system. Even so, his concern with welfare bore some resemblance to that of modern welfare economists. He sought both justice in exchange and justice in distribution. He did not, however, accept the view that justice would or could be realized under conditions of laissez faire or pure competition. For he believed that justice would be realized only in proportion as expression was given to the virtues (which may be looked upon also as ultimate values or value attitudes), and such expression was more likely of realization under some forms of constitution than under others. Because acceptance of these virtues as ends entailed a playing down of the role of wealth or instrumental goods, Aristotle's system, despite its emphasis on merit, was not very conducive to material progress, though more favorable thereto than the set of values endorsed by the Cynics, the Epicureans, and the Stoics.

E. Roman Response to Greek Economic Thought

After Aristotle's death conditions became less favorable to his conception of economics and economic justice both in Greece and in Rome where the Roman essayists, Cicero and Seneca, "made the Hellenistic philosophers presentable and intelligible."[142] Both were more favorable to the thought of Aristotle and Plato than were the Cynics and Epicureans even though Cicero, translator of Xenophon's *Oeconomicus*, and Seneca were less critical of business.[143]

Responsible for the change in attitude toward Aristotle were a number of conditions. The replacement of the polis or city-state by the larger state or empire "stripped the individual of the insulated shelter of his little city-state and forced him to come to terms and find a place in an enormously expanded polity."[144] Within Greece the opposition of political liberalism to conservative Greek classicism became much stronger.[145] The role of the state was redefined and the belief that men were equal in

---

[141] *Nic. Eth.* 4.2.

[142] Moses Hadas, *The Stoic Philosophy Of Seneca*, p. 3.

[143] Seneca apparently approved the definition of "economics" as "the science of administering private property." See Hadas, p. 222.

[144] Ibid., p. 20.

[145] Havelock, esp. ch. 13.

some respects was strengthened.[146] The Cynics rejected distinctions which differentiated men, saying that all were subject only to the law of virtue and that man's capacity for happiness was independent of human institutions. Similarly, the original Stoics had no place for institutions, economic or otherwise, in their ideal society. These early Stoics developed the view that equality in a world order founded upon universal law could be achieved by the wise, irrespective of their worldly stations, if they lived justly and according to right reason. Eventually, Panaetius, drawing upon Plato and Aristotle as well as upon the Stoics, reinstated health, property, etc., as goods (saying that men should rationalize rather than extirpate their normal inclinations), redefined law, described justice as the bond of the state, and declared all men equal in that they possess "a common humanity, a common affinity to the divine reason, and a common subjection to the eternal principles of right and justice."[147] The Stoic conception of natural law became integrated with the *jus gentium*, or law common to divers peoples, giving rise to "a body of legal principles which are at once in general use and also represent the dictates of equity, reason, and justice."[148] Since the Stoics were not reformers, any more than were the Cynics or the Epicureans, the material state of slaves was not improved except insofar as masters were moved by the counsel of humanity.[149]

[146] Recently Rifkin (pp. 276–83), while admitting A. J. Carlyle's view that Cicero and Seneca gave expression to the beginnings of the theory of human nature and society which eventually became "liberty, equality, and fraternity," rejects his view that the most complete change in political theory between Aristotle's time and that of Cicero was the rise in the belief in the equality of mankind. Rifkin finds considerable evidence of a belief in equality in Aristotle's time and discovers even in his works concern with questions of equality. Such is also Havelock's view.

[147] Sabine and Smith, p. 31, also pp. 17–30. See also Diogenes Laertius, *Lives of Eminent Philosophers in Ten Books*, 6.102–5, 7; H. D. Oakeley, pp. 199–215. Epicureanism was an escape philosophy just as was Cynicism and early Stoicism. Epicurus described "natural justice" as an "expression of expediency, to prevent one man from harming or being harmed by another." Justice is arrived at through covenant and is the same for all, though its content varies with the locality and the circumstances under which it is applied. There is nothing apparently on exchange or distribution beyond statements that while pleasure is the end of life, its attainment is largely independent of the possession of material goods. See Diog. L. *Lives* 10. On the Stoics see also Ferguson, passim; Havelock, passim.

[148] Sabine and Smith, pp. 36–37.

[149] In time the treatment of slaves improved, perhaps in part as a result of Cicero's urging that slaves be treated justly and Seneca's that they be treated as friends, and as a consequence of the disappearance of the theory of natural inequality and the development of the view that slavery is "an institution of the *jus gentium* and contrary to nature." See Carlyle, *Medieval Political Theory*. 1:47–51;

Into Cicero's conceptions of the commonwealth, law, and justice entered principally the views of Plato, Aristotle, and the Stoics. The Commonwealth was not the result of convention or compact designed to escape a Hobbesian world; it came into being in consequence of "a kind of social instinct natural to man."[150] Cicero took exception to inferences drawn from the observation that the content of law and justice varied greatly in time and space, saying there was but one law and justice, both existing in Nature and based upon universal reason, by which society was bound together and in the light of which men were equal. Men are summoned to the performance of their duties and to the aversion of wrongdoing by "a true law—namely, right reason—which is in accordance with nature, applies to all men, and is unchangeable and eternal." With this law, of which God is the author, interpreter, and sponsor, it is not morally permissible for the agencies of the state to interfere.[151] Justice, which is "right reason applied to command and prohibition" and which exists "in Nature" and inheres in "human nature," is essential to the existence of the commonwealth, producing good conduct and harmony and serving to bind men together.[152]

Cicero refers a number of times to proportional justice, which became the Roman legal principle *jus suum cuique tribuere*, and on at least one occasion, under the influence of the Stoics, went beyond it. The "equality" found in a democracy "is inequitable in that it does not recognize degrees of merit."[153] Justice "gives to every man his own and preserves

also Cicero *De Officiis* 1.41 and *De Republica* 3.25; Seneca *De Beneficiis* 3.18–20, 28.

[150]*De rep.* 1:25–26, 3.13; see also *De Finibus* 5.23; also A. Litman, *Cicero's Doctrine of Nature and Man*, p. 21. The historian Polybius explained the origin of political society and of notions of justice (among them the apportioning of rewards and penalties according to desert) in social-evolutionary terms. See *Histories* 6.5–7). He employed the idea of rising and declining generations to account in part for changes in values and the "cycle" of constitutions (6.9). Honors and punishment hold society together (6.14). Polybius has little to say about economic questions as such.

[151]*De rep.* 3.22, also 1.31–32, 3.10–12; *De Inventione* 160–61; *De Legibus* 1.6–7, 15. Cicero described a political career as more honorable than a life of (Aristotle's) tranquility and a duty on the part of those whom Nature had suitable endowed (*De Officiis*, 1.21); also Litman, pp. 28–29, 32. Cicero's views on law, the state, and the role of statesmen are treated in Sabine and Smith, pp. 79ff., 90ff., 94ff.

[152]*De rep.* 1.44, 2.42, 3.7–8; *De leg.* 12, 14–15; *De fin.* 2.18, 5.23; *De off.* 1.4–5, 7. "The first office of justice is to keep one man from doing harm to another, unless provoked by wrong; and the next is to lead men to use common interests, private property for their own." See *De off.* 1.7, 20.

[153]*De rep.* 1.27.

fair dealing in all human relationships."[154] Rendering "unto everything its deserts is said to be the mark of a good and just man."[155] Justice teaches one "to consider the interests of the human race, to render to each his own, and not to tamper with that which is sacred, that which is public, and that which belongs to another."[156] "This sentiment, assigning to each his own and maintaining with generosity and equity that human solidarity and alliance of which I speak, is termed Justice: connected with it are dutiful affection, kindness, liberality, good-will, courtesy and the other graces of the same kind."[157] In one place, under the influence of the Stoics, he defines justice as rendering more than that which is due. "For justice—assuming that it exists—is the only virtue preeminently unselfish and generous, and only a man who is inspired by justice prefers the interests of all men to his own and is born to serve others rather than himself."[158] To the argument that men would find it more advantageous to themselves to act from motives of utility and self-interest and hence go contrary to the dictates of justice, Cicero replied that self-interest is not the only motive to action, that elements of all virtues are innate and susceptible of strengthening through education, that the sense of shame acts as a justice-producing sanction, and that in general men act from an innate sociability which develops as men grow up and which underlies justice as well as other virtues.[159]

Cicero was not opposed to engagement in business conducted in keeping with justice. "As for property, it is a duty to make money, but only by honorable means; it is a duty also to save it and increase it by care and thrift."[160] What he has to say about exchange and distribution somewhat

[154] *De rep.* 3.7; *De off.* 1.15.

[155] *De rep.* 3.11.

[156] *De rep.* 3.15; *De off.* 1.5.

[157] *De fin.* 5.23. According to Cicero, moral rectitude sprang from four sources or virtues: prudence, justice or "social instinct," courage, and temperance, even though wisdom is described as "the foremost of all virtues." See *De off.* 1.43–45, also 5.28. See also *De fin.* 5.23; *De leg.* 1.16. Actually Cicero esteemed justice and the duties flowing from it above wisdom and duties flowing from it, according to Litman (p. 35).

[158] *De rep.* 3.8; also 7; also p. 203, and pp. 49–50 on equity and (good) faith which, originating in Nature as does justice, apparently reenforce it. In *De off.* 2.18, 64, he says it befits a gentleman "to be at the same time liberal in giving and not inconsiderate in exacting his dues, but in every business relation . . . to be fair, reasonable, often freely yielding much of his own right and keeping out of litigation as far as his interests will permit and perhaps even a little farther."

[159] See *De rep.* 1.25, 3.27, 5.4; *De off.* 1.16; *De fin.* 2.14; Sabine and Smith, pp. 219, 246 nn. Much of Cicero's argument is translatable into terms of Pareto's sentiments, or of Talcott Parsons's value-attitudes.

[160] *De off.* 2.40, 87. Here he refers to Xenophon's similar view.

anticipates later medieval views. Asserting that only what is moral is expedient,[161] he states that a vendor is obliged to inform purchasers of known defects in objects of sale, to avoid misrepresentation, and to refrain from concealing information that affects the value set upon something by a prospective purchaser. Whether, however, just prices would be approximated if all relevant facts were known to buyer and seller and few elements of monopoly were present, is not clear.[162] Respecting distribution he says that reward should be according to merit,[163] and that avarice, love of wealth and luxury are to be condemned.[164]

Cicero condemned the use of excessive doles on the part of the state, together with extravagant public expenditures, though he recognized the "duty of charity" to the unfortunate.[165] "The chief purpose in the establishment of constitutional and municipal governments was that individual property rights might be secured." Hence agrarian laws were to be avoided and a property tax resorted to only in time of dire need.[166] While he criticized movements to distribute property equally,[167] he said that a man may claim things as his own, not through civil law but by "virtue of that right which inheres in wisdom," by "virtue of that general law of nature which forbids that anything should belong to any one, except to a man who knows how to use and employ it wisely."[168] It was essential that

[161] *De off.* 3.11–15, 6.27–32, 34, 68–72, 101, 120, 119.

[162] When he is describing the liberal professions, agriculture, and large-scale wholesale trade as suitable occupations for gentlemen, and tax-gathering, money-lending, and retail and service trades as unsuitable, he remarks that retailers "would get no profits without a great deal of downright lying." See *De off.* 1.42.

[163] *De rep.* 1.27.

[164] *De off.* 1.7–8, 21, 30, 34, 2.22, 3.5, 18.

[165] *De off.* 2.56, 60–64, 72, 3.30–31; also on the proper use of riches, 1.25–27, 68, 3.24.

[166] *De off.* 2.12–24, 78–82.

[167] *De off.* 2.72–87. When urging measures to prevent indebtedness which may "endanger the public safety," he indicates that the repudiation of debts is at the expense of property-holders (2.84–85).

[168] *De rep.* 1.17; also p. 122, on the Stoic origin of this view. The Stoics held that "everything the earth produces is created for man's use." See *De off.* 1.7.22, 16.51. While Seneca's theory of human nature resembled Cicero's, his views of property and institutions differed somewhat. Private property was necessary, but it was not necessary that individual holdings exceed what was needed to prevent poverty (*De Tranquilitate*, 8). Seneca went far beyond Cicero in stressing the corruptness of human nature, finding therein the origin of private property and coercive government, institutions which, however unnecessary in an ideal world, served, in an imperfect world, to hold man's evil tendencies in check. See *De tran.* 8; Carlyle, *Medieval Political Theory*, 1: 24–26, 61–62. This view anticipates both the Christian view that finds in sin the origin of various institutions, and the

property had been "honesty acquired," increased only "by wisdom, industry, and thrift," and "made available for the use of as many as possible (if only they are worthy) and be at the service of generosity and beneficence rather than of sensuality and excess. By observing these rules, one may live in magnificence, dignity, and independence, and yet in honour, truth, and charity toward all."[169] Cicero counselled generosity on the part of those able to distribute money or contribute services, subject to the qualification that the generosity hurt no one, could be afforded by the donor, and benefitted the meritorious.[170] He supposed presumably that generosity would cushion the impact of want in a world marked by great inequality. Cicero's work helped to shift philosophy from emphasis upon intellectual interests to emphasis upon moral interests, and to rest moral behavior upon the performance of duty instead of upon compliance with reason.[171]

It may be noted in closing that Cicero's sentiments as represented differ somewhat from those manifested in his *De Imperio Cn. Pompeii*. There he reveals great insight into the economic structure of the Roman world. An imperialist who recognizes that the fortunes of Roman citizens "are dependent upon the political power of the state" and that "Roman society rests economically on a small group of wealthy citizens," he had "no genuine sympathy for the exploited *provinciales*" or for "Romans running small-scale business in the provinces."[172]

F. Conclusion

Of the classical authors whose work has been passed in review, Aristotle remains the most influential, the most stimulative of the classical authors, and the one the spirit of whose work is most in keeping with that of the modern social scientist.

Perhaps the major point to be made against Aristotle's approach to economics within the framework of the city-state is his neglect of the market,

---

analogous views of later writers, such as T. R. Malthus, that institutions are necessary to curb man's socially unfavorable forms of behavior.

[169] *De off.* 1.26; also 2.24.87, where he says that "it is a duty to make money, but only by honourable means," and to save it and "increase it by care and thrift." He refers to Xenophon's *Oeconomicus*. Property is not private by nature but becomes such through long occupance, conquest, due process of law, bargain, purchase, or allotment. *De off.* 1.7.21.

[170] *De off.* 1.14–15, 2.15–20. Also *De leg.* 1.18.

[171] See Litman, pp. 37–39, 41, also pp. 28–29 on Cicero's interest in knowledge that led to action.

[172] E. J. Jonkers, *Social and Economic Commentary on Cicero's De Imperio Cn. Pompeii*, pp. 51–53.

whether free or less than free, and its role in allocating gross national product and gross income. Yet, as Thomas J. Lewis has shown recently, even Aristotle's case against the market is defensible if it is recognized that Aristotle may not have been attempting an analysis of market exchange but "was concerned with the problem of acquisition in a non-market context."[173] Lewis reasons that Aristotle's case against market exchange is based on the incompatibility of market activity and human virtue "due to market-generated anxiety about livelihood and the concomitant destruction of the possibility of friendship and citizenship." Lewis also suggests that the "irrelevance of Aristotle's economic ideas to contemporary economics may be in part due to the difficulty of submitting to the standards required by non-market exchange."[174]

Another instance of the relevance of one of Aristotle's theories—his theory of revolution—is his case for the proposition that a sufficient separation of political and economic power entails political disorder and possibly revolution.[175] Kort's analysis suggests that many propositions present in Aristotle's works may be identified and examined in respect to their validity.

[173] Thomas J. Lewis, pp. 69–70. See also Karl Polanyi, "Aristotle Discovers the Economy," in *Trade and Market in the Early Empires*, eds. Karl Polanyi, C. M. Arensberg, and H. W. Pearson.

[174] Lewis, p. 69.

[175] Fred Kort, "The Quantification of Aristotle's Theory of Revolution," *American Political Science Review* 19:486–93.

[176] See *Four Comedies of Aristophanes*, edited by Andrew Oneappe, p. 110.

6

Political Economy and Ethics

*If men agree on rights, the problem of social order
is largely resolved.*
James M. Buchanan, *Public Choice*

*A society is properly arranged when its institu-
tions maximize the net balance of satisfaction.*
John Rawls, *A Theory of Justice*

*A community which fails to preserve the discipline
of competition exposes itself to the discipline of absolute authority.*
Henry C. Simons, *Journal of Political Economy*

A great increase in interest on the part of economists and students of
ethics in the interrelations of economics and ethics has occurred during
the past decade. For this increase the seminal works of John Rawls and
Robert Nozick (essentially a critic of Rawls' conception of distributive
justice), together with the work of James M. Buchanan and Gordon Tul-
lock on "public choice," are responsible. According to Rawls, "the principles of justice may serve as part of the doctrine of political economy,"
having "embedded in them a certain ideal of social institutions."[1] Nozick,

---

[1] John Rawls, *A Theory of Justice*, p. 258. Having stated his first principle of
justice—"each person is to have an equal right to the most basic liberty compatible with similar liberty for others"—Rawls formulates the second of the principles of justice: "Social and economic inequalities are to be arranged so that they
are both (a) reasonably expected to be to everyone's advantage, and (b) attached
to positions and offices open to all" (p. 60). Elsewhere (pp. 12–13, 576–77) Rawls
defines "justice as fairness" in that it conveys the idea "that the principles of
justice are agreed to in an initial situation that is fair." While he rejects deduc-
tively rational and nonmoral justification of ethical principles, he associates justice
as fairness with rational choice and "contract" (pp. 15–17, 477–87). Daniel Orr
and Wolfhard Ramner describe as "both important and persistent" the problem
of "balance between liberty and equality," a problem for which Rawls proposes
solutions; they point to the need for economists to deal with this problem and

having examined distributive justice in the light of the "minimal state" and the state "beyond the minimal," concludes that the framework for utopia "is equivalent to the minimal state."[2] In what follows we do not touch upon the discussion precipitated by the work of Rawls and Nozick and the literature of "public choice" but upon much earlier interaction between ethical and economic discussion, together with the formal characteristics of their interaction.

Although discussion of economic matter has been mixed with the discussion of ethical matter for more than four millennia, intermixture of the discussion of economic *science* and ethics is of relatively recent origin. For economics in the sense of a conceptualized, systematized, and generalization-yielding science did not come into being until the seventeenth century. Scientific discussion of economic matter therefore lagged behind that of ethical matter, more so than discussion of political matter with its greater emphasis upon "public interest" and less explicit emphasis upon "self interest."[3] Always, however, there was some overlap between ethics and economics, in substantive concern and in emerging analytical orientation. The analytical parallel is evident. Economics enables us to contrive a set of rules, compliance with which maximizes the aggregate output to be gotten from a fixed budget of resources, and permits a society of men to choose the best of the growth paths available. Ethics, as A. J. Lotka pointed out, functions as "a *regulator of conduct* in close analogy to the manner in which logic functions as a *regulator of thought*";

---

programmatic approaches to it. See "Rawls' Justice and Classical Liberalism: Ethics and Welfare Economics," *Economic Inquiry* 12:377–97.

[2] Robert Nozick, *Anarchy, State, and Utopia*, pt. 2, esp. ch. 7 and ch. 10, pp. 333–34. See also James M. Buchanan's critique of several of Nozick's theories, among them his "entitlement theory of justice," in "Utopia: The Minimal State, and Entitlement," *Public Choice* 23:121–26; also his *The Limits of Liberty: Between Anarchy and Leviathan*.

[3] "In politics, primary emphasis has traditionally been placed on political obligation, on the duty of the individual to act in the 'public interest'." Political scientists, therefore, have relied mainly on policies designed to increase the valuation which the individual puts on the utilities of others. Economists, by contrast, "have assumed that individuals act in accordance with quite narrowly-defined self-interest" and "have developed policy norms" based upon this underlying behavioral postulate. Meanwhile political scientists devote more attention "to the prospects of making institutional changes that channel private choice in the direction of producing more desirable social results." See James M. Buchanan, *Cost and Choice*, p. 80 n. Practical administrators throughout the centuries have relied upon so tilting the structure of penalties and rewards as to incline subjects to behaving as administrators expect. So run manuals of government. See my "Kautilya, Plato, Lord Shang: Comparative Political Economy," *Proceedings of the American Philosophical Society* 113:450–57.

then, given compliance with the rules of ethics, welfare defined in a certain way will be maximized, subject to the constraints flowing from the economy, together with how rationally it is administered. The animus to ethical behavior flows from within the individual in greater measure than does the animus to compliance with economic principles since the latter reflects markedly the pressure each member of the relevant group experiences from other economically behaving members. Temporarily stable economic outcomes are not very likely, however, to coincide with what may be described as an ethical optimum.

In the history of social thought ethics and economics converged in the realm of law and jurisprudence. For even though ethics was treated as a "science mainly of duties" binding on the conscience, while laws referred to general rules "of external human action enforced by a sovereign political authority," ethics could function as a source of criteria in the light of which to judge the moral quality of these general rules. In a parallel fashion economics could function as a source of criteria for judging the impact of these rules on the growth of wealth. The roles of ethics and economics thus became somewhat parallel to each other and to that of jurisprudence, the concern of which was the means by which the Law subserved its purposes and sought "its ultimate object . . . the highest well-being of society."[4]

In the world of affairs ethical, economic, and legal considerations often became comingled. Not surprisingly, therefore, ethical and economic concerns often were viewed as related and, upon the emergence of economics as an independent science, it was viewed as a moral science and given something of a moral orientation.[5] With the greater formalization of ethics and economics, it was recognized that metawelfare principles might be necessary to reduce formal incompatibility between economic and ethical considerations and between the ethical order and the political and economic orders. In this chapter we confine our inquiry into the interrelations of ethics and economics in the Western World.

[4]On this paragraph see T. E. Holland, *The Elements of Jurisprudence*, 12th ed., chs. 1–3, 6–7, esp. pp. 24–31, 40–42, 79–82. On A. J. Lotka's comment see his *Elements of Physical Biology*, p. 412. See also H. T. Buckner, "Transformation of Reality in the Legal Process," *Social Research* 37:88–101.

[5]S. Moos, "Laissez-faire, Planning, and Ethics," *Economic Journal* 55:17–27. E.g., John Locke, seventeenth-century contributor to the development of economic science, declared that the "same law of Nature" that gave man property in that with which he mixed his labor also limited his right to acquire property. "As much as anyone can make use of to any advantage of life before it spoils, so much may he by his labour fix a property in. Whatever is beyond this is more than his share, and belongs to others." *Of Civil Government: The Two Treatises of Government* (1690), bk. 2, ch. 5, p. 131.

A. *Interrelations as Such*

The realm of economics may be treated, at least theoretically, as may the realm of ethics, as a component or subsystem of a larger and more inclusive societal system of which the legal, the political, and yet other subsystems are members. Indeed, the legal and the political subsystems originated, as did the economic system, in areas of scarcity, in the absence of which none would have a raison d'etre. Hence a fruitful source of information regarding the development of man's economic thinking at particular times is the set of laws and customs he created in order to cope with what we call economic scarcity.[6] Given the parallel origins of these interrelated subsystems, change in the ethical realm has affected the economic realm directly as well as indirectly, through direct impact upon the economic realm as such and through indirect impact via the legal, political, and other components of the societal system. It is not easy (if at all possible), therefore, to identify and estimate with precision the effect of changes in the economic realm upon the ethical, in part because these changes may be cushioned or accentuated by the intervention of other components of the societal system.

Definitional problems need to be avoided, inasmuch as definitions have changed over time as the content of ethics and/or economics, never universally agreed upon, as changed. Both deal with choice, preference, and as a rule, cost.[7] Definitions along these lines may prove too confining,

[6] See Talcott Parsons and Neil J. Smelser, *Economy and Society*; James Bonar, *Philosophy and Political Economy*, 3rd ed. On the greatness of the contents common to both a people's "moral consciousness" and its legal system and the similarity of the principles underlying both its legal rights and duties and its "moral consciousness," see W. D. Lamont, *The Principles of Moral Judgment*, p. 32. Since many ties connect the economy and the legal system, the legal system may serve as a link between the ethical and the economic realms.

[7] R. M. Hare describes ethics as "the logical study of the language of morals." *The Language of Morals*, p. v; cf. H. Kellner, "On the Sociolinguistic Perspective of the Communication Situation," *Social Research* 37:71–87. G. H. von Wright describes the "concept of preference" as of "pivotal importance to the theory of value in general and to its principal branches—aesthetics, economics, and ethics." "Ethics, or moral philosophy, is a special study of concepts of all three groups," of the normative (notions of right and duty, command, permission, and prohibition"), of value concepts ("ideas of good and evil, and the comparative notion of bitterness"), and of the "anthropological" ("Notions of need and want, decision and choice, motive, end and action"). Normative notions "do not admit of *degrees*" whereas value-concepts do. *The Logic of Preference*, pp. 5, 7, 9. W. D. Lamont observes that three main problems fall under the history of moral philosophy, "the problem of goodness or value, the problem of duty or obligation, and the problem of responsibility or freedom." *The Value Judgment*, p. xi. See also I. M. D. Little, on value judgments and welfare economics in *A Critique of*

however. Accordingly, we shall assume the ethical realm to consist of three elements: (1) the "science" of ethics; (2) the "moralities" that exist empirically or, though mainly ideational in character, may be under consideration; and (3) what may be called the welfare index implicit in each morality. Let us identify (1) with the symbol E_s, or "ethical theories," as "reflective attempts to understand and help guide morality." The second element, morality, E_m, is essentially regulative in character and embracing "many qualities and processes: rules enjoining or forbidding selected types of action, selected character-traits cultivated or avoided, selected patterns of goals and means."[8] Then the objective of a morality is realization of what we may call an ethical welfare function E_i. Ethical science enables men to consider alternative moralities and relate them to alternative or potentially optimum welfare index values. Legal systems or codes, being parts of moralities, are examined by ethical science along with other elements of moralities. The economic realm may be defined in a manner parallel to the ethical realm. Politicoeconomic science P_s consists in the principles and techniques utilized to analyze the behavior of economies and establish sets of arrangements P_m (parallel to E_m) and is designed to realize an optimum value for welfare function P_i. It thus bears some resemblance to what H. A. Simon calls a science of the artificial, that is, a science of designing or creating the artificial (e.g., engineering, medicine).[9]

Definition of E_i and P_i presents a problem. We may suppose that P_i is essentially a shorthand expression of the outcome of P_m whereas E_i is a shorthand expression of E_m plus allowance for improvement in E_i in the direction of an ideal ethical index. In reality, however, the conditions implicit in an ideal index, even if definable, could not be achieved. Most populations are too heterogeneous, with differing and probably instable norms, some of which entail one group's taking advantage of other groups. Indeed, in most societies definition of the content of an ideal index differs with group, and in such wise that the several indices resulting are not transformable into a single index equally satisfactory to each group.

Difficulties surrounding the definition of E_i and P_i in sufficiently persuasive terms must have contributed to the development of belief in a higher "natural law," a repository of superior man- and society-transcend-

---

Welfare Economics, 2nd ed., ch. 5; also Abram Bergson, *Essays in Normative Economics*; A. C. Zijderveld, "Rationality and Irrationality in Pluralistic Society," *Social Research* 37:23–47.

[8] Abraham Edel, *Science and the Structure of Ethics (International Encyclopedia of Unified Science*, vol. 2, no. 3), pp. 7–8.

[9] *The Sciences of the Artificial*, ch. 3.

ing rules and constraints, of divine or transcendental origin, "to which the ordinary civil rules made by man must conform and which necessarily place limits on the operation of such rules."[10] The development of such a belief was not confined to the West. *Tao* long performed this role in Chinese ethical philosophy, though its precepts seem to have been honored more in the breach than in the observance; *Dharma* so functioned in ancient India; and in ancient Sumer and later in Israel, ideal prescriptions were represented as of transcendental origin.[11] Several millennia later, in the eighteenth century, before utilitarianism had undermined natural-rights philosophy, natural law was undergirding American political theory and physiocratic legal theory,[12] only to become vulnerable to the winds of change sweeping in with the century that followed.

Several circumstances contributed to decline in the belief in the availability of a transcendental source of optimum solutions. An axiomatic approach was subject to limitation, as Gödel showed in another connection,[13] while search for nonarbitrary finality was subject to infinite regress. Transformation of the derivative doctrine of natural rights in the modern period probably weakened its appeal,[14] as did the lowness of the rate of social change and level of expectations associated with natural law but no longer found acceptable when men's aspirations, aroused by accelerating material progress, began to grow more rapidly than natural-law philosophy seemed to imply.[15] Of greater significance in respect to the relation between the economic and the ethical realms was the emergence of utilitarianism, together with individualism,[16] only to succumb a

[10]Charles Grove Haines, *The Revival of Natural Law Concepts*, p. 3. Ancient and medieval natural law theories are described in ch. 1. Haines includes a large amount of bibliographical matter. See also Frederick Copleston, S.J., *A History of Philosophy*; Otto F. von Gierke, *Natural Law and the Theory of Society, 1500–1800*; R. G. Collingwood, *The Idea of Nature*, pp. 1–91; Holland, passim.

[11]See Fung Yu-lan, *A History of Chinese Philosophy*, 1, ch. 8, John Spellman, *Political Theory of Ancient India*, and S. Radhakrishnan, *Eastern Religious and Western Thought*; J. A. Wilson, *The Burden of Egypt*, pp. 48–50; S. N. Kramer, *History Begins at Sumer*, chs. 8, 13–14, 23, 27; A. L. Oppenheim, *Ancient Mesopotamia*.

[12]B. F. Wright, Jr., *American Interpretations of Natural Law*; Mario Einaudi, *The Physiocratic Doctrine of Judicial Control*. The "state of nature" was sometimes designed to serve as a model. E.g., see M. Einaudi, *The Early Rousseau*, pp. 4–5, 8, 116, 123–30, 234, 245, 264–65.

[13]Ernest Nagel and J. R. Newman, *Gödels Proof*.

[14]See Leo Strauss, *Natural Right and History*.

[15]E.g., see J. W. Hurst, *Law and the Conditions of Freedom in the Nineteenth Century*, ch. 3.

[16]E.g., see E. Halévy, *The Growth of Philosophical Radicalism*, pp. 174–81, 257, 431–32, 473–78.

century later to its deficiencies and incompatibilities[17] and give place to a survivalist ethic such as was associated with theories of natural and social selection[18] or to an ethic entailing a growing demand for state intervention in socioeconomic affairs.[19]

Both economic and ethical theory may be treated as more or less but not entirely free of ideology. It is virtually impossible to strip a so-called social science completely of ideological content.[20] When the possibility of the presence of ideological content is recognized, however, the degree of bias resulting should prove reducible. Moreover, recognized adverse consequences of bias tend to result in its correction and reduction.

Several kinds of interaction are possible between the economic realm and the ethical realm. Application of economic science may yield results or indications at variance with those of ethical science; then E_s and P_s generate results that are at variance and perhaps quite incompatible. Similarly, dissatisfaction with the adequacy of E_m or P_m, given objectives E_i or P_i, may require changes in E_m or P_m. Changes in objectives E_i and P_i may also give rise to changes in E_m and P_m and possibly to changes in E_s and P_s as well. The initial changes in E_s or P_s, in E_m or P_m, or E_i or P_i, may originate *within* any one of these subcomponents, though mainly, as a rule, within E_s or P_s, inasmuch as the formulators and custodians of a science are likely to be more prone to change than administrators concerned with arrangements or high priests committed to preserving welfare functions.

The economic realm has been more sensitive to change than the ethical, in part because technological and other changes in the external world have modified P_m and sometimes P_i and thereby tended to stimulate change in P_s, already prone to some change as a result of change in the external world. The proneness of P_s to change has greatly increased, of course, as a result of the multiplication of economists in this century, the intensification of international communication, and the premium placed upon the modification or at least the restatement of elements included

[17] E.g., see Talcott Parsons, *The Structure of Social Action*, pp. 64–67, 344ff., 368ff., 390ff., 698–702.

[18] R. Hofstadter, *Social Darwinisim in American Thought, 1860–1915*.

[19] Illustrative is the increasing interest in German Idealism in late nineteenth-century Britain. E.g., see T. H. Green, *Lectures on the Principles of Political Obligation*; Bernard Bosanquet, *The Philosophical Theory of the State*. See also Jacob Viner, "The Intellectual History of Laissez Faire," *Journal of Law and Economics* 3:45–69; Sidney Fine, *Laissez Faire and the General-Welfare State*.

[20] W. A. Weisskopf, *The Psychology of Economics*. On the adverse effects of disguising value judgments as cognitive judgments see Karl Brunner, "Knowledge, Values and the Choice of Economic Organization," *Kyklos* 23:558–79.

within the economic realm.[21] It may be noted that the proneness of E_s to change has been increased by parallel changes affecting the ethical realm. Feedback mechanisms within P_s and P_m and between P_m and P_s are more sensitive and powerful than corresponding mechanisms in the ethical realm.

There is, of course, what amounts to a greater propensity to stability and constancy within the ethical realm than outside it, in part because the circumstances or forces making for commitment to E_m and E_i are strong, if only because group survival depends upon the avoidance of too much instability in E_m and E_i.[22] Ideological circumstances may also be present or emerge to reenforce this stability, sometimes with the result that even the stability of P_s (e.g., Physiocracy, Marxism) may be strengthened.[23] Stability may also be supported through recourse to informal courses of action when E_m or E_i stand in the way of the performance of functions which are viewed as indispensable outside the ethical realm;[24] illustrations will be encountered later in respect of usury. Even when verbal change takes place in E_s and E_m, it may represent little substantive change; for the universe of ethical discourse and manner of expression may change notably, even though the underlying content of the themes constituting this universe change little. As in Molière's play, men may be speaking prose though not aware of it, changing the verbal guise but not the substance.

The stability of the ethical realm is subject to greater immediate threat from P_m and P_i than from P_s, given that the social and institutional bulwarks supporting E_m and E_i are not powerful enough to repel threats against the ethical realm. The concerns of users of P_s consist in the analy-

---

[21] See my "Economics: Its History, Themes, Approaches;" also A. O. Hirschman, "The Search for Paradigms as a Hindrance to Understanding," World Politics 22:329–43.

[22] "In a world which exists by the balance of Antagonisms, the respective merit of the Conservator and the Innovator must ever remain debatable." So wrote Thomas Carlyle on "Boswell's Life of Johnson," Critical and Miscellaneous Essays 3:130. On inventive excess and premature obsolescence see Sir Josiah Stamp, The Science of Social Adjustment, pp. 29–37, 58–60.

[23] Y. Chu Wang compares the Marxist-Leninist system to the Confucian system which he describes as "highly resistant to cultural infiltration." See "Ideas and Men in Traditional China," Monumenta Serica 19:269, 274–75.

[24] E.g., see R. K. Merton, Social Theory and Social Structure, esp. pp. 31–38. Cf. how the cambium maratimum contract could conceal usury. See Raymond De Roover, "The Cambium Maratimum Contract According To The Genoise Notarial Records Of The Twelfth And Thirteenth Centuries," Explorations in Economic History 7:15–33.

sis of pricing, variations in levels of activity, response of the economy to impacts from outside, and the creation or modification of institutions realizing P_m and designed to bring about P_i; they are therefore strongly oriented to if not swamped by material considerations. These concerns do not, however, disturb the ethical realm until they both sanction and generate policies, actions, etc., within P_m that are at variance with E_m and perhaps also with E_i. Then either E_m and E_i remain ascendant and constrict P_m in such wise as to reduce the realizability of P_i or should P_m and P_i prove overriding, as has often happened, ethical considerations are subordinated to economic, or are modified and redefined to be more compatible with the economic realm. In reality, of course, P_m is seldom as well set up as P_s indicates it need be if P_i is to be realized. As a result incompatibility with the ethical realm is likely to be accentuated, since suboptimal performance within the economic realm is unlikely to reduce disparity.

Prescriptive principles of ethical origin tend to constrain economic practice and relations, today[25] as in earlier times when prohibition of usury[26] limited economic activity and when economic striving had to be shown to be in keeping with religious precept instead of opposed to it.[27] These principles may increase.[28] or decrease the efficiency with which an economic system works. They will have such effect in some degree if they are merely internalized in man's person and enforced only by the sanction of his conscience, of his hopes and fears. They will have such effect in greater degree if they are enforced by legal as well as by private, personal sanctions, by the threat of punishment at the hands of the community or some agency of the state. Prescriptive principles will increase an economy's efficiency if they rule out monopolistic practice, favor competition, condemn inflationary practice as well as wasteful public and private consumption, clothe labor with dignity, outlaw dishonesty, and so on. These principles will produce an opposite effect if they sanction un-

[25] "The basic objective of corporate business in the private sector is to maximize the long-term return opportunities for the shareholders within the constraints implied by law and generally accepted ethical standards." D. A. Hayes, "Management Goals in a Crisis Society," *Michigan Business Review* 22:7.

[26] See Benjamin Nelson, *The Idea of Usury from Tribal Brotherhood to Universal Otherhood*, 2nd. ed.; also A. I. Qureshi, *Islam and the Theory of Interest*.

[27] E.g., see S. D. Goitein, *Studies in Islamic History and Institutions*, pp. 220–41.

[28] For example, Nicole Oresme expressed a not uncommon ethical opinion when he condemned the altering of money, a practice corresponding to recourse to inflationary financing by irresponsible present-day governments. See *Traictie de la première invention des monnoies* (c. 1360), chs. 7–22. The Theodosian Code prescribed capital punishment for coin-debasing (bk. 9, title 22).

economic practices, or if they depreciate material objects and thisworldly concerns and attach excessive weight to transcendental and otherworldly aspirations. Ethical principles may, of course, transform the general environment in ways favorable to economic welfare even though they produce some uneconomic consequences. Illustrative are some concomitants of the emergence of great peace-favoring religions (e.g., Buddhism, Christianity, Confucianism) which condemned strife and thus probably more than offset economically adverse consequences of some of their principles.

B. Temporal Setting

The interrelations of the ethical and the economic vary over time as settings change. These settings did not differ greatly from one another before the nineteenth century, either in the degree to which men thought it proper to devote attention to *both* economic and ethical considerations, or in the degree to which settings at one period resembled those at an earlier period. Historical settings change both in the wake of problem-affecting changes in technology and empirical environment and as a result of modification of the ideational and/or ideological environment and hence of the vision men form of their world, its challenges, and the range of responses at their disposal. No attempt is here made to trace the genesis of these changes or to express them in terms of a Markov chain or an analogous pattern. We shall concentrate initially upon Aristotle and Thomas Aquinas, each of whom viewed society as an organism, thus neglecting Roman legal influence. The organismic view of society was largely displaced by a mechanistic view of society emerging in the wake of nominalism and of influences given release in the Renaissance and Reformation periods, together with the development of full-bodied utilitarianism and individualism. Of course, just as one found some defense of a mechanistic conception of society in classical Greece, so one finds defense of at least quasi-organismic conceptions of society in the current and recent centuries and hence always the possibility that the ruling conception will be displaced by the alternative conception.[29] In what follows attention will be focused mainly on the *direct* bearing of ethical principles upon the moral evaluation of individual economic behavior and second-

---

[29] E.g., see Werner Stark, *The Fundamental Forms of Social Thought; The Sociology of Knowledge;* and *Social Theory and Christian Thought;* Ferdinand Tönnies, *Community and Society;* Eric A. Havelock, *The Liberal Temper in Greek Politics;* R. B. Perry, *General Theory of Value,* chs. 14–17; Talcott Parsons, *The Structure of Social Action,* pp. 31–35 and passim; P. A. Sorokin, *Social and Cultural Dynamics,* passim on ethical, organismic, and nonorganismic theories.

arily on the indirect influence which these principles exercised via the medium of the regnant type of state (i.e., mainly the organic and the mechanistic contractual types).

The nineteenth century witnessed a marked acceleration of the rate of progress, a movement earlier couched in terms more of wish than of reality,[30] an acceleration so pronounced as to swamp earlier perspectives and eventually arouse concern at the prospective course of events.[31] The setting in which ethical and economical ideas were expressed therefore changed, with the result that some authors came to look upon "the 'propensity to variation' . . . as the principle of progress" and upon survival itself as evidence of meritoriousness, and economists to limit sharply the degree to which they might attend to ethical issues.[32] The implications of ethical considerations for economics continued, however, to receive some attention in the early twentieth century,[33] even though ethical thought had not yet become adjusted to the great changes in setting. Of these changes A. N. Whitehead wrote: "We are living in the first period of human history for which this assumption ["that each generation will substantially live amid the conditions governing the lives of its fathers, and transmit those conditions to the succeeding generation"] is false."[34] And Stamp observed, "The price of pace is peace. Man must move by stages in which he enjoys for a space a settled idea, and thus there must always be something which is rather delayed in its introduction, and the source of sectional scientific scorn."[35] The burden of adjustment to ideational change, Bagehot implied, was accentuated by the increase in energy being placed at man's disposal and a resultant increase in abstract and contradictory speculation. "The superfluous energy of mankind has

[30] See John Bury, *The Idea of Progress*; G. H. Hildebrand, ed., *The Idea of Progress: A Collection of Readings*.

[31] See chapters 24–25, written in 1904, on "A Dynamic Theory of History" and "A Law of Acceleration," in Henry Adams, *The Education of Henry Adams*; also Josiah Stamp, *Social Adjustment*.

[32] For example, Walter Bagehot, in a critique of criticisms directed against "economical writers" by "uncultured moralists," points out that "the economical writers under consideration did not mean (and rightly did not mean) to deal with ethics at all." See his "The Preliminaries of Political Economy," in *The Works of Walter Bagehot* 5:322. On Bagehot's view of variation see his *Lombard Street* 5:9; also *Physics and Politics*, in *Works* 4:514. See also my "Evolutionism in American Economics, 1800–1946," and W. F. Quillian's "Evolution and Moral Theory in America," in Stow Persons, ed., *Evolutionary Thought in America*.

[33] E.g., see Sir Josiah Stamp, *The Christian Ethic As An Economic Factor*.

[34] Cited by Stamp in *Social Adjustment*, p. 54.

[35] Ibid., p. 58.

flowed over into philosophy, and has worked into big systems what should have been left as little suggestions."[36]

Bernard Bosanquet observed that the significance of man's membership in the community as a whole was devalued as a result of the ascendance of the conception of the world as one of finite individuals environed by a moral order "bounded by rights and duties, claims and counterclaims."[37] Increasing awareness of change resulted in the replacement of the old view of society as subject to little change by a new view emphasizing change, sometimes to the extent of making change for the sake of change a criterion of the desirable. Associated with this new emphasis has been decreasing stress upon ends and upon the subordination of the course of change to the implications of these ends. Instead, means to change have become stressed at the expense of ends, with the result that technological solutions have increasingly been sought not only for problems which are technological in character but also for those which are fundamentally moral in character and hence in need of moral solutions.

C. Greek Thought

Greek thought bearing upon economic matter not only dealt with the role of virtue but also focused on fundamental issues respecting what belonged to each individual though without discussion of related problems of measurement. Greek thought dwelt also upon the role of the virtues describable as corresponding in some degree to what Parsons calls values or value-attitudes;[38] they were grounded on habit or intellect and were expected to function as regulators of man's economic and other relations with his fellow men.[39] These values became a part of the stream of

---

[36]*Physics and Politics*, in *Works* 4:568. Capacity for using energy that otherwise goes to waste gives man or any other species an evolutionary advantage. Lotka, *Physical Biology*, pp. 356–58.

[37]See Bosanquet, *The Value and Destiny of the Individual*, Lecture 5; also F. H. Bradley, *Ethical Studies* (1876), chs. 2–3; also W. D. Lamont, *The Principles of Moral Judgment*, ch. 6, on "ideal morality," p. 163.

[38]Parsons, *Social Action*, passim. "Virtue, then, is a state of character concerned with choice, lying in a mean, i.e., the mean relative to us, this being determined by a rational principle;" it was distinguishable from "passions" and "faculties." See Aristotle, *Nic. Eth.* 1105^b, 1106^b.

[39]E.g., Aristotle states (*Nic. Eth.* 1103^a) that "intellectual virtue in the main owes its birth and growth to teaching, . . . while moral virtue comes about as a result of habit." In *Pol.* 1332^b the contribution of "education" is noted as well. "In educating the young we steer them by the rudders of pleasure and pain." (*Nic. Eth.* 1172^a; see also 1180^a–1180^b). St. Thomas Aquinas also viewed virtues as good habits. See Copleston, 2:405ff.

ethics, with analysis of them contributing to the development of a science of ethics, and with their relation to economics and economic welfare undergoing change as economic science developed and economic values increased in relative importance. It was not always taken into account that the regulatory impact of values or virtues based on habit or reason often depended upon their incorporation in institutions; nor was it adequately recognized that, when bonds between man and society were severed, social institutions might become goals in themselves.[40] Full recognition of the need for regulation by a polity quite distinct from an economy tended to be corollary to the emergence of stress upon the multicomponent character of society and an egoistic ethic.[41]

One finds two main bases for the evaluation and/or control of economic behavior in Aristotle's works, one based upon his conception of the role of virtue and the other based upon his essentially organic conception of the "state." The virtues, described mainly in Aristotle's chief work on ethics, evolved out of values present in earlier Greek society and literature[42] and found renewed life in medieval ethical literature, especially in the work of St. Thomas Aquinas. Interpersonal economic relationships were influenced far more by "justice" than by other moral virtues, none of which played so important a role as "friendship," described as "a virtue" or implying "virtue" but not included in Aristotle's list of virtues (N.E. 1155[a]), even though friendship involved various exchange relationships and performed functions quite similar to some performed by justice, among them that of holding "states together." (N.E. 1155[a], 1158[b]–1160[b]).[43] Of these other moral virtues, several had some significance for

[40]Neglect of institutional support of values persists. Illustrative is Myron L. Joseph's observation regarding wage and price guideposts: "an effective guidepost policy requires an institutionalized process for creating an atmosphere of public opinion in which noninflationary wage-and-price behavior is more likely to occur." See "Requiem for A Lightweight: A Critical Historical Sketch," in *Prices: Issues in Theory, Practice and Public Policy*, ed. A. Phillips and O. E. Williamson, p. 61. On institutions become goals see Zijderveld, pp. 37–39.

[41]R. D. Cumming, *Human Nature and History*, vol. 2, pt. 4. See also R. M. MacIver, *The Web of Government*; Parsons and Smelser, *Economy and Society*.

[42]Counterparts of some of the virtues of which Aristotle and other Greeks wrote are found in Chinese, Indian, and Middle Eastern philosophical literature. E.g., see Fung Yu-lan, *Chinese Philosophy*; A. L. Basham, *The Wonder That Was India*, pp. 167, 170, 276, 283–87, 293–94, 338–42; S. Radhakrishnan, *Eastern Religions and Western Thought*; John Ferguson, *Moral Values in the Ancient World*, pp. 42, 212–26, on differences and similarities between Greek and Hebrew concepts.

[43]On the development of Greek thought on friendship and its standing in later Epicurean and Stoic thought see Ferguson, *Moral Values*, ch. 4. On the social

economic behavior, especially those concerned with money (i.e., "liber-ality" and "magnificence" and their opposites) and bearing heavily upon how man handles his "wealth," or "things whose value is measured by money," together with "equity,"[44] which may be said to have some resem-blance to liberality, at least on grounds of motive, in that the equitable man "tends to take less" than he is entitled to under the law (*N.E.* 1138ᵃ, 1143ᵃ). Of the intellectual virtues, most relevant is "practical wisdom," having to do with man's "capacity to act with regard to human goods," to "things that are good or bad for man," and the acceptance or rejection of which is subject to deliberation and choice (*N.E.* 1140ᵃ–1140ᵇ).

The scale of values to which Aristotle subscribed led him to play down and sharply limit the importance to be attached to material wealth. He not only condemned those who "take more than they ought and from wrong sources" (e.g., "those who lend small sums and at high rates,") (*N.E.* 1121ᵇ–1122ᵃ). He also set very great store by "activity in accordance with virtue," that is, by activity which "is contemplative," together with what amounts to spiritual self-sufficiency and material self-sufficiency in the sense of being "equipped with bodily health" and with "the necessar-ies" in sufficient but not superabundant measure (*N.E.* 1177ᵃ–1179ᵃ). These values entailed not only moderate consumption at the individual level and "finance" limited to a household's needs, but also an ideal po-litical milieu within which the *summum bonum* could be pursued in rela-tive freedom from dependence upon foreign countries (*Pol.* bks. 1, 7–8).[45] Aristotle thus wrote primarily as a philosopher who, as Gordon observes, found solution for scarcity, not in multiplying and judiciously allocating means, "but by reorienting human demands" in light of the means avail-able.[46]

Connections between Aristotle's ethical and economic views are found mainly in his discussion of state and justice, discussion that played down material ends and hence was out of keeping with materials ends and Greek economic practice except insofar as noncitizens relieved citizens of economic activities normally pursued in what was then a relatively

---

role of exchange see my "Allocation and Development, Economic and Political," in R. Braibanti, *Political and Administrative Development*, pp. 632–37.

[44]"He is liberal who spends according to his substance and on the right objects" while he is "magnificent" who, possessed of considerable means, spends in the right amount on the right objects. *N.E.* 1120ᵃ–1123ᵃ. On justice, equity, and vir-tues see also Aristotle *Rhetoric* bks. 1–2.

[45]On the "triumph of autarchy" or self-sufficiency in Greek moral thought see Ferguson, *Moral Values*, ch. 8.

[46]B. J. Gordon, "Aristotle and Hesiod: The Economic Problem in Greek Thought," pp. 147–56, esp. pp. 152–56.

"modern" society.[47] After all, ethical principles guide behavior in societies only insofar as they are imbedded in man's conduct-determining value structure and internalized, or insofar as they are enforced by state police power, or insofar as exchange and negotiation on the part of a society's inhabitants reveal that compliance with these principles yields utility to all or most.

Aristotle reasoned that all of man's needs, together with the highest good, were to be sought within the state, highest form of community and prior to individual and household in the order of Nature (*Pol.* 1252ª). The state satisfied man's social instinct, produced good character, and fitted him for the good life (*Pol.* 1278ᵇ–1279ª; *N.E.* 1099ᵇ). The "best life, both for individuals and states, is the life of virtue, when virtue has external goods enough for the performance of good actions," (*Pol.* 1323ᵇ–1324ª) and essential to happiness. Possession of "external goods" in excess of this limit was either useless or harmful (*Pol.* 1323ᵇ). Accordingly, while property was an indispensable substratum to the household, wealth was not to be accumulated for its own sake, through trade or otherwise. Indeed, as Soudek observes, when Aristotle is writing of exchange he usually has in view "isolated exchange between individuals" and not a market composed of many buyers and sellers.[48] The purpose of trading was not to produce unlimited wealth and riches but, as part of the "natural art of acquisition," to facilitate satisfaction of the needs of household and state through the "useful parts of wealth-getting" (*Pol.* 1256ᵇ–1258ᵇ). All this called for restraint, since the desires of some were "unlimited" (*Pol.* 1258ª).

Much of the *Politics* was therefore devoted to aspects of the "ideal state," one designed to make possible realization of the *summum bonum*—sufficient territory to support a small but numerically and racially adequate citizen population, good situation, a noncitizen population to carry on trade, agriculture, and mechanical activities, a sufficiently large middle-class, and an ideal educational system (*Pol.* 1295ᵇ–1296ᵇ, 1326ª–1341ª). It was necessary, therefore, to avoid communism, great inequality, pauperism, excessive numbers, and the known causes of revolution (*Pol.* Bks. 2–5). Essential also was the avoidance of injustice since it was "by proportionate requittal that a city holds together" (*N.E.* 1132ᵇ).

The virtue of justice, especially in the shape of the three modes of particular justice, thus played a critical part in Aristotle's ethical theory,

[47] E.g., see my "Herodotus on the Subject Matter of Economics," pp. 276–85; B. J. Gordon, "Aristotle and The Development of Value Theory," pp. 115–28; J. Soudek, "Aristotle's Theory of Exchange," pp. 45–75; Havelock, passim.
    [48] Soudek, p. 46.

given dependence of the state's continuity upon the behavior of its citizenry compatibly with the rules of justice. "Justice" made "people disposed to do what is just and act justly and wish for what is just" (*N.E.* 1129ª). Distributive justice, he observed when discussing "friendship," was based upon the principle to each his own, and rested in part upon a class basis. "We ought to render to each class what is appropriate and becoming.. . . . To every . . . class one should always try to assign what is appropriate, and to compare the claims of each class with respect to nearness of relation and to virtue or usefulness. The comparison is easier when persons belong to the same class" (*N.E.* 1165ª). In Book 5 on justice Aristotle states that what was distributed should be distributed "according to merit in some sense," with merit defined in keeping with the criteria accepted in a society (*N.E.* 1131ª–1131ᵇ). Justice in "transactions between man and man," by contrast, was a "sort of equality" (*N.E.* 1132ª). Given money to make goods commensurate, exchange took place between two persons when the four-fold coincidence essential to barter was present and presumably each party to the exchange stood to benefit (1133ª–1133ᵇ). There being then a just exchange ratio or range of ratios, exchange outside this range was unjust (*N.E.* 1133ᵇ–1134ª). Aside from playing down the importance of material wealth, Aristotle ruled out the taking of interest (*N.E.* 1121ᵇ; *Pol.* 1258ᵇ) and charging more than what later writers considered the just price (*N.E.* 1132ᵇ–1134ª).[49] He looked upon money, in both hard and conventional forms, as a store of value as well as a means of exchange, but did not suggest that injustice might flow from great change in the value of money, perhaps since its value "tends to be steadier" than that of goods (*N.E.* 1133ᵇ; *Pol.* 1257ª–1257ᵇ).

D. Pre-Reformation Christian Thought

While the concept of just price passed into Roman Law and the commentaries of such authors as St. Augustine, later to be refined through reexamination of Aristotle's discussion of justice, the concept of usury as treated by the Church Fathers was essentially of Judaic origin, though later refined under the influence of Aristotle.[50] These developments are not here considered, however, my discussion being limited to some views of St. Thomas Aquinas, Catholic continuator of Aristotle. Nor is attention given to the views of the Epicureans and Stoics or to the ab-

---

[49] See my "Aristotle on Economic Imputation And Related Matters"; also Soudek.

[50] Both prices and interest rates were subject to control in the Mesopotamian world, but this control was not so philosophically undergirded as that later supported by the works of Plato and Aristotle.

sorption of these and other Greek as well as Judaic ethical and related views into Christian thought.[51] It should be noted, however, that Stoic philosophy contributed notably—more so than the Epicurean—to the cosmopolitanization of men's outlook and thereby facilitated the replacement of the state-oriented religion and philosophy of Imperial Rome by the world-embracing philosophy and religion of the Christians.[52] It also made men more aware of the nature of the relation of the individual to the state and other institutional components of society or the cosmic order.[53] Undoubtedly Stoic philosophy, though it did not set great store by material goods and devoted little attention to economics,[54] helped increase both the scope of voluntary interindividual relations and the autonomy of voluntarily established institutions, thereby contributing to the emergence and hence the discussion of private economic relations.

Cicero, disciple of the Stoics, supported the principle of "rendering to every man his due"[55]—*suum cuique tribuere*—taken from Greek philosophy into Roman Law[56] where it was given greater precision and whence it passed into scholastic and other conceptions of justice as "the everlasting maxim, unicuique suum."[57] This principle, together with attempts at giving it empirical and (sometimes) quantitative meaning, continued to command juristic attention. This principle, component of moral law which regulates the life of the individual and is supported by juristic law which regulates the life of a people, was recognized as determining the distribution of things valued by men appropriately and in keeping with "divine justice;"[58] it served, along with attempts to give it empirical con-

---

[51] C. N. Cochrane, *Christianity and Classical Culture*; Ferguson, *Moral Values*, chs. 11–12; also David Knowles, *The Evolution of Medieval Thought*, pts. 1–2; Bernard W. Dempsey, *The Functional Economy*, ch. 21.

[52] On the Hellenic conception of "Cosmopolis," see A. Toynbee, 4:332–38, also pp. 365–69. See also A. MacIntyre, *A Short History of Ethics*, pp. 106–9, 107–19.

[53] See George H. Sabine, *A History of Political Theory*, chs. 7–10; Henry Sidgwick, *Outlines of the History of Ethics*, pp. 70–103.

[54] E.g., see Moses Hadas, *The Stoic Philosophy of Seneca*. Cicero, however, declared the property owner duty-bound "to make money, but only by honourable means" and "to save it and increase it by care and thrift." *De Officiis* 2.34.87.

[55] *De Officiis* 1.5.15.

[56] Wrote Ulpian: "*Justitia est constans et perpetua voluntas jus suum cuique tribuendi.*" See next note.

[57] On the Greek origins and subsequent history of this principle see Giorgio del Vecchio, *Justice*, pp. 55, 219, also pp. 26, 32–33, 56, 72–73, 75–76, 112, 121–25.

[58] See Rudolph Sohm. *The Institutes*, on the history and system of Roman private law, pp. 22–25. The principle of *suum cuique* determines the relation of individual to group in that "law apportions to each individual that which is due him as a member of the people, and due to him, moreover, for the sake of the people" (p. 24). On the distinction between ethics, the science of duties, and

tent, to focus the attention of philosophical and politicoeconomic writers on distributive justice and change in its empirical content.

St. Thomas's tightly knit discussion of the relations between economics and ethics proceeds along Aristotelian lines—lines that became well-known in the West only in the 13th century.[59] In place of Aristotle's *summum bonum*—virtuous life inclusive of speculation and practical activity—St. Thomas put the "vision of the Divine Essence," or, as S. T. Worland restates St. Thomas, "the intellectual perception of the essence of God."[60] Whence the value of means, together with the ordering of means, derives from their contribution to the realization of St. Thomas's *summum bonum*. Accordingly, nonpecuniary "wealth" or "exterior goods" were found of importance only insofar as they supported life itself, the performance of virtuous acts, and the individual's station in life, together (as we note below) with the "common good" and a virtue-fostering social environment. Man, qua sole individual, was insufficient, incapable of achieving a virtuous life outside the environs of domestic and civil society, coupled with a state designed to realize the "common good." Hence "exterior goods" were required for the support of domestic and civil society along with the state. The importance attached to wealth-getting was quite circumscribed, therefore, as also were the approved modes of wealth-getting. Limited also were the amounts allocable to the various approved uses of exterior goods.

Responsibility for the production of exterior goods, for wealth-getting, belonged to individuals and not to the state. Private management and administration—hence a system of private property, one entailing stewardship and limited returns—were more efficient than collective management and administration. Private activity needed, however, to be compatible with realization of the common good. To this compatibility liberality on the part of those with more goods than they needed should contribute. Essential also, particularly given functional specialization, was beneficent cooperation-assuring exchange within the community—that is, exchange in keeping with commutative justice, with the principle of just price.[61]

St. Thomas therefore faced a problem making for ambiguity in Aris-

---

nomology, the science of rules regarding which legislation is possible, see T. E. Holland, *The Elements of Jurisprudence*, 12th ed., pp. 26–31; also pp. 31–42, on the role of "the law of nature." On Roman Law and the Christian Fathers, see George Catlin, *The Story of the Political Philosophers*, ch. 5.

[59] E.g., see David Knowles, pt. 3.

[60] *Scholasticism and Welfare Economics*, ch. 2, p. 31. Cf. Perry, ch. 22, on "highest good," also chs. 14–17 on social integration.

[61] Worland, chs. 2, 7–9; also Catlin, pp. 259–71.

totle's discussion of just price, that of reconciling distributive and (what the scholastics later called) commutative justice. For the just price will depend upon the prices at which inputs are fixed in keeping with distributive justice. Whence, if excessive prices were put upon some inputs—e.g., those of the services of persons of high status, of high position in the socioeconomic hierarchy—the exchange ratio resulting would be unjust to one party to a bargain. This problem is examined by Worland who, unlike some interpreters of St. Thomas's analysis, concludes that the "just price" of a commodity corresponds (i) to its "long-run normal value as determined by cost and 'need' or (ii) to its market price as the latter fluctuates, in response to local short-run factors, around long-run normal value."[62] While this interpretation is acceptable in respect to the pricing of commodities, it does not resolve the problem of the pricing of services, probably more affected by "force" in St. Thomas's day than today.[63]

Given St. Thomas's prescriptive framework—the framework of a society and state viewed as an organism to which its component parts were subordinate[64]—and its emphasis upon the *means*-character of economic activity, both the significance and the permissible modes of their activity were restricted. The charging of prices that were excessive or monopolistic was declared unjust and condemnable.[65] Usury was condemned as well, but on grounds other than the charging of excessive prices, namely, on natural law grounds regarding which medieval authors differed.[66] St. Thomas also condemned[67] contraception and recourse to positions not "fit" in intercourse though he was not a populationist in the sense of later critics of celibacy and advocates of pronatalist legislation.

The views to which St. Thomas gave expression underwent change. Changing conditions, discussion, and rejection of his organismic philosophy were responsible at least in part. The small city-state which he seems to have envisaged and which contributed to the revival of urban civilization, though in lesser measure than did the later Roman Empire's semi-

[62] Worland, ch. 8, esp. pp. 230–31. See also chs. 7–9 for a fuller discussion.

[63] However, see my "The Cost of Specialization in a Service Economy," *Social Science Quarterly* 51:237–62.

[64] Cp. Stark, *Social Thought*, also *Social Theory and Christian Thought*, pp. 1–30. On nineteenth-century theories see F. W. Coker, *Organismic Theories of the State*.

[65] E.g., see J. T. Noonan, Jr., *The Scholastic Analysis of Usury*, pp. 88–89.

[66] Ibid., ch. 3; Bernard W. Dempsey, *Interest and Usury*, ch. 8. In his encyclical letter *Quod provinciale* (Aug. 10, 1754) Pope Benedict XIV falls back on "the so-called Clause of Commutative Justice" in ruling out usury. Anne Fremantle, *The Papal Encyclicals*, pp. 107–8.

[67] John T. Noonan, *Contraception*, pp. 285, 290, 300, 305–8, 333.

sovereign and self-sufficient *civitates*,[68] was superseded or dominated by an emerging national state as were the Greek city-states by the Hellenistic and Roman empires. With the development of this national state, predecessor of the modern state,[69] were associated changes in the circumstances that made St. Thomas's economic philosophy less acceptable even as the decline of the Greek city state had made Aristotle's economic philosophy less acceptable. Accordingly, as will be noted later, the organismic view of the state lost support as well[70] but never entirely.[71] The doctrine of just price continued to have support, sometimes in the guise of condemnation of monopoly pricing. The concrete definition of usury changed as authors became aware of the varied circumstances surrounding loans.[72] Emphasis upon the need for distributive justice has, however, been accompanied by questions regarding the tenability of arguments supporting interest-taking.[73] Views relating to contraception and based upon natural law have undergone little change.[74] The importance attached to income and wealth, though still constrained, has greatly increased as men have become richer.

E. Post-Thomistic Thought

Events, based largely upon theory, modifications of which often constitute the most important source of social change, shifted the center of ethical constraint upon economic activity from that stressed by St. Thomas. Of these changes in theory, two appear to be most important, the spread of nominalism and the partial replacement of Catholic doctrine by Protestant doctrine.

While vestiges of nominalism are found in Plato's *Crito* as well as in Democritus and Epicurus, this view of society as of the world did not begin to reorient the sociopolitcal and ideational environs of economic

[68] Cochrane, pp. 144ff.

[69] J. R. Strayer, *On the Medieval Origins of the Modern State*, cf. MacIntyre, pp. 115–16.

[70] See Stark, *Social Thought*.

[71] Dempsey, *The Functional Economy*; also the encyclical letters of Pope Leo XIII in Etienne Gilson, ed., *The Church Speaks to the Modern World*; Coker.

[72] E.g., see Noonan, *Scholastic Analysis*; Dempsey, *Interest and Usury*; Nelson, *The Idea of Usury*. For review of recent literature on the scholastic doctrine of usury and a critique of it in terms of modern economics see Jacques Melitz, "Some Further Reassessment of the Scholastic Doctrine of Usury," *Kyklos* 24: 473–91.

[73] J. W. Ryan, *Distributive Justice*; also the views of Pope Leo XIII, in Gilson, pp. 140–245.

[74] Noonan, *Contraception*.

activity until in the fourteenth century, when William of Ockham and Marsilius of Padua began to become influential. The contribution attributable to them and their followers was the substitution of the conception of society as a mechanism for the Aristotelian-Thomistic conception of it as an organism. Society as well as the world at large is now viewed as a collection of individual units or atoms, free of *demonstrable* causal connexion as well as of organic or holistic constraint. These individuals are held together in mechanical systems by contractual and related ties which reflect or give rise to equilibria, sometimes stable and sometimes not. In consequence, the focus of attention, the source of action, becomes the individual; variations significantly distinguishing one from another are mainly of environmental origin.[75] The heightened attention to the individual contributed to the conception of man, in the Renaissance period following the emergence of nominalism, as an autonomous individual, and hence to the formulation of individualistic philosophy.[76] Nominalism and (sometimes) contractualism were reflected in the philosophy of Hobbes, Locke, Berkeley, Hume, Hamilton, and Mill, and in classical political economy generally.[77] Indeed, the development of free-enterprise capitalism, a concomitant of nominalism, reenforced nominalism and contractualism by providing, not a "preexistent-social pattern" as in feudal times, but an essentially contractual society within which the individual must find his own way. Society came to resemble, in conception even if not in fact, a collection of individuals bound together mainly by contract and cash nexus instead of a community of superiors and inferiors bound together in a network of reciprocity.[78]

Turning now to the Protestant revolution, in part the product of nominalist philosophy[79] and, at least in its Calvinist form, a strong proponent of "private judgment" and associational organization,[80] we find it to have produced several effects favorable to a nominalist ethic. It separated Church and Religion and Church and State with the eventual result that religion was possible outside the Church and independent of the state.

---

[75] E.g., on nominalism see Stark, *Social Thought*, pp. 2, 117–20, 142, 172, 190, 207, 209, and ch. 12; M. H. Carré, *Realists and Nominalists*, pp. 118–19, 121–22, 125 and ch. 3 on Saint Thomas. On the impact of nominalism in the fourteenth century see Copleston, 3:1–16 and pt. 1; Knowles, pp. 325, 335, 338–41.

[76] Copleston, 2:18–19, 208–9.

[77] Carré, pp. 123–24; Stark, *Social Thought*, ch. 12.

[78] Stark, *The Sociology of Knowledge*, pp. 37–41; MacIntyre, pp. 155–56.

[79] Luther "hailed Ockham as his master" when attacking the "edifice of Catholic belief." Carré, p. 122; also MacIntyre, pp. 121–22.

[80] Stark, *Sociology*, p. 81; *Social Theory*, p. 132; Macintyre, pp. 124–26, 166–67; Talcott Parsons, *The Structure of Social Action*, pp. 52–56; R. Bendix, *Max Weber*, pp. 50–79, 71.

As a result Morality could be established on natural instead of religious foundations and hence divorced from religion and made freer of state control.[81] Among the consequences of these changes may be included a weakening of the religious sanctions underlying observance of ethical principles and increase in the importance attached to material and this-worldy ends.[82] Of equal importance was the sharpened awareness of the distinction between society and its agent, the state, and hence of the great dependence of the prevailing system of property upon the prevailing system of government and of the corollary that producing change in the distribution of property entails prior change in the prevailing systems of government and the associated class structure.[83] Economic "reform" thus was capable of accomplishing little in the absence of corresponding political "reform."

The seventeenth century witnessed increase in the ideational support given, at least conditionally, to individual autonomy, and at the same time to improvement in the living conditions of many individuals which strengthened their disposition to avail themselves of greater autonomy, greater freedom from otherworldly constraints, and the doctrine that man qua man had a natural right to certain freedoms, a claim to natural rights that could be relinquished through a contractual arrangement.[84] This doctrine, initially designed, as was natural law doctrine, to guard the individual against the state, later was mobilized as well in support of the common man's right to subsistence or work.[85]

F. Eighteenth-Century and Early Nineteenth-Century Thought

The eighteenth century witnessed two major developments. First was the emergence of the philosophical revolution and its vision of the Heavenly City,[86] together with its belief in the solubility of man's problems through the removal or modification of his main institutions—a belief

---

[81] F. K. Chaplin, *The Effects of the Reformation on Ideals of Life and Conduct*. See also C. J. Friedrich, *Transcendent Justice*, chs. 2–3.

[82] Cf. Chaplin, ch. 4.

[83] R. M. MacIver, pt. 2, esp. ch. 6. Cf. on state and society the differing view of organismic theorists. Coker, ch. 5.

[84] MacIntyre, ch. 11; Sidgwick, *Ethics*, pp. 169ff. W. Windelband, *A History of Philosophy*, pp. 397, 431–36.

[85] Bonar, pp. 140–45 and ch. 9; MacIntyre, ch. 12; E. Cassirer, *The Philosophy of the Enlightenment*, ch. 6; my "Right to Work: A Backward Glance," *Journal of Economic History* 28:171–96.

[86] Cf. Carl Becker, *The Heavenly City of the Eighteenth-Century Philosophers*; also F. A. Hayek, *The Counter-Revolution of Science*, pt. 1, and *Individualism and Economic Order*, (London, 1949), chs. 1–6.

that prompted William Godwin to reject utilitarianism.[87] Second was the growth of individualism and the accentuation of several problems, always present in a society. (1) The end of law and morality needed to be defined in keeping with a society composed of individuals, bound together by contractual or comparable ties. This end was initially declared to be the general good or happiness;[88] it was later transformed into the meaningless formula or ideal ascribed to Francis Hutchison and popularized by Jeremy Bentham, that of *"the greatest happiness of the greatest number,"*[89] the *"watch-word of Utilitarianism."* In the hands of Jeremy Bentham this formula became closely associated with political economy, in an alliance that subsequently had widespread acceptance in Great Britain and Western Europe.[90] (2) The realization of this ideal was found more difficult when the main point of departure in ethical and related analysis ceased to be the individual qua member of an organic network of reciprocity and instead became the relatively autonomous individual. This shift in point of departure, given most current ethical theories, generated a conflict in need of resolution. For how could the behavior of essentially autonomous individuals be coordinated in such a way as to make possible realization of whatever *collective* objective (e.g., common good, socioeconomic welfare, stability) was compatible with their *private* objectives. For heterogeneity of ends or purposes presupposed (a) the presence of a technical or social mechanism (or unseen hand) capable of coordinating diverse purposes and (b) sufficient motivation on the part of the individuals composing a society to make this mechanism work.

Condition (a), it was generally supposed in orthodox economic circles, could be met and would be met; denial issued mainly from the Marxists until, in the present century, it was argued (mainly by J. M. Keynes and his anticipators) that something like "full employment" would not necessarily result, even given a competitive economy and a free market. Collective intervention might, therefore, be necessary. In time, of course, men also questioned the belief in an automatic, self-regulating mechanism "which operated so that the pursuit by each individual of his own

---

[87] William Godwin, *Enquiry Concerning Political Justice* (1793) 3:26–27, 35, 37.

[88] E.g., H. Höffding, *A History of Modern Philosophy* 1: 368, 395; Windelband, pp. 513ff.

[89] Ibid., p. 513; Sidgwick, *Ethics*, pp. 203–4; J. S. Mill, *Utilitarianism, Liberty, Representative Government*, ch. 1; C. M. Douglas, ed., *The Ethics of John Stuart Mill*.

[90] Bonar, bk. 3, ch. 2–3, pp. 385–88; Sidgwick, *Ethics*, pp. 224, 236–50, 300–303; MacIntyre, pp. 234–43. "Philosophy is never more worthily occupied, than when affording her assistances to the economy of common life." Jeremy Bentham wrote in *Jeremy Bentham's Economic Writings* 1: 81. See W. Stark, "Jeremy Bentham as an Economist," *Economic Journal* 51:56–79, 56:583–608.

self-interest and private ends would result in the greatest possible satis-faction of the wants of all."[91] For essential to the effective functioning of such a mechanism were suitable institutions and values which had been neglected by the utilitarians.[92]

Condition (b) was questioned from the start, already by Hobbes in his *Leviathan*, by Locke, Hume, Smith, and others. Would self-regarding individuals, persons animated by self-love, so behave as to insure the maximum realizable happiness or good of their fellows? This was doubted. Hence sanctions were indicated.[93] There might be recourse to the sovereign or government as Hobbes, Locke, and others suggested. Or one might argue, as did Smith, that if the state did not intervene pursuit of private purpose would support the ends of others. Or one might argue as did Herbert Spencer that "opposition between eogism and altriusm" would disappear. Or one might seek, as did Bentham, to bring public and private objectives in line with one another. In general, the use of sanctions was counted upon. Some, however, believed man to be endowed with a "moral sense" that would bring public and private concerns in line, or to be duty-bound to behave appropriately.[94]

It may be noted in passing that Bentham's utilitarianism presents two types of problems, one relating to his assumptions and influence, and the other to the concrete processes whereby divergent interests, or self-love and social need, are made to converge. Here we refer only to the first, prompted by G. Myrdal's assertion that Bentham had to assume a natural harmony of individual interests and that very philosophy of natural law which, in apparent keeping with his utilitarianism, he rejected when he denied the doctrines of rational natural law and natural rights. The har-mony doctrine, initially lent only partial support by Leibniz's *Theodicy* (1710) and his view that this is the best of possible worlds, must have contributed to the support of laissez faire in the nineteenth and early twentieth centuries. More persuasive than Myrdal's interpretation is the view that Bentham, given his belief that human purpose could be ho-mogenized into happiness, recognized the presence of conflict of inter-ests and hence the need to devise essentially political rather than market-oriented arrangements to reconcile and minimize conflicting interests.[95]

---

[91] Talcott Parsons, *Social Action*, p. 4.

[92] Ibid., passim.

[93] Windelband, p. 515; Basil Willey, *The Eighteenth-Century Background*. See also R. B. Perry on interests and value, chs. 3–10, 18–19.

[94] Höffding, 1:394–97, 451; Sidgwick, *Ethics*, p. 189; MacIntyre, pp. 163, 192–94, 197–98; Herbert Spencer, *The Data of Ethics*, ch. 14.

[95] See L. J. Hume, "Myrdal or Jeremy Bentham: Laissez Faire and Harmony of Interests," *Economica* 36:297–303. Excellent bibliography is included. See also A. O. Lovejoy, *The Great Chain of Being*, chs. 6–7.

G. Late Nineteenth-Century and Early Twentieth-Century Thought

Despite these difficulties—difficulties eventually enhanced by the substitution of power blocs and alliances between blocs and the state[96]—the economist remained inclined to continue in the tradition of utilitarianism. This may have been due initially to the lack of an alternative framework, together with the increasingly material character of the economist's definition of ends. Subsequently, with the marginal revolution of the 1870s and the reenforcement of its utilitarian and other early nineteenth-century forerunners, the economist could satisfy more fully what inclination he had to deal with the quantifiable, the manipulable, and the maximizable.[97] The transition is reflected in Henry Sidgwick's *Principles of Political Economy* (1883, 1887), a work designed to restate, with "due recognition," the "traditional doctrines" and hence, one might say, bring John Stuart Mill up to date. He noted that resources were not optimally allocated by the competitive system and that "distributive justice" was less fully realized than was possible, but observed that "political economy can only assist in showing how 'fairness' arbitrarily defined is to be maintained under changing conditions."[98] He found "moral value" in "Cooperation," a movement popular in England in the last third of the nineteenth century, in that it tended to counteract the "egoistic influences of the individualistic organization of industry."[99] Pigou was to develop fully the divergences Sidgwick observed between social and private net products.

Of the continuators, most prominent was A. C. Pigou who developed the welfare theory present in Alfred Marshall's *Principles*,[100] a theory already subject to effective criticism.[101] Pigou treats welfare as that part of

[96] See my "Power Blocs and the Formation and Content of Economic Decisions," *American Economic Review, Proceedings* 40:413–30.

[97] See Hla Myint, *Theories of Welfare Economics*; also F. Y. Edgeworth, *Mathematical Psychics*.

[98] Sidgwick, *Political Economy*, bk. 3, chs. 6, 7, 9. It may be noted, as our government never has, that the English or American conception of fair play is profoundly different from that found in Asia. See Dennis Bloodworth, *An Eye for the Dragon: Southeast Asia Observed*.

[99] *Political Economy*, pp. xxiv, 592–93. While Sidgwick has been described as a utilitarian, Hayward is probably correct in treating him and his *Methods of Ethics* (1874ff.) as based upon egoism and the "defence of self-love." F. H. Hayward, *The Ethical Philosophy of Sidgwick*, esp. chs. 5, 8–9.

[100] See Pigou, *Economics of Welfare*. On Marshall's misgivings see Parsons, *Social Action*, pp. 129–40, 702–3. For Marshall's unpublished reactions to Pigou's scheme for increasing welfare see Krishna Bharadwaj, "Marshall on Pigou's *Wealth and Welfare*," *Economica* 39:32–46.

[101] The best statement appears in Lionel Robbins, *Essay on the Nature and Significance of Economic Science*.

total welfare measurable in terms of money and hence as susceptible to increase through bettering the distribution of resources among uses— optimizing the conditions of production and exchange—and through some reduction in the inequality with which the national dividend is distributed. As Little points out, Pigou's assumptions regarding the addibility of satisfactions and the interpersonal comparability of satisfactions were subject to criticism. Moreover, his utilitarian scheme was not objective and free of value or ethical judgments, any more than alternative schemes.[102] Accordingly, although welfare economics could be useful in the assessment of change, given realistic enough factual assumptions, the conclusions drawn would remain matters of opinion.[103] It may be noted in passing, however, that the institutionalization of an inequality-reducing social security program in Great Britian, usually identified with the name of Sir William Beveridge, was in fact traceable mainly to the growing influence of the Fabian movement.[104]

Utilitarianism and the utilitarian system were attacked from several points of view, on Idealist grounds by T. H. Green, F. H. Bradley, and Bernard Bosanquet, by those who stressed the corporate or sui generis character of society, and by those who found the system weakly constructed. Green did not reject so completely as Bentham the doctrine of natural rights,[105] but he found the system of laissez faire wanting and the theory of social contract (e.g., as in Hobbes) oblivious to the fact that rights and obligations exist *within*, not outside society.[106] His approach was that of a collectivist whose views were more restrained than those of the Fabians and the Marxists, but yet quite contributive to the develop-

[102] Pigou, ch. 1, on welfare measurable in money; Little, chs. 2–5, 15. Cf. Milton Friedman's critique of A. Lerner's argument in support of less unequal distribution of income. *Essays in Positive Economics*, pp. 307–19.

[103] Little, pp. 275–79.

[104] E.g., see A. H. Hobbs, "Welfarism and Orwell's Reversal," *The Intercollegiate Review* 6:105–12.

[105] See Green, *Lectures on the Principles of Political Obligation*, pp. 31–33, 38–43; W. D. Lamont, *Moral Judgment*, ch. 6, and *Introduction to Green's Moral Philosophy*, pt. 3. See also Bradley; Bosanquet, *Philosophical Theory*; Stark, *Social Thought*, pt. 1. On German and French post-1800 organismic theories directed against individualism see Coker, and compare these with the medieval theories described by Otto von Gierke in *Political Theories of the Middle Age*. See also Othmar Spann, *The History of Economics*, pp. 53–65, 279–84, and ch. 8.

[106] Green, pp. 5–7, 63–67, 138, 154–274. A state, Green adds, "is not an aggregate of individuals under a sovereign, but a society in which the rights of men already associated in families and tribes are defined and harmonised," Lectures (pp. xvi, 139). See also J. R. Rodman's introduction to his *The Political Theory of T. H. Green*.

ment of the democratic Welfare State that was to come into being after his death.[107] Parsons shows, on the basis of the work of leading early twentieth-century social scientists, that the utilitarian system implied the ends of action to be random. Yet in reality "the actions of the members of a society are to a significant degree oriented to a single integrated system of ultimate ends common to these members;" a common value element pervades both a society's "ultimate ends" and its "value attitudes" and may underlie its normative rules.[108]

The German historical school, however, apparently under the influence of German organismic theories, devoted attention to ethical considerations, while the Austrian marginalists and others supposed that the spheres of ethics and economics did not overlap.[109] J. N. Keynes subdivided the matter at issue by distinguishing the "ethics of political economy," concerned with determining "economic ideals," from the "art of political economy," concerned with formulating "economic precepts" and realizing ideals, and the "positive science of political economy," concerned with establishing "economic uniformities."[110] Political economy qua "positive science" was "independent of ethics" and unsuited to pass ethical judgment, but "applied economics," concerned with solving problems, needed to take "ethical aspects" and "moral considerations" into account. Accordingly, the "ethics of political economy," a "branch of applied ethics," was charged with examining the bearing of "the general principles of morality" upon "economic activities" and the production and distribution of wealth.[111]

Perhaps the major change taking place within the realm of orthodox economics was recognition that the optimum state associated with competitive economic equilibrium did not coincide with what might be called the welfare-optimum state for a community. Walras, having defined competitive economic equilibrium, recognized this disparity; but it remained

---

[107] Ibid.

[108] *Social Action*, pp. 59–60, 707, 710. See also pp. 702–3, 718–19, also p. 715 on Marx's utilitarian orientation; also Bendix, *Max Weber*, pp. 486–94.

[109] On views such as those of the German historical school see J. N. Keynes, *The Scope and Method of Political Economy*, 4th ed., pp. 23, 25, 26, 37–38; Coker; Cf. Leo Ward, ed., *Ethics and the Social Sciences*. On the Austrian view see K. Menger, *Problems of Economics and Sociology*, pp. 87–89, 235–37. See also T. Suranyi-Unger, *Economics in the Twentieth Century*, and *Wirtschaftsphilosphie des 20 Jahrhunderts*, chs. 1, 4, 15.

[110] *Political Economy*, pp. 36, 46–59.

[111] Ibid., pp. 60–63. On distinguishing the role of economist qua economist from his role as an evaluating agent see my "Have Values a Place in Economics?" *International Journal of Ethics* 44:313–31.

for Pareto to develop it in his treatise on sociology. Therein he distinguishes between the maximum of ophelimity *for* a collectivity and the maximum of ophelimity *of* the collectivity, thus recognizing the latter to be, as Parsons notes, "a reality *sui generis*" with its own distributive norms. Accordingly, while Pareto dismisses individual ethics, he is aware of the great importance of community norms perhaps in need of support of force.[112] Pareto thus lays the groundwork for modern collective welfare theory, but on a broader base than that underlying Alfred Marshall's concept of "Maximum Satisfaction."

Frank Knight's critique of the ethical implications which some economists attach to competitive equilibirum could be fitted into the stream of criticism running from John Ruskin and Matthew Arnold to their contemporary counterparts. Knight pointed out that Christian, Aristotelian, and other conceptions of "good" were antithetical to the conception of competition which permeated economic analysis, and that there was no "really ethical basis" on which to rest approval of "competitive" in the sense either of motive or of ideal human relations. An "ethics of power," such as "nineteenth-century utilitarianism was in essence," had nothing to say about "the true problem of ethics," namely, "the purposes for which power ought to be used;" it was content to accept "the fact of desire . . . as the essence of value."[113]While economics stressed efficiency, it could not distinguish between economic and other wants, or between true and false values; it could not provide standards for comparing and selecting ends or deal with the substance of human conduct.[114] Knight himself draws attention to what he considers to be notable shortcomings of the sportlike aspects of the "competitive game," shortcomings characteristic as well of so-called business game theory.[115]

One of the most fundamental examinations of valuation as carried out by the ethicist and the economist, respectively, is that of W. D. Lamont.[116] He distinguishes the "moral judgment" from "the value judgment" as well as from the "efficiency" and the "aesthetic" judgments.[117] Since what is valued is demanded and hence entails cost, the study of

---

[112]*Trattato di Sociologia generale* (1916), translated by A. Livingston as *The Mind and Society*, vol. 4, ch. 12, paragraphs 2126–47. See also T. Parsons's fine analysis in *The Structure of Social Action*, pp. 241–49, 264–68. See also Léon Walras, *Elements of Pure Economics*, Lesson 22.

[113]Knight, *The Ethics of Competition*, pp. 61–75. On the background against which Knight was writing see Hla Myint, pt. 3.

[114]Knight, pp. 33–40, 72–73.

[115]Ibid., pp. 74–75.

[116]*The Value Judgment.*

[117]Ibid., pp. 3–22; also ch. 10.

valuation entails the study of demand and cost from the economic point of view.[118] Valuation cannot usefully be based upon a *summum bonum* since the assumption of such an absolute end is unnecessary to the act of valuation.[119] The "ultimate ground of the comparative value judgment is the principle of Economy," for it is that principle which, given "common demand," drives us "to evaluate" and "also operates to generate common demand, if such does not already exist, without which valuation cannot take place."[120] Having established the ultimate ground of the "attribution of goodness,"[121] Lamont inquires into the bases of moral judgment, among them the operation of the judicial process and distinctions between moral judgment and both legal and value judgments.[122] In effect he shows how economics and jurisprudence, having developed historically out of moral philosophy, embody problems bound up with those of ethics and can contribute to the solution of questions traditional in ethical theory and perhaps best understood as a result of inquiry into the "activity of 'valuation' and the 'attribution of goodness.'"[123]

Conclusion

The shortcomings of welfare economics reenforce the opinion that ethics, although distinct from economics, has much to contribute to social practice. Let us, therefore, note first the shortcomings imputed to welfare economics, that branch of economics with certain concerns similar to those of ethics. Little concludes that "economic welfare is a subject in which rigour and refinement are probably worse than useless. Rough theory, or good common sense, is, in practice, what we require." We must not forget that the reality of a "rigorous logical system" of welfare theory "is obviously limited" with the "degree of such reality. . . . a matter of judgement and opinion."[124] Mishan goes much further. The "study of welfare," as carried out by economists, is "positively misleading." "The things on which happiness ultimately depends, friendship, faith, the perception of beauty and so on, are outside its range; only the most obstinate pursuit of formalism would endeavor to bring them into relation with the measuring rod of money; and then to no practical effect. Thus, the triumphant achievements of modern technology . . . may be exacting a fearful

---

[118] Ibid., chs. 1–5.
[119] Ibid., ch 6, esp. pp. 198–202. Relevant also are the difficulties that beset giving meaning to a "summum bonum."
[120] Ibid., pp. 202–6, esp. pp. 203, 206.
[121] Ibid., ch. 9.
[122] Ibid., ch. 10.
[123] Ibid., preface.
[124] Little, p. 279.

toll in terms of human happiness. But the formal elegance of welfare economics will never reveal it."[125]

Mishan's comments on the yield of welfare economics recalls Knowles's comments upon "the erection of logic and dialectic as the sole training and method behind every intellectual discipline," to the exclusion of literature, in the twelfth and thirteenth centuries. There resulted "a divorce between thought and life, and between dialectic and the muses. Life and the universe no longer continued to supply the philosopher with impetus for thought" and thought itself began to "wither" while "definitions and conclusions" escaped the control of varied "human experience."[126] Or, as Stark has put it, until the Renaissance "man, seen in his social relations, had been the focus of interest; from then onward, man in his relation to the world of things."[127]

It may be true that economics qua economics cannot tell us anything about the comparative merits of ends, though it does illuminate the valuation process[128] and facilitate isolation of the material or resource costs of realizing ends, together with at least some of their benefits. It may therefore be true that regarding the comparative merit of the ends, the contribution of the economist is restricted largely if not completely to his role qua economist. It does, however, follow as a corollary that close cooperation on the part of economist, political scientist, jurist, and ethicist is essential. Moreover, examination of contemporary literature relating to politicoeconomic policy shows that ethical issues probably command more attention today than ever before. Responsible, of course, is the increasing role played by the state in economic life, that is, by a state whose apparatus necessarily serves the interests of those who dominate it. Recourse to ethical principles, together with their implementation and institutionalization, is essential, therefore, to the protection of the underlying population.

Illustrative is Feldman's conclusion that economists need to base their policy-oriented arguments on distributive justice and not on efficiency, since otherwise politicians will not listen. The principle that "factors of production receive their marginal product, and their rights to use and disposal without interference" when markets function well puts in the hands of individuals, not the state, control of redistribution of wealth from rich to poor. Then assistance of government is indicated only when externalities and market imperfections are present. Recourse to arbitrary

---

[125] "A Survey of Welfare Economics, 1939–59," in *Surveys of Economic Theory*, prepared for the American Economic Association and Royal Economic Society 1:213. See also Mishan, *Welfare Economics*.

[126] Knowles, pp. 339–40.

[127] *Social Thought*, p. 259.

[128] E.g., see Stark, *Social Thought*, pt. 3.

social welfare functions is not indicated.[129] Of course, when rights of property have not been well defined or assigned, the courts may have to define these rights. Moreover, there may be need for governmental action to remove restraints on the movement of factors. Public expenditures will be justifiable, however, not on grounds of efficiency but by whether taxpayers find the benefit to the *whole* of society sufficient to warrant such expenditures.

Of growing importance is the ethical aspect of family planning.[130] Most writers argue that individuals have the right to freedom of procreative choice, though subject to the obligation to respect the freedom of others and the requirements of the "common good." Major emphasis tends to be put on an actor's freedom of choice, usually to the neglect of externalities, of spillover costs, and so on. Accordingly, ethics seems to require that a principle stressing freedom run in terms both of the freedom of actor and of others, so that reproductive freedom becomes subject to the condition that all costs and benefits associated with its exercise be internalized. At present there is too much emphasis on freedom and too little on externalities which increase as a society becomes more complex and population becomes more dense.

Economic behavior—that is individual response to changes in price structure or in income—is conditioned by the ruling noneconomic parameters and changes with changes in these parameters. Thus, if we write $b = f(p, y, V)$ where b denotes an individual's response to change in p or y (designating price and income, respectively), the change in b will be conditioned by the nature of V, the value structure ruling in the community and variously reflected in individual members of the community. V may embody ethical orientations internalized as values in the individual. Accordingly, because it usually is values rather than ethical principles as such that condition the response of b to changes in p or y, it is not easy to relate these principles to concrete behavior.[131]

When the results produced by the market mechanism are found not to be in accord with the desires of a community or people, recourse is most often to the political process to redress the imbalance between the economic results and the pattern of wants. While this imbalance may be the product of eliminatable deficiencies in the market mechanism as it is actually functioning, it usually flows from disparity between economic re-

---

[129] Paul Feldman, "Efficiency, Distribution, and the Role of Government in a Market Economy," *Journal of Political Economy* 79:508–26.

[130] Daniel Callahan, *Ethics and Population*.

[131] Somewhat relevant is J. Davis, "Morals and Backwardness," *Comparative Studies in Society and History* 41;340–53 and Edward Banfield's critique of Davis's paper, pp. 353ff.

sults and that which current value attitudes sanction. The issue, however, is political rather than ethical.[132] Bringing both economic and political considerations to bear on this and related or parallel issues discussed under the head of collective and public goods, externalities, and "public choice," involves solution of various technical problems in the realm of *Public Choice*.

[132] Cf. R. A. Musgrave's discussion of what income distribution *should* be in his *Theory of Public Finance*, pp. 10–11, 19.

Bibliography

Index

Bibliography

Adams, Henry. *The Education of Henry Adams*. New York: Random House, Modern Library, 1931.

Adams, Robert M. "Anthropologial Perspectives on Ancient Trade." *Current Anthropology* 15 (September 1974).

———. "Strategies of Maximization, Stability, and Resilience in Mesopotamian Society, Settlement and Agriculture." *Proceedings of the American Philosophical Society* 122 (1978).

———, and H. J. Nissen. *The Uruk Countryside*. Chicago: University of Chicago Press, 1972.

Ahmad, A. J., "Irrigation in Relation to State Power in Middle Asia." *International Studies* 1 (April 1960).

Aristophanes. *Ecclesiazusae*. Edited by R. G. Usher. Oxford: Clarendon Press, 1972.

Aristotle. *Basic Works*. Edited with introduction by Richard McKeon. New York: Random House, 1941.

———. *Politics*. Translated by Ernest Barker. Oxford: Clarendon Press, 1946.

Arndt, H. W. "Prestige Economics." *Economic Record* 48 (1972).

Astour, M. C. *Hellenosemitica*. Leiden: Brill, 1965.

Bagehot, Walter, The Works of Walter Bagehot. Edited by Forest Morgan. Hartford, 1889.

Banico, Hermelindo. "Kauṭilya and the Legalist Concept of State and Government: A Comparative Study." *Asian Studies* 9 (1971).

Barker, Ernest. *Greek Political Theory: Plato and His Predecessors*, 2nd ed. London: Methuen, 1925, 1947.

Barth, Frederik. *Models of Social Organization*. London: Royal Anthropological Institute, 1966, 1971.

Basham, A. L. *The Wonder That Was India*. New York: Macmillan, 1954.

Becker, Carl. *The Heavenly City of the Eighteenth-Century Philosophers*. New Haven: Yale University Press, 1959.

Bendix, R. *Max Weber*. Garden City, N.Y.: Doubleday, 1962.

Bentham, Jeremy. *Jeremy Bentham's Economic Writings*, vol. 1. Edited by W. Stark. London: Allen and Unwin, 1952.

Bergson, Abram. *Essays in Normative Economics*. Cambridge, Mass.: Harvard University Press, 1966.

Bernardelli, Harro. "The Origins of Modern Economic Theory." *Economic Record* 37 (1961).

Bevan, E. R. *Ancient Mesopotamia*. Chicago: University of Chicago Press, 1918.

Bharadwaj. Krishna. "Marshall on Pigou's *Wealth and Welfare*." *Economica* 39 (1972).

Blitz, R. C., and Millard Long. "The Economics of Usury Regulation." *Journal of Political Economy* 83 (1965).

Bloch, Marc. *Feudal Society*. Chicago: University of Chicago Press, 1961.

Bloodworth, Dennis. *An Eye for the Dragon: Southeast Asia Observed*. New York: Farrar, Straus and Giroux, 1970.

Bodde, Derk. "Basic Concepts of Chinese Law: The Genesis and Evolution of Legal Thought in China." *Proceedings of the American Philosophical Society* 107 (1963).

————. *China's First Unifier: A Study of the Ch'in Dynasty as Seen in the Life of Li Ssŭ* (280?–208, B.C). Leiden: Brill, 1938.

————. *"Henry A. Wallace and the Ever-Normal Granary."* *Far Eastern Quarterly* 5 (1946).

————. "Harmony and Conflict in Chinese Philosophy." In *Studies in Chinese Thought*, edited by Arthur F. Wright. Chicago: University of Chicago Press, 1953.

————, and Clarence Morris. *Law in Imperial China*. Cambridge, Mass.: Harvard University Press, 1967.

Bogaert, Raymond, *Les origins antiques de la banque de depot; Une mise au point accompagnée d'une esquisse des operations de banque en Mesopotamie*. Leiden: Sijthoff, 1966.

Bogardus, Emory. *A History of Social Thought*. Los Angeles: University of Southern California Press, 1924.

Bolkestein, H. *Economic Life in Greece's Golden Age*. Leiden: Brill, 1958.

Boman, Thorlief. *Hebrew Thought Compared with Greek*. London: SCM. Press, 1960.

Bonar, James. *Philosophy and Political Economy*. 3rd ed. London: Allen and Unwin, 1927.

Bosanquet, Bernard. *The Value and Destiny of the Individual*. London: Macmillan, 1913.

————. *The Philosophical Theory of the State*. London: Macmillan, 1899.

Boyer, C. B. *A History of Mathematics*. New York: Wiley, 1968.

Bradley, F. H. *Ethical Studies (1876)*. London: Oxford University Press, 1962.

Bibliography

Braibanti, Ralph. *Political and Administrative Development*. Durham: Duke University Press, 1969.

————, and J. J. Spengler, eds. *Administration and Economic Development in India*. Durham: Duke University Press, 1963.

Brainerd, Charles J. "The Origins of Number Concepts." *Scientific American* 233 (March 1973).

Broughton, T. R. S. "New Evidence on Temple Estates in Asia Minor." In *Studies in Roman Economic and Social History*, edited by P. R. Coleman-Norton. Princeton: Princeton University Press, 1951

Brunner, Karl. "Knowledge, Values and Choice of Economic Organization." *Kyklos* 23 (1970).

Buch, Magan A. *Zoroastrian Ethics*. Baroda, India: A. G. Widgery, 1919.

Buchanan, James M. *Cost and Choice*. Chicago: Markham, 1969.

————. *The Limits of Liberty: Between Anarchy and Leviathan*. Chicago: University of Chicago Press, 1975.

————. "Utopia: The Minimal State, and Entitlement." *Public Choice* 23 (1974).

————. "What Should Economists Do?" *Southern Economic Journal* 30 (1964).

Buckner, H. T. "Transformation of Reality in the Legal Process." *Social Research* 37 (1970).

Burnet, John. *Early Greek Philosophy*. 4th ed. London: Black, 1945.

————. *Essays and Addresses*. New York: Macmillan 1930.

————. *The Ethics of Aristotle*. London: Methuen, 1960.

————. *Greek Philosophy*, part 1. London: Black, 1928.

Bury, John. *The Idea of Progress*. London: Macmillan, 1924, 1944.

Callahan, Daniel. *Ethics and Population*. New York: Occasional Paper, Population Council, 1971.

Carlyle, R. W., and A. J. Carlyle. *A History of Medieval Political Theory In the West*, vol. 1. 2nd ed. London: Blackwood, 1927.

Carlyle, Thomas. "Boswell's Life of Johnson." *Critical and Miscellaneous Essays*. Vol. 3. Boston, 1861.

Carmichael, R. D. "Motives for the Cultivation of Mathematics." *Scientific Monthly*, September 1950.

Carré, M. H. *Realists and Nominalists*. London: Oxford University Press, 1946.

Cassirer, E. *The Philosophy of the Enlightenment*. Boston: Beacon Press, 1951.

Catlin, George. *The Story of the Political Philosophers*. New York: McGraw-Hill, 1939.

Cato (the Censor). *On Farming*. Translated by E. Brehaut. New York: Columbia University Press, 1933.

Chai, Ch'u, and Winberg Chai, eds. *The Sacred Books of Confucius and*

Other Confucian Classics. New York: University Books, 1965.

Chaplin, F. K. *The Effects of the Reformation on Ideals of Life and Conduct*. Cambridge: W. Heffer, 1927.

Charlesworth, M. P. "Romano Trade with India: A Resurvey." In *Studies in Roman Economic and Social History*. Edited by P. R. Coleman-Norton. Princeton: Princeton University Press, 1951.

Chen Huan-chang. *The Economic Principles of Confuscius and His School*. New York: Columbia University Press, 1911.

Ch'ien Ssŭ-ma. *Records of the Grand Historian*. Translated by Burton Watson. New York: Columbia University Press, 1961

Chiera, Edward. *They Wrote on Clay*. Chicago: University of Chicago Press, 1938.

Ching, Julia. "Truth and Ideology: The Confucian Way (Tao) and Its Transmission." *Journal of the History of Ideas* 35 (1974).

Choudhary, Radhakrishna. Kauṭilya's Political Ideas and Institutions. Varanasi-l (India): Chowkhamba Sanskrit Series Office, 1971.

Cicero. *De Officiis*. Loeb Classical Library. Cambridge, Mass.: Harvard University Press, 1947.

Cicero, Marcus Tullius. *De Republica: or On The Commonwealth*. Translated with notes and introduction by George H. Sabine and Stanley B. Smith. Columbus: Ohio State University Press, 1929.

Clark, Colin, and M. R. Haswell. *The Economics of Subsistence Agriculture*. London: Macmillan, 1964.

Coase, R. H. "The Nature of the Firm." *Economica* 4 (1937).

Cochrane, Charles N. *Christianity and Classical Culture*. New York: Oxford University Press, 1944.

Coker, F. W. *Organismic Theories of the State*. New York: Longmans, Green for Columbia University, 1910.

Coleman-Norton, P. R., ed. *Studies in Roman Economic and Social History*. Princeton: Princeton University Press, 1951.

Collingwood, R. G. *The Idea of Nature*. Oxford: Clarendon Press, 1945, 1960.

Commons, J. R. *Institutional Economics*. New York: Macmillan, 1934.

———. *Legal Foundations of Capitalism*. New York: Macmillan, 1924.

Cook, R. M. "Ionia and Greece in the Eighth and Seventh Centuries, B.C." *Journal of Hellenic Studies* 66 (1946).

Cook, S. A. *The Laws of Moses and the Code of Hammurabi*. London: Black, 1903.

Copeland, M. A. "Concerning the Origin of a Money Economy." *The American Journal of Economics and Sociology* 33 (1974).

———. "Foreign Exchange in the 4th Century, B.C." *The American Journal of Economics and Sociology* 36 (1977).

Copleston, Frederick, S. J. *A History of Philosophy*. rev. ed. 8 vols. Westminster, Maryland: Newman Press, 1957ff.

Cornford, F. M. *From Religion to Philosophy*. New York: Harper, 1957.

Creel, Herrlee G. *Chinese Thought from Confucius to Mao Tsê-tung*. Chicago: University of Chicago Press, 1953.

———. *The Origins of Statecraft in China*. Vol. I *The Western Chou Empire*. Chicago: University of Chicago Press, 1970.

Cumming, R. D. *Human Nature and History*. Vol. 2. Chicago: University of Chicago Press, 1969.

Dalton, George. "Theoretical Issues in Economic Anthropology." *Current Anthropology* 10 (1969).

———, ed. *Primitive, Archaic, and Modern Economies: Essays of Karl Polanyi*. New York: Anchor Books, 1968.

Davis, J. "Morals and Backwardness." *Comparative Studies in Society and History* 12 (1970).

De Burgh, W. G. *The Legacy of the Ancient World*. Baltimore: Penguin Books, 1953.

del Vecchio, Giorgia. *Justice*. Edited by A. H. Campbell. Edinburgh: University Press, 1956.

Dempsey, Bernard W. *The Functional Economy*. Englewood Cliffs: Prentice-Hall, 1958.

———. *Interest and Usury*. Washington: American Council on Public Affairs, 1942.

De Roover, Raymond. "The Cambium Maratimum Contract According to the Genoise Notarial Records of the Twelfth and Thirteenth Centuries." *Explorations In Economic History* 7 (1969).

———. "Scholastic Economics: Survival and Lasting Influences from the Sixteenth Century to Adam Smith." *Quarterly Journal of Economics* 69 (1955).

Diankonoff, I. M., ed. *Ancient Mesopotamia*. Moscow: Nauka Publishing House, 1969.

Douglas, C. M., ed. *The Ethics of John Stuart Mill*. Edinburgh: University Press, 1897.

Driver, G. R., and J. C. Miles. *The Babylonian Laws*. Oxford: Clarendon Press, 1956.

Dubs, Homer H. *Hsüntze, The Moulder of Ancient Confucianism*. London: Probsthain, 1927.

———, trans. *The History of the Former Han Dynasty*. Translation of Pan Ku's *Han Shu*. 3 vols. Baltimore: Waverly Press, 1938–55.

Dumont, Louis. *From Mandeville to Marx: The Genesis and Triumph of Economic Ideology*. Chicago: University of Chicago Press, 1977.

———. *Homo hierarchicus: An Essay on the Caste System*. Translated by Mark Sainsbury. Chicago: University of Chicago Press, 1970.

———"On the Comparative Understanding of Non-Modern Civilization." *Daedalus* 104 (Spring 1975).

Duncan-Jones, Richard. *The Economy of the Roman Empire: Quantita-*

tive Studies. Cambridge: University Press, 1974.

Durand, John. "The Population Statistics of China, A.D. 2–1953." *Population Studies* 13 (1960).

Duyvendak, J. L. *The Book of Lord Shang*. Chicago: University of Chicago Press, 1963.

Edel, Abraham. *Science and the Structure of Ethics. International Encyclopedia of Unified Science*. Chicago: University of Chicago Press, 1961.

Edgeworth, F. Y. *Mathematical Psychics*. London: C. K. Paul and Co., 1881.

Ehrenberg, Victor. *Alexander and the Greeks*. Oxford: Blackwell, 1938.

———. *The People of Aristophanes*. Oxford: Blackwell, 1951.

———. "When Did the Polis Rise?" *Journal of Hellenic Studies* 57 (1937).

Eicholz, D. W. "The Pseudo-Platonic Dialogue ERYXIAS." *Classical Quarterly* 29 (1935).

Einaudi, Mario. *The Early Rousseau*. Ithaca: Cornell University Press, 1967.

———. *The Physiocratic Doctrine of Judicial Control*. Cambridge, Mass.: Harvard University Press, 1938.

Escarra, Jean. *Le droit Chinois*. Pekin: Librairie du Recueil Sirey, 1936.

Fairbank, John K. *The United States and China*. Cambridge, Mass.: Harvard University Press, 1959.

Fee, Jerome. "Maupertius and the Principle of Least Action." *Scientific Monthly* 52 (1941).

Feldman, Paul, "Efficiency, Distribution and the Role of Government in a Market Economy." *Journal of Political Economy* 79 (1971).

Ferguson, John. Moral Values in the Ancient World. London: Methuen, 1958.

Ferguson, Wallace K. *The Renaissance*. New York: H. Holt, 1940.

Fine, Sidney. *Laissez Faire and the General-Welfare State*. Ann Arbor: University of Michigan Press, 1964.

Finkelstein, J. J. "Mesopotamian Historiography." *Proceedings of the American Philosophical Society* 107 (1963).

Finley, M. I. *The Ancient Economy*. Berkeley: University of California Press, 1973.

———. "Aristotle and Economic Analysis." *Past and Present* 47 (1970).

Firth, Raymond. *Themes in Economic Anthropology*. London: Tavistock, 1967.

Fisher, Irving, *The Theory of Interest*. New York: Macmillan, 1930.

Foley, Vernard. "The Division of Labor in Plato and Smith." *History of Political Economy* 6 (1974).

————. "Smith and the Greeks." *History of Political Economy* 7 (1975).

Frankfort, Henri; H. A. Frankfort; J. A. Wilson; and Thorkild Jacobsen. *Before Philosophy*. Harmondsworth, Eng.: Penguin Books. 1951.

Fredericksen, M. W. "Theory, Evidence and the Ancient Economy." *Journal of Roman Studies* 65 (1975).

Freeman, Kathleen. *Ancilla to the Pre-Socratic Philosophers*. Cambridge, Mass.: Harvard University Press, 1948.

————. *Greek City States*. New York: Norton, 1950.

————. *The Pre-Socratic Philosophers*, Cambridge, Mass.: Harvard University Press, 1946.

————. *The Work and Life of Solon*. London: Melford, 1926.

Fremantle, Anne. *The Papal Encyclicals*. New York: Mentor, 1956.

French, A. *The Growth of the Athenian Economy*. London: Routledge and Kegan Paul, 1964.

————. "Solon and the Megarian Question." *Journal of Hellenic Studies* 77 (1957), pt. 2.

Friedman, Milton. *Essays in Positive Economics*. Chicago: University of Chicago Press, 1953.

————. *Price Theory: A Provisional Text*. Chicago: Aldine, 1967.

Friedrich, C. J. *Transcendent Justice*. Durham: Duke University Press. 1964.

Fung Yu-lan. *A History of Chinese Philosophy*. 2 vols. Princeton: Princeton University Press, 1952–53.

Gale, Esson M. ed., *Discourses on Salt and Iron*. Leiden: Brill, 1931.

Garelli, Paul. "The Changing Facets of Conservative Mesopotamian Thought," *Daedalus* 104 (Spring 1975).

George, C. S., Jr. *History of Management Thought*. Englewood Cliffs: Prentice-Hall, 1968.

Georgescu-Roegen, N. "Economic Theory and Agrarian Economics." reprinted in his *Analytical Economics*. Cambridge, Mass.: Harvard University Press, 1966.

————. *The Entropy Law and the Economic Process*. Cambridge, Mass.: Harvard University Press, 1971.

Ghisshman, R. *Iran*. Harmondsworth: Penguin Books, 1954.

Gierke, Otto F. von. *Natural Law and the Theory of Society, 1500–1800*. Boston: Beacon Press, 1957.

————. *Political Theories of the Middle Age*. Cambridge: Cambridge University Press, 1900.

Giles, H. A. *Confucianism and Its Rivals*. London: Williams and Norgate, 1925.

Giles, Lionel. *The Book of Mencius* (abridged). London: John Murray, 1949.

Gilson, Etienne, ed. *The Church Speaks to the Modern World*. Garden City, N. Y.: Doubleday, 1954.

Ginzberg, Eli. "Studies in the Economics of the Bible." *Jewish Quarterly Review* 22 (1932).

Godwin, William. *Enquiry Concerning Political Justice*. Ed. F. E. I. Priestly. Toronto: University of Toronto Press, 1946.

Goitein, S. D. *A Mediterranean Society*. Berkeley: University of California Press, 1967.

————. *Studies in Islamic History and Institutions*. Leiden: Brill, 1966.

Gonioran, Hillel. "The Biblical Law Against Loans on Interest," *Journal of Near Eastern Studies* 30 (1971):

Gordon, Barry. "Aristotle and Hesiod: The Economic Problem in Greek Thought." *Review of Social Economy* 21 (1963).

————. "Aristotle and the Development of Value Theory." *Quarterly Journal of Economics* 78 (1964).

————. *Economic Analysis Before Adam Smith: Hesiod to Lessius*. New York: Barnes and Nobel, 1975.

Goy-Sterboul, Sylvie. "Confucius, ses disciples et la population." *Population* 29 (1974).

————. "Mo-Tseu: Les idées d'un non Confucien sur la population." *Population* 33 (1978).

Green, T. H. *Lectures on the Principles of Political Obligation*. London: Longmans, Green, 1917.

Grousset, René. *The Rise and Splendour of the Chinese Empire*. Berkeley: University of California Press, 1959.

Guibal, M. P. *De l'influence de la philosophie sur le droit romain et la jurisprudence de l'époque classique*. Paris: Libraire du Recueil Sirey, 1937.

Hacker, L. M. "Food Supply." *Encyclopedia of the Social Sciences*. New York: Macmillan, 1934.

Hadas, Moses. *The Stoic Philosophy of Seneca*. Garden City, N. Y.: Doubleday, 1958.

Haines, C. G. *The Revival of Natural Law Concepts*. Harvard Studies in Jurisprudence, vol. 4. Cambridge, Mass.: Harvard University Press, 1930.

Halévy, E. *The Growth of Philosophical Radicalism*. New York: Kelley, 1949.

Hamburger, Max. *Morals and Law*. New Haven: Yale University Press, 1951.

Hammond, Mason. *The City in the Ancient World*. Cambridge, Mass.: Harvard University Press, 1972.

————. *City-State and World-State in Greek and Roman Political Theory Until Augustus*. Cambridge, Mass.: Harvard University Press, 1951.

Hammond, N. G. L. "Land Treasure in Athens and Solon's Seisachteia." *Journal of Hellenic Studies* 81 (1961).

Han Fei Tzŭ. *Basic Writings*. Translated by Burton Watson. New York: Columbia University Press, 1964.

———. *The Complete Works*. Translated by M. K. Liao. London: Arthur Probsthain, 1939.

Hare, R. M. *The Language of Morals*. Oxford: Clarendon Press, 1952.

Haring, H. A. "Warehousing," *Encyclopedia of the Social Sciences*. New York: Macmillan, 1934.

Harper, R. F. *The Code of Hammurabi, King of Babylon*. Chicago: University of Chicago Press, 1904.

Havelock, E. A. *The Liberal Temper in Greek Politics*. London: Jonathan Cape, 1957.

Hawkes, J. *The First Great Civilizations*. New York: Knopf, 1973.

Hayek, F. A. *The Counter-Revolution of Science*. Glencoe: Free Press, 1952.

———. *Individualism and Economic Order*. London: Routledge and Kegan Paul, 1949.

Hayes, D. A. "Management Goals in a Crisis Society." *Michigan Business Review* 22 (1970).

Hayward, F. H. *The Ethical Philosophy of Sidgwick*. London: Swan Sonnenschein, 1901.

Heichelheim, F. M. *An Ancient Economic History*. Leiden: Sijthoff, 1957–58.

Hesiod. "Works and Days." *The Homeric Hymns and Homerica*. New York: Loeb Classical Library, 1924.

Hildebrand, G. H., and F. J. Teggart, eds. *The Idea of Progress: A Collection of Readings*. Berkeley: University of California Press, 1949.

Hirschman, A. O. "The Search for Paradigms as a Hindrance to Understanding." *World Politics* 22 (1970).

Ho Ping-ti. *The Cradle of the East*. Chicago: University of Chicago Press, 1976.

———. *Ladder of Success in Imperial China*. New York: Wiley and Sons, 1964.

———. *Studies on the Population of China, 1368–1911*. Cambridge, Mass.: Harvard University Press, 1959.

Hobbs, A. H. "Welfarism and Orwell's Reversal." *The Intercollegiate Review* 6 (1970).

Hodges, Henry. *Technology in the Ancient World*. New York: Knopf, 1970.

Höffding, H. *A History of Modern Philosophy*, vol. 1. New York: Dover, 1955.

Hofstadter, R. *Social Darwinism in American Thought, 1860–1915*. Philadelphia: University of Pennsylvania Press, 1944.

Hogben, Lancelot. *The Wonderful World of Mathematics*. Garden City, N. Y.: Doubleday, 1955.

Holland, T. E. *The Elements of Jurisprudence*, 12th edition. New York: Oxford University Press, 1917.

Homer, Sidney. *A History of Interest Rates*. New Brunswick: Rutgers University Press, 1963.

Household, H. W. *Hellas the Forerunner*. 2nd ed. London: J. M. Dent, 1928.

Hsu Cho-yun. *Ancient China in Transition*. Stanford: Stanford University Press, 1965.

Hucker, Charles O. *China's Imperial Past*. Stanford: Stanford University Press, 1975.

Hughes, E. R. *Chinese Philosophy in Classical Times*. New York: E. P. Dutton, 1942.

Hume, L. J. "Myrdal or Jeremy Bentham: Laissez Faire and Harmony of Interest." *Economica* 36 (1969).

Humphreys, S. C. "'Transcendence' and Intellectual Roles: The Ancient Greek Case." *Daedalus* 104 (Spring 1975).

Hurst, J. W. *Law and the Conditions of Freedom in the Nineteenth Century*. Madison: University of Wisconsin Press, 1956.

Ibbetson, Sir Denzil. *Punjab Castes*. Lahore: Punjab Government Printing Office, 1916.

Jacobsen, Thorkild. "Ancient Mesopotamian Religion: The Central Concerns." *Proceedings of the American Philosophical Society* 107 (1963).

———. *Toward the Image of Tammuz*. Edited by W. L. Moran. Cambridge, Mass.: Harvard University Press, 1970.

———, and R. M. Adam. "Salt and Silt in Ancient Mesopotamian Agriculture." *Science* 128 (November 21, 1958).

Jaeger, Werner. *Aristotle*, 2nd ed. Oxford: Clarendon Press, 1950.

———. *Paideia: The Ideals of Greek Culture*. 2nd ed. New York: Oxford University Press, 1945.

Jastrow, Morris, Jr. *The Civilization of Babylonia and Assyria*. Philadelphia: Lippincott, 1915.

Jawad, A. J. *The Advent of the Era of Townships in Northern Mesopotamia*. Leiden: Brill, 1965.

Johns, C. H. W. *Babylonian and Assyrian Laws, Contracts and Letters*. New York: C. Scribner and Sons, 1904.

Johnson, D. Gale. *World Food Problems and Prospects*. Washington, D. C.: American Enterprise Institute, 1975.

Jones, A. H. M. *The Roman Economy*. Oxford: Blackwell, 1974.

Jones, T. B., and J. W. Snyder. *Sumerian Economic Texts from the Third Ur Dynasty*. Minneapolis: University of Minnesota Press, 1961.

Jonkers, E. J. *Social and Economic Commentary on Cicero's De Imperio Cn. Pompeii*. Leiden: Brill, 1939.

Joseph, M. L. "Requiem for A Lightweight: A Critical Historical Sketch." In *Prices: Issues in Theory, Practice and Public Policy*. Edited by A. Phillips and O. E. Williamson. Philadelphia: University of Pennsylvania Press, 1967.

Kane, P. S. V. *History of Dharmaśāstra*, 5 vols. Poona, India: Bhandarkar Oriental Research Institute, 1930–62.

Kang, Shin T. *Sumerian Economic Texts From the Drehem Archive*. Urbana: University of Illinois Press, 1972.

Kangle, R. P. *The Kauṭiliya Arthaśāstra*. Bombay: University of Bombay, 1963.

Keith, A. B. *A History of Sanskrit Literature*. Oxford: Clarendon Press, 1928.

Kellner, H. "On the Sociolinguistic Perspective of the Communication Situation." *Social Research* 37 (1970).

Keynes, J. M. *Essays in Persuasion*. New York: Norton, 1930.

————. *The General Theory of Employment, Interest, and Money*. New York: Harcourt Brace, 1936.

Keynes, J. N. *The Scope and Method of Political Economy*. 4th ed. London: Macmillan, 1917.

Kirby, E. S. *Economic History of China*. London: Allen and Unwin, 1954.

Kline, Morris. *Mathematics in Western Culture*. New York: Oxford University Press, 1953.

Kluckhohn, Clyde. *Anthropology and the Classics*. Providence: Brown University Press, 1961.

Knight, Frank. *The Ethics of Competition*. New York: Harper, 1935.

Knowles, David. *The Evolution of Medieval Thought*. Baltimore: Helico Press, 1962.

Kohl, Phillip L. "The Balance of Trade in Southwestern Asia in the Mid-Third Millennium, B.C." *Current Anthropology* 19 (1978).

Kohler, O. "The Ability of Birds to Count." In *The World of Mathematics*. Edited by James R. Newman. New York: Simon and Schuster, 1956.

Kort, Fred. "The Quantification of Aristotle's Theory of Revolution." *American Political Science Review* 19 (1952).

Kraus, Oskar. "Die Aristotelische Werttheorie in ihren Beziehungen zu den Lehren der modernen Psychologenschule." *Zeitschrift für die gesamte Staatswissenschaft* 61 (1905).

————. *Die Werttheorien*. Brno: Fudolf M. Rohrer, 1938.

Kramer, S. N. *From the Tablets of Sumer*. Indian Hills, Colo.: Falcon's Wing Press, 1956.

————. *History Begins at Sumer*. Garden City, N. Y.: Doubleday, 1959.

Laertius, Diogenes. *Lives of Eminent Philosophers*. New York: Putnam, 1925.

Laistner, M. L. W., ed., *Greek Economics*. New York: Dutton, 1923.

Lambert, W. G. *Babylonian Wisdom Literature*. Oxford: Clarendon Press, 1960.

Lamont, W. D. *Introduction to Green's Moral Philosophy*. London: Allen and Unwin, 1934.

————. *The Principles of Moral Judgment*. Oxford: Clarendon Press, 1946.

————. *The Value Judgment*. Edinburgh: The University Press, 1956.

Lancaster, K. J. "A New Approach to Consumer Theory." *Journal of Political Economy* 74 (1966).

Ledisma, L. S. "The Concept of Sovereignty in Pre-Modern Asia." Asian Studies 9 (1971).

Lee, H. D. P. "The Legal Background of Two Passages in the Nichomachean Ethics." *Classical Quarterly* 31 (1937).

Lee, Mabel Ping-Hua. *The Economic History of China with Special Reference to Agriculture*. New York: Columbia University Press, 1921.

Leemans, W. F. *Foreign Trade in the Old-Babylonian Period*. Leiden: Brill, 1960.

————. *The Old-Babylonian Merchant*. Leiden: Brill, 1950.

————. "The Role of Landlease in Mesopotamia in the Early Second Millennium." *Journal of the Economic and Social History of the Orient* 18 (June 1975).

Letwin, William. *The Origins of Scientific Economy: English Economic Thought 1660–1776*. London: Methuen, 1963.

Levy, Marion. "Contrasting Factors in the Modernization of China and Japan." In *Economic Growth: Brazil, India, Japan*. Edited by Simon Kuznets, Wilbert E. Moore, and J. J. Spengler. Durham: Duke University Press, 1955.

————. *Modernization and the Structure of Society*. Princeton: Princeton University Press, 1966.

Lewis, Thomas J. "Acquisition and Anxiety: Aristotle's Case Against the Market." *Canadian Journal of Economics* 11 (1978).

Liang Ch'i-ch'ao. *History of Chinese Political Thought*. New York: Harcourt Brace, 1930.

————. *La conception de la loi et les theories des Legistes à la veille des Tsin*. Peking: Chinese Booksellers, 1926.

Liang En-yuan. "The Legalist School Was the Product of Great Social

Change in the Spring and Autumn and Warring States Periods." *Chinese Studies in Philosophy* 8 (1976).

Limet, H. "Les metaux à l'epoque d'Agade." *Journal of the Economic and Social History of the Orient* 25 (June 1972).

Lin Yutang. *The Wisdom of China and India*. New York: Random House, 1942.

———. *The Wisdom of Confucius*. New York: Random House, 1938.

Litman, A. *Cicero's Doctrine of Nature and Man*. New York: Columbia University Press, 1930.

Little, I. M. D. *A Critique of Welfare Economics*. 2nd ed. Oxford: Clarendon Press, 1960.

Locke, John. *Of Civil Government: The Two Treatises of Government* (1960). New York: Everyman's Library, 1936.

Lopez, R. S. "Stars and Spices: The Earliest Italian Manual of Commercial Practice." In *Economy, Society, and Government in Medieval Italy*. Edited by David Herlihy et al. Kent: Kent State University Press, 1969.

———, and I. W. Raymond. *Medieval Trade in the Mediterranean World*. New York: Columbia University Press, 1955.

Lotka, A. J. *Elements of Physical Biology*. Baltimore: Williams and Wilkins, 1925.

Lovejoy, Arthur O. et al. *A Documentary History of Primitivism and Related Ideas*. Baltimore: Johns Hopkins Press, 1936.

———. *Essays in the History of Ideas*. New York: Putnam, 1948.

———. *The Great Chain of Being*. Cambridge, Mass.: Harvard University Press, 1953.

Lowry, S. Todd. "Aristotle's Mathematical Analysis of Exchange." *History of Political Economy* 1 (1969).

———. "Aristotle's 'Natural Limit' and the Economics of Price Regulation." *Greek, Roman, and Byzantine Studies* 15 (1974).

———. "The Classical Greek Theory of Natural Resource Economics." *Land Economics* 41 (1964).

———. "Recent Literature on Ancient Greek Economic Thought." *Journal of Economic Literature* 17 (1979).

Machlup, Fritz. "Homo Oeconomicus and His Classmates." In *Phenomenology and Social Reality*. Edited by Maurice Natanson. The Hague: Nijhoff, 1970.

MacIntyre, A. C. *A Short History of Ethics*. New York: Macmillan, 1966.

MacIver, R. M. *The Web of Government*. New York: Macmillan, 1947.

Mair, Lucy. *Primitive Government*. Baltimore: Penguin Books, 1962.

Mallowan, M. E. L. *Early Mesopotamia and Iran*. New York: McGraw-Hill, 1965.

Manu. *The Laws of Manu*. Translated by G. Bühler. In *Sacred Books of the East*. Vol. 25. Oxford: Oxford University Press, 1886.

Margueron, Jean-Claude. *Mesopotamia*. Cleveland: World, 1965.

Marrou, H. F. *A History of Education in Antiquity*. New York: Sheed and Ward, 1946.

Maverick, Lewis. *China: A Model for Europe*. San Antonio: Anderson, 1946.

————. ed., *Economic Dialogues in Ancient China: The Kuan Tzŭ*. New Haven: Far Eastern Publications, 1954.

Mauss, Marcel. *The Gift*. Glencoe: Free Press, 1954.

McNulty, Paul J. "A Note on the Division of Labor in Plato and Smith." *History of Political Economy* 7 (1974).

Melitz, Jacques, "Some Further Reassessment of the Scholastic Doctrine of Usury." *Kyklos* 24 (1971).

Menger, K. *Problems of Economics and Sociology*. Urbana: University of Illinois Press, 1963.

Menninger, Karl. *Number Words and Number Symbols*. Cambridge, Mass.: M.I.T. Press, 1970.

Merton, R. K. *Social Theory and Social Structure*. Glencoe: Free Press, 1949.

Michell, H. *The Economics of Ancient Greece*. Cambridge: Cambridge University Press, 1940.

Miles, J. C. *The Babylonian Laws*, vol. 1. Oxford: Clarendon Press, 1956.

Mill, J. S. *Utilitarianism, Liberty, Representative Government*. New York: Everyman's Library, 1920.

Minar, E. L. *Early Pythagorean Politics*. Baltimore: Waverly Press, 1942.

Mishan, E. J. "A Survey of Welfare Economics, 1939–59." *Surveys of Economic Theory*, vol. 1. London: Macmillan, 1965.

————. *Welfare Economics*. New York: Random House, 1964.

Moos, S. "Laissez-faire, Planning, and Ethics." *Economic Journal* 55 (1945).

Morrison, J. S. "The Place of Protagoras in Athenian Public Life." *Classical Quarterly* 35 (1941).

Munro, Donald J. *The Concept of Man in Early China*. Stanford: Stanford University Press, 1969.

Murray, Gilbert. "Reactions to the Peloponnesian War." *Journal of Hellenic Studies* 63 (1943).

Musgrave, R. A. *Theory of Public Finance*. New York: McGraw-Hill, 1959.

Myint, Hla. *Theories of Welfare Economics*. Cambridge; Mass.: Harvard University Press, 1948.

Myres, John L. *Herodotus: Father of History*. Chicago: Henry Regnery Co., 1971.

Nagel, Ernest, and J. R. Newman. *Gödels Proof*. New York: New York University Press, 1960.

Needham, Joseph. *Science and Civilisation in China*. Cambridge: University Press, 1956.

Nelson, Benjamin. *The Idea of Usury from Tribal Brotherhood to Universal Otherhood*. 2nd ed. Chicago: University of Chicago Press, 1969.

Neugebauer, O. "The Survival of Babylonian Methods in the Exact Sciences of Antiquity and Middle Ages." In *Proceedings of the American Philosophical Society* 107 (1963).

Neumann, John Von, "The Mathematician." In *The World of Mathematics*, edited by James R. Newman. New York: Simon and Schuster, 1956.

Newman, James R., ed., *The World of Mathematics*. 4 vols. New York: Simon and Schuster, 1956.

Noonan, J. T. *Contraception: A History of its Treatment by Catholic Theologians and Canonists*. Cambridge, Mass.: Harvard University Press, 1965.

————. *Scholastic Analysis of Usury*. Cambridge, Mass.: Harvard University Press, 1957.

Nozick, Robert. *Anarchy, State, and Utopia*. New York: Basic Books, 1974.

Oakeley, Hilda D., ed. *Greek Ethical Thought from Homer to the Stoics*. Boston: Beacon Press, 1950.

Olmsted, A. T. *History of the Persian Empire*. Chicago: University of Chicago Press, 1959.

Oneappe, Andrew, ed., *Four Comedies of Aristophanes*. Garden City, N. Y.: Doubleday, 1955.

Oppenheim, A. L. *Ancient Mesopotamia*. Rev. ed. Chicago: University of Chicago Press, 1977.

————. *Letters from Mesopotamia*. Chicago: University of Chicago Press, 1967.

————. "The Position of the Intellectual in Mesopotamian Society." *Daedalus* 104 (Spring 1975).

————. "The Seafaring Merchants of Ur." *Journal of American Oriental Studies* 74 (1954).

Oresme, Nicole, *Traictie de la première invention des monnoies*. Paris: Wolowski, 1864.

Orr, Daniel, and Wolfhard Ramner. "Rawls' Justice and Classical Liberalism: Ethics and Welfare Economics." *Economic Inquiry* 12 (1974).

"Outlines of Lectures on the History of Chinese Philosophy." *Chinese Studies in Philosophy* 8 (1977).

Pan Ku. *See* Dubs, Homer H.; Swann, Nancy Lee

Parento, V. *The Mind and Society*. New York: Harcourt Brace, 1935.

Parsons, Talcott. *The Social System*. Glencoe: Free Press, 1951.

——. *Sociological Theory and Modern Society*. New York: Macmillan, 1967.

——. *The Structure of Social Action*. New York: McGraw-Hill, 1937.

——, and Neil J. Smelser. *Economy and Society*. Glencoe: Free Press, 1956.

Perry, R. B. *General Theory of Value*. Cambridge, Mass.: Harvard University Press, 1926.

Persons, Stow, ed. *Evolutionary Thought in America*. New Haven: Yale University Press, 1950.

Phillips, A., and O. E. Williamson, eds. *Prices: Issues in Theory, Practice and Public Policy*. Philadelphia: University of Pennsylvania Press, 1967.

Pigou, A. C. *Economics of Welfare*. 5th ed. London: Macmillan, 1932.

Plutarch. *The Lives of the Noble Grecians and Romans*. Translated by John Dryden and revised by Arthur Hugh Clough. New York: Random House, The Modern Library, 1932.

Polanyi, Karl, "Aristotle Discovers The Economy" and "The Economy as Instituted Process." In *Trade and Market in the Early Empires*. Edited by Karl Polanyi, C. M. Arensberg, and H. W. Pearson. New York: Free Press, 1957.

——, ed. *Primitive, Archaic, and Modern Economies*. Introduction by George Kalton. Garden City, N. Y.: Doubleday, 1968.

Polybius. *The Histories*. Translated by Mortimer Chambers and edited by H. R. Trevor-Roper. New York: Washington Square Press, 1968.

Popper, K. R. *The Open Society and Its Enemies*. London: G. Routledge, 1957.

Priestley, F. E. I., ed. *Enquiry Concerning Political Justice*. Toronto: University of Toronto Press, 1946.

Pritchard, James B., ed. *Ancient Near Eastern Texts Relating to the Old Testament*. Princeton: Princeton University Press, 1955.

Pryor, F. L. *The Origins of the Economy*. New York: Academic Press, 1977.

Ptah-Hotep, *The Instruction of Ptah-Hotep and the Instruction of Ke'gemini: The Oldest Books in the World*. Translated by B. C. Gunn. London: J. Murray, 1908.

Quesnay, F. *Le Despotisme de la Chine*. *See* Maverick, *China*.

Qureshi, A. I. *Islam and the Theory of Interest*. Lahore: Shaikh M. Ashraf, 1946.

Radhakrishnan, S. *Eastern Religious and Western Thought*. Oxford: Clarendon Press, 1939.

Rawls, John. *A Theory of Justice*. Cambridge, Mass.: Harvard University Press, 1971.

Renfrew, Colin. *Before Civilization*. New York: Knopf, 1974.

Rickett, W. Allyn, *Kuan Tzŭ*. Hong Kong: Hong Kong University Press, 1965.

Rifkin, L. H. "Aristotle on Equality: Criticism of A. J. Carlyle's Theory." *Journal of the History of Ideas* 14 (1953)

Robbins, Lionel, *Essay on the Nature and Significance of Economic Science*. London: Macmillan, 1933.

Robertson, H. M. "Robinson Crusoe Economics." *South African Journal of Economics* 1 (March 1933).

Rodman, J. R., ed. *The Political Theory of T. H. Green*. New York: Crafts Classics Series, 1964.

Ross, W. D. *Aristotle*. 5th ed. London: Methuen, 1953.

––––––. *The Works of Aristotle*. London: Oxford University Press, 1911–52.

Rostovtzeff, Michael. *The Social and Economic History of the Hellenistic World*. Oxford: Clarendon Press, 1941.

––––––. *A Large Estate in Egypt in the Third Century B.C.* Madison: University of Wisconsin Studies in the Social Sciences and History, no. 6, 1922.

Ryan, J. W. *Distributive Justice*. New York: Macmillan, 1922.

Sabine, G. H. *A History of Political Theory*. New York: Henry Holt, 1937.

Sabine, George H., and Stanley P. Smith. *See* Cicero, Marcus Tullius

Sabloff, J. A., and C. C. Lamberg-Karlovsky, eds. *Ancient Civilization and Trade*. Sante Fe: University of New Mexico Press, 1975.

Sahlins, Marshall D. "On the Sociology of Primitive Exchange." In *The Relevance of Models for Social Anthropology*. Edited by M. Banton. London: Travistock, 1965.

––––––. *Stone Age Economics*. Chicago: Aldine-Atherton, 1972.

Samuelson, P. A. *Foundations of Economic Analysis*. Cambridge, Mass.: Harvard University Press, 1947.

Schulz, Fritz. *History of Roman Legal Science*. Oxford: Clarendon Press, 1946.

Schumpeter, J. A. "Science and Ideology." *American Economic Review* 39 (March, 1939).

Schwartz, Benjamin I. "The Age of Transcendence." In *Wisdom, Revelation, and Doubt: Perspectives on the First Millennium B.C.*, constituting *Daedalus* 104 (Spring 1975).

Schwartz, R. A. "Personal Philanthropic Institutions." *Journal of Political Economy* 88 (1970).

Sharma, P. Gopal. "Problems of Hindi Terminology." *Asian Studies* 6 (1968).

Sidgwick, Henry. *Outlines of the History of Ethics*. (Additional Chapter by A. G. Widgery). London: Macmillan, 1939.

——. *Principles of Political Economy*. 2nd ed. London: Macmillan, 1887.

Simon, H. A. *Models of Man*. New York: Wiley, 1957.

——. *The Sciences of the Artificial*. Cambridge: M.I.T. Press, 1969.

Singer, Kurt. "Oikonomia: An Inquiry into Beginnings of Economic Thought and Language." *Kyklos* 11 (1958).

Skeel, C. A. J. *Travel in the First Century After Christ*. Cambridge: University Press, 1901.

Smelser, Neil J., and S. M. Lipset, eds. *Social Structure and Mobility in Economic Development*. Chicago: Aldine, 1966.

Smeltzer, Donald. *Man and Number*. London: Black, 1953.

Smith, D. E., and Yoshio Mikami. *A History of Japanese Mathematics*. Chicago: Open Court Publishing Co., 1914.

Sohm, Rudolph. *The Institutes*. 3rd ed. Translated by J. C. Leslie. Oxford: Clarendon Press, 1907.

Sorokin, P. A. *Social and Cultural Dynamics*. New York: American Book Co., 1937–41.

Soss, Neal M. "Old Testament Law and Economic Society." *Journal of the History of Ideas* 34 (1973).

Soudek, Josef. "Aristotle's Theory of Exchange: An Inquiry Into the Origin of Economic Analysis." *Proceedings of the American Philosophical Society* 96 (1952).

Southard, Frank A. "Famine," *Encyclopedia of the Social Sciences*. New York: Macmillan, 1934.

Spann, Othmar. *The History of Economics*. New York: Norton, 1930.

Speiser, E. A. "Cuneiform Law and the History of Civilization." *Proceedings of the American Philosophical Society* 107 (1963).

——. "Early Law and Civilization." *The Canadian Bar Review* 31 (1953).

Spellman, John. *Political Theory of Ancient India*. Oxford: Clarendon Press, 1964.

Spencer, Herbert. *The Data of Ethics*. London: Williams and Northgate, 1890.

Spengler, J. J. "Aristotle on Economic Imputation and Related Matters." *Southern Economic Journal* 21 (1955).

——. "Arthaśāstra Economics." In *Administration and Economic Development in India*. Edited by Braibanti and Spengler. Durham, Duke University Press, 1963.

——. "The Cost of Specialization in a Service Economy." *Social Science Quarterly* 51 (1970).

————. "Economic Thought in Islam: Ibn Khaldun." *Comparative Studies in Society and History* 6 (1964).

————. "Economics: Its History, Themes, Approaches." *Journal of Economic Issues* 2 (1968).

————. "Evolutionism in American Economics, 1800–1946." In *Evolutionary Thought in America*. Edited by Stow Persons. New Haven: Yale University Press, 1950.

————. "Have Values a Place in Economics?" *International Journal of Ethics* 44 (1934).

————. "Herodotus on the Subject Matter of Economics." *Scientific Monthly* 81 (1955).

————. *Indian Economic Thought: A Preface to Its History*. Durham: Duke University Press, 1971.

————. "Kauṭilya, Plato, Lord Shang: Comparative Political Economy." *Proceedings of the American Philosophical Society*. 113 (1969).

————. "Laissez Faire and Intervention: A Potential Source of Historical Error." *Journal of Political Economy* 57 (1959).

————. "Notes on the International Transmission of Economic Ideas." *The History of Political Economy* 2 (1970).

————. "Population Phenomena and Population Theory." In *Research in Population Economics*. Edited by Julius Simon. New York: JAI Press, 1978.

————. "Power Blocs and the Formation and Content of Economic Decisions." *American Economic Review, Proceedings* 40 (1950).

————. "Right to Work: A Backward Glance." *Journal of Economic History* 18 (1968).

————. "Ssŭ-ma Ch'ien, Unsuccessful Exponent of Laissez Faire." *Southern Economic Journal* 30 (1964).

Ssŭ-ma Ch'ien. *See* Ch'ien Ssŭ-ma.

Stamp, Sir Josiah. *The Christian Ethic as an Economic Factor*. London: Epworth Press, 1926.

————. *The Science of Social Adjustment*. London: Macmillan, 1937.

Stark, Werner. *The Fundamental Forms of Social Thought*. London: Routledge and Kegan Paul, 1962.

————. "Jeremy Bentham as an Economist." *Economic Journal* 51 (1941); 56 (1946).

————. *Social Theory and Christian Thought*. London: Routledge and Kegan Paul, 1959.

————. *The Sociology of Knowledge*. Glencoe: Free Press, 1958.

Strauss, Leo. *Natural Right and History*. Chicago: University of Chicago Press, 1953.

————. "The Spirit of Sparta or the Taste of Xenophon." *Social Research* 6 (1939).

————. *Xenophon's Socratic Discourse*. Ithaca: Cornell University Press, 1970.

Strayer, J. R. *On the Medieval Origins of the Modern State*. Princeton: Princeton University Press, 1971.

Struik, D. J. *A Concise History of Mathematics*. New York: Dover, 1948.

Sun Tzŭ. *The Art of War*. Translated by S. B. Griffith. Oxford: Clarendon Press, 1963.

Suranyi-Unger, T. *Economics in the Twentieth Century*. New York: Norton, 1931.

————. *Wirtschaftsphilosphie des 20 Jahrhunderts*. Stuttgart: G. Fischer, 1967.

Swann, Nancy Lee, trans. *Food and Money in Ancient China:* Han Shu of Pan Ku. Princeton: Princeton University Press, 1950.

Sylvester, J. J. "The Study That Knows Nothing of Observation." In *The World of Mathematics*. Edited by James R. Newman. New York: Simon and Schuster, 1956.

T'ang Hsiao-wen. "Why Is Hsün Tzŭ Called a Legalist?" *Chinese Studies in Philosophy* 8 (1976).

Taylor, H. O. *Ancient Ideals*. New York: Macmillan, 1921.

Teggart, F. J. "The Argument of Hesiod's Works and Days." *Journal of the History of Ideas* 8 (1947).

Thakur, Upendra. "Early-Indian Mints." *Journal of the Economic and Social History of the Orient* 16 (1973).

————. "A Study in Barter and Exchange in Ancient India." *Journal of the Economic and Social History of the Orient* 15 (1972).

Thapar, Romila. "A Possible Identification of Meluhha, Dilmun and Makan." *Journal of the Economic and Social History of the Orient* 18 (1975).

Thomas, E. D. *Chinese Political Thought*. New York: Prentice-Hall, 1927.

Thucydides. *The Complete Writings*. Translated by R. Crawley. New York: Random House, Modern Library, 1934.

Tönnies, Ferdinand. *Community and Society*. East Lansing: Michigan State University Press, 1957.

Toynbee, Arnold J. *A Study of History*. London: Oxford University Press, 1939.

Trautmann, T. R. *Kauṭīliya and the Arthaśāstra*. Leiden: Brill, 1976.

Treistman, J. M. *The Pre-history of China*. New York: Natural History Press, 1972.

Tregear, T. R. *A Geography of China*. Chicago: Aldine, 1965.

Vecchio, Giorgio del. *Justice*. Edited by A. H. Campbell. Edinburgh: University Press, 1956.

Usher, A. P. *Early History of Deposit Banking in Mediterranean Europe*. Cambridge, Mass.: Harvard University Press, 1943.

Veenhof, K. R. *Aspects of Old Assyrian Trade and Its Terminology*. Leiden: Brill, 1972.

Viner, Jacob. "The Intellectual History of Laissez Faire." *Journal of Law and Economics* 3 (1960).

Vinogradoff, Paul. *Outlines of Historical Jurisprudence*. Vol. 2. Oxford: Oxford University Press, 1922.

Vlaemminck, Joseph H. *Histoire et doctrines de la comptabilité*. Paris: Dunod, 1956.

Walbank, F. W. "The Causes of Greek Decline." *Journal of Hellenic Studies* 63 (1943).

Walras, Léon. *Elements of Pure Economics*. Translated by William Jaffé. London: Allen and Unwin, 1954.

Wang, Y. Chu. "Ideas and Men in Traditional China." *Journal of Oriental Studies*. Monumenta Serica 19 (1960).

Ward, Leo, ed. *Ethics and the Social Sciences*. South Bend: University of Notre Dame Press, 1959.

Waters, K. H. "Solon's 'Price Equalisation'." *Journal of Hellenic Studies* 80 (1960).

Weil, Eric. "What Is a Breakthrough in History?" *Daedalus* 104 (Spring 1975).

Weisskopf, W. A. "The Image of Man in Economics." *Social Research* 40 (1973).

————. *The Psychology of Economics*. London: Routledge and Kegan Paul, 1955.

Welles, C. B. "The Economic Background of Plato's Communism." *Journal of Economic History*. Supplement 8 (1948).

White, Leslie A., "The Locus of Mathematical Reality: An Anthropological Footnote. In *The World of Mathematics*. Edited by James R. Newman. New York: Simon and Schuster, 1956.

Whitehead, A. N. *Science and the Modern World*. New York: Macmillan, 1947.

Wicksteed, P. H. *The Common Sense of Political Economy*. London: Routledge and Sons, 1933.

Wilder, Raymond L. *Evolution of Mathematical Concepts*. New York: Wiley, 1969.

Willey, Basil. *The Eighteenth-Century Background*. London: Chatto and Windus, 1940.

Wilson, George W. "The Economics of the Just Price." *History of Political Economy* 7 (1976).

Wilson, John A. *The Burden of Egypt*. Chicago: University of Chicago Press, 1954.

Windelband, W. *A History of Philosophy*. New York: Macmillan, 1901.

Winspear, A. W. *The Genesis of Plato's Thought*. New York: S. A. Russell, 1956.

Worland, S. T. *Scholasticism and Welfare Economics*. South Bend: University of Notre Dame Press, 1967.

Wright, Arthur F., ed. "The Chinese Language and Foreign Ideas." In *Studies in Chinese Thought*. Edited by A. F. Wright. Chicago: University of Chicago Press, 1953.

Wright, B. F., Jr. *American Interpretations of Natural Law*. Cambridge, Mass.: Harvard University Press, 1931.

Wright, G. H. von. *The Logic of Preference*. Edinburgh: University Press, 1963.

Wu Kuo-cheng. *Ancient Chinese Political Theories*. Shanghai: Commercial Press, 1928.

Xenophon. *Cyropaedia*. London: Macmillan, 1914.

———. *Oeconomicus*. In *Xenophon's Socratic Discourse*. Edited by Leo Strauss, Ithaca: Cornell University Press, 1970.

———. *Scripta Minora*. Cambridge, Mass.: Harvard University Press, 1956.

Zijderveld, A. C. "Rationality and Irrationality in Pluralistic Society." *Social Research* 37 (1970).

Index

Age of transcendence: B. I. Schwartz and economic relationships in the, xii
Agriculture: Cato on, 28; Mesopotamian, 35–36; Sumerian, 35–38
Alexander, 78
Anaximander, 80–81
Aquinas, St. Thomas: 129; on relations between economics and ethics, 131–33; and the renewed life in medieval ethical literature, 126; and society as an organism, 123
Archimedes: scientific mentality of, xi
Archytas: view of, 82–84
Aristophenes, 87
Aristotle: approach to economics within the framework of the city-state, 112–13; conception of economics, 93–107; endowed with full scientific mentality, xi; and importance of justice, 77; list of virtues, 126; on man's natural resources, 74; and man's needs, 128; and the meaning of justice, 82; plays down material wealth, 127; on preconditions of justice, 29; and universal justice, 96–97; and views on society as an organism, 123
Arthaśāstra: Kauṭilya and the guidelines of the, 39–45
Augustine, St., 129
Authoritarianism: Hsün Tzǔ's defense of, 62–63

Bacon, Roger: and the existence of natural order, xi
Behavior: maximizing and satisficing, 3–4, 6–7, 50
Bureaucracy: economy based on, 41

Capitalism: emergence of, 10; flourished in the Western world, 4; free-enterprise of, 134
Cato, 28. *See also* Agriculture
Ch'ien Ssǔ-ma, 52, 57, 57nn. 38, 39

China: Confucianism in, 49–63, 68–70; Han Fei Tzǔ and, 67–68; *Kuan Tzǔ* thought and policy in, 65–67; laissez faire voice in, 38; Legalist thought and counsel in, 63–65. *See also* Confucianism
Chou dynasty, 56
Christian thought: Judaic origin of, 129
Cicero: and his conceptions of the commonwealth, 109–12; preconditions of justice by, 29; principle of, 130; refers to proportional justice, 109–10
Class structure, 38
Classical economics: rules and trade pricing becoming basis for, 7–8
Commercial exchange: economics and, 8–9
Communism, 128
Confucianism: and concept of man, 54–55; and justice, 70; and laissez faire, 53, 56, 57, 60, 68–70; and Legalism, 62; and the well-field system, 55–56
Contractualism: reflected in classical political economy, 134
Cosmic order: conceptions of, 8
Credit: development of, associated with exchange, 29
Credit customs: in the ancient world, 37–38

Democritus: 97, 133; views of, 82–83
Dharmaśāstra: Manu and his guidelines for the individual in the, 46–48
Distributive justice. *See* Justice, distributive

Economic affairs: a laissez faire state of, 57
Economic analysis: ambiguity of terminology an impairment to, xiv
Economic behavior: in China, 49; discussed in Aristotle's works, 126; early manifestations of, 22; and exchange, 21; and moral virtues, 126–27; in the polis,

Index

Index

Index

Philosophical revolution: emergence of, 135

Plato: attitude toward justice, 29, 77, 82, 83; conception of economics, 84–93; and division of labor, 72; on earth's periodic disasters, 14–15; on the need for "communion of mind," 86; views with respect to economic welfare, 91

Plutarch, 72–73

Polis: Aristotle's and Plato's views of, 94–95, 128–29; and instrumental economic activities, 77–78; law of the, 81

Political economy: qua "positive science," 140; and utilitarianism, 136

Political science, 8

Political stability: development of, 28–29; Greek thought on matters pertaining to, 9–10

Politicoeconomic behavior: beliefs on stabilization of, 14; impact of universals on, 8–12

Politicoeconomic science, 118

Polybius, 12, 71, 109

Polytheism: Hebrews eliminated, 32

Preconditions: to the coming of economics, 19–23

Price-system: conception of a market-oriented, 4–5

Private enterprise: economy of, 41

Private ownership: economic scope for, 42–43

Productivity-favoring institutions: Carl Menger and the existence of, xii–xiii

Propensity: universality of defined, 4

Proportionate equality, 88

Propriety: importance of, 60

Protoeconomics: conditions of, xiii–xiv; economic behaviorial propensities in, 3–5; evolved into wisdom, 28

Protoeconomic thought: exchange and, 21

Protestant revolution: a part of nominalist philosophy, 134–35

Ptah-Hotep, 11

Rationalism, 32

Remuneration: distribution of, 43

Revolution: philosophical. See Philosophical revolution: emergence of

Revolution, Protestant. See Protestant revolution: a part of nominalist philosophy

Right: conception of an enforceable, xi

Satisficing: role of exchange in terms of, 21; versus maximizing, 50

Scarcity: presence of, 8

Shang Yang, 64–65

Societal system: economics and ethics as components in a, 117

Solon: set the "Solonian Economic Revolution," 72

Ssŭ Li. See Li Ssŭ

Ssŭ-ma Ch'ien. See Ch'ien Ssŭ-ma

State: magnitude of the parameters of, 11; policy of, 69–70

Storage economy, 36, 65–66

Sun Tzŭ, 54

Taoism: and laissez faire, 52, 56–57

Taxation, 41; and a state's financial support, 43

Thucydides, 46, 75, 79–81

Trade: dynamic role of as influenced by exchange, 21

Tsing Tien System: beginning of, 55–56; Mencius's views on, 61

Tyrtaeus, 78

Ulpian, 96

Universal factors: labor and land as, 12

Usury: concept of, 129

Utilitarianism: 23; contribution to support of laissez faire, 137–41; economist continued in the tradition of, 138; emergence of, 119; emphasis of the Legalists upon, 50; in the present century, 141–42; rejection of, 136; as supported by Mo Tzŭ, 63

Utilitarian objectives, 56

Value-attitudes. See Virtues: role of

Virtues: role of, 125

Wang Mang, 52–53, 56, 69–70

Wealth: material, 129; science of, 41

Weights and measures: development of, 56

Welfare maximization, 138–41, 142–44

Welfare theory: as developed by A. C. Pigou, 138–39

Well-field system: productive restrictions of, 65; revival of, 63. See also Confucianism, and the well-field system; Tsing Tien System

William of Ockham: influence of, 134

Wisdom, economic: managerial skill and, 5; and protoeconomic, 6–7

Xenophanes, 82

Xenophon: 89, 110, 112; deals with husbandry, 74; describes the division of occupations, 73